HORROR IN THE CINEMA

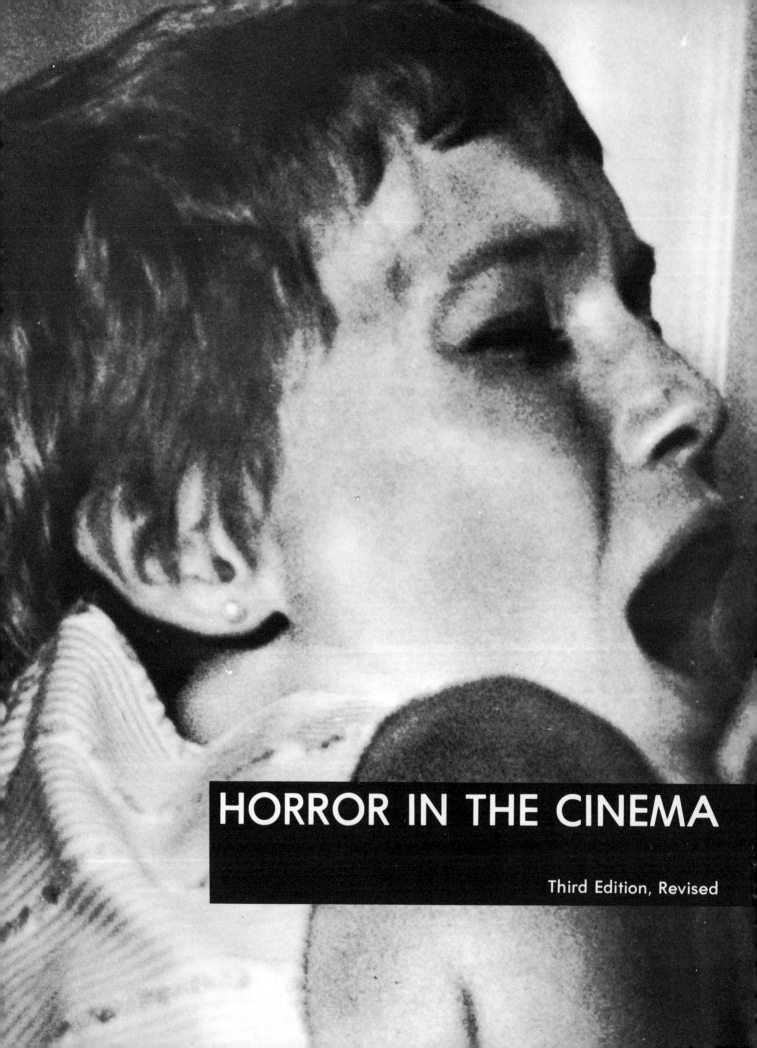

HORROR IN THE CINEMA

Third Edition, Revised

Ivan Butler

South Brunswick and New York: A. S. Barnes and Company
London: Thomas Yoseloff Ltd

© 1979 by A. S. Barnes and Company, Inc.

A. S. Barnes and Co., Inc.
Cranbury, New Jersey 08512

The Tantivy Press
Magdalen House
136-148 Tooley Street
London SE1 2TT, England

Library of Congress Cataloging in Publication Data

Butler, Ivan.
    Horror in the cinema.

    Bibliography: p.
    Includes index.
    1. Horror films—History and criticism. I. Title.
PN1995.9.H6B8 1978   791.43'0969'16   77-84787
ISBN 0-498-02137-8

PRINTED IN THE UNITED STATES OF AMERICA

for Gillian and Francis

Contents

Acknowledgments

I should like to express my thanks to Peter Cowie (The Tantivy Press) and Maurice Speed for the loan of stills. Other stills are reproduced by courtesy of: American-International, Amicus Films, Border Films, Avco-Embassy, Cinerama Releasing, Columbia, Columbia-Warner, EMI, Fox-Rank, Hamner Films, MGM-EMI, Miracle Films, National Film Archive, Paramount, Rank Organisation, 20th Century-Fox, United Artists, Universal-International, Warner-Pathé.

1. Introduction

When it was first suggested that I should prepare a revised edition of *Horror in the Cinema* to replace the edition which was selling out, I hesitated. In 1967, under its original title, *The Horror Film* was a pioneer in its field. Since that time so many books have appeared, so much has been written on all aspects of the subject, that it was necessary to consider whether there would be a call for the reappearance of an old trail-blazer brought up to date and in a new dress. However, during its lifetime the little book seems to have made quite a large number of friends (one kind reader recently described it, with undoubted but gratifying hyperbole, as his bible), and so there is perhaps reason to hope that it may still find a welcome among devotees of the macabre and the frightening in the cinema.

It occurred to me that one reason for its past popularity may have been the fact that—the writer being a film enthusiast of fairly long standing—a fair share of attention was given to earlier films, many of them seen at the time of their first release. With the continuing flood of "old movies" across the television screen many of these films are no longer museum pieces mouldering away in dusty archives, but might be made available to millions any late evening on the small screen.

Bearing this in mind, I have left much of the early part of the text unchanged, making only minor amendments and cuts. In most cases, also, personal opinions have been retained as they were when written. There is a vogue at the moment for the "revaluation" of past films. This may be an entertaining exercise, but is also rather a pointless (indeed one might almost say an arrogant) one. A film is made for the time when it was made: to suit the public of that time, to reflect the attitudes of that time, to record the opinions of that time, to present itself to the critical judgements of that time. It is rooted in the conventions of that time, and is bound by the technical limitations of that time. In order to assess the film later with any justice or accuracy it is necessary for the viewer—critical or otherwise—to "think" himself or herself as far as possible into its own period, rather than deliberately to drag it into a period of which it could know nothing, and care less.

It is, of course, extremely difficult to achieve this frame of mind completely, and there are probably instances that can be quoted back at me from my own book, particularly in regard to films that were made in the very early years. However, in only one significant instance have I altered an opinion given on a film that was recent when the previous edition of the book appeared. In it (the subject was a Dracula film) I expressed the view that a certain scene was "merely disgusting." The scene in question is so mild in comparison with what has been smeared across many a cinema screen since, and filmgoers have become so used to swallowing what would only a short time ago have made them retch, that I have expunged that remark made in a less "permissive" but slightly less tarnished era.

The other main alteration in this new edition is the omission of a number of films which, while not coming into the category of Horror Films, contained horrific moments. By no means all such films have been left out. No study of Horror in the Cinema could omit, for instance, the nightmare sequence from Ingmar Bergman's *Wild Strawberries* or the Chabrol episode from *Six in Paris;* but, if only for reasons of space, some cuts have been made in this area.

The latest popular *genre,* Disaster Films—the earthquakes, fires, floods, tempests, big fishes and other destructive phenomena—have in general been excluded. Their function is not so much to horrify as to excite, dismay—and perhaps to warn.

The boundary between the horror and the science fiction film is notoriously shadowy, and frequently does not exist at all. It could, of course, be said that the two streams are neatly identified in the two most famous characters of each: Dracula, the "natural" monster, and Frankenstein, creator of the man-made monster. But to exclude the Frankenstein series, and other films where the horrific has been brought about by the human "scientist" or "doctor" (both generally demented) would be absurd, as would be the exclusion of other "creatures," "blobs" and "things" of bizarre appearance and eccentric habits brought into being by some form of human fooling around with the universe. Such films, indeed, are generally made in order to bring about precisely that sense of the dreadful which the term Horror Film implies. The guiding principle here must surely be the evident intention of the film-maker.

With reluctance, television horror plays are also omitted, not least because of the tragically ephemeral nature of the medium. The number of quite brilliant plays and films which are made for this voracious medium and then literally wiped out after one, or at most two, showings, is shameful—a destruction which makes many other forms of vandalism seem mild in comparison. In November 1976, for instance, two superb essays in the macabre were shown, both written by Nigel Kneale—author of the Quatermass films, which also had their origins in television. The first, *At Barty's Party,* concerned an invasion of rats into private houses. Not a single rodent was seen, but the effect was incalculably more terrifying than the rat-ridden film *Willard.* The second, *The Dummy,* was an outstandingly original treatment of the monster theme, using the actual production of a horror film

as the basis of a story of the most subtle pity and terror. Above all is Jonathan Miller's unforgettable version of the famous M.R. James ghost story, *O, Whistle and I'll Come to You, My Lad;* the most terrifying half-hour that has ever sent a viewer, shaken and shattered, from the television set, wholly reluctant to turn out the light for the rest of the night. These are only the three finest examples among many others—but, sadly, to discuss them is merely to tantalise, when there is precious little likelihood of those who missed them ever being lucky enough to have another chance.

The balance between the horrific and the ludicrous is a delicate one—far more so than that between tragedy and comedy. The slightest false touch (even one brought about through no fault of the director—a disturbance in the audience, a failure on the soundtrack) can destroy the most carefully built-up tension and terror. Time alone can work this ruin, as witness the effect on some present-day audiences of silent or early sound thrillers. As indicated above, an intelligent attempt should be made to regard films in the conventions of their period and the impact they had on the audiences of their day. In years to come we shall undoubtedly be glad of such indulgence, such reasonable respect, towards our contemporary "masterpieces."

The sense of horror is a very personal one. As Dilys Powell pointed out some years ago (*Diversion,* 1950) ". . .one man's *frisson* is another man's guffaw." A study such as this, therefore, must inevitably be based on personal reactions, and the reader is clearly entitled to exclaim: "Well, I saw that, and it didn't frighten *me!*" The general basis must be the evident intention of the director, and such intention remains constant, whatever the effect on individual audiences.

2. Horror through the Ages

Like one that on a lonesome road
Doth walk in fear and dread,
And having once turned round, walks on
And turns no more his head;
Because he knows a frightful fiend
Doth close behind him tread.
    The Ancient Mariner (S. T.
    Coleridge)

Horror has always been honourable coinage in the currency of the arts, In literature its presence is obvious. It also has its place in painting, from the infernos of Hieronymous Bosch to Fuseli's nightmares, the silent-screaming faces of Munch, and the terrifying figures depicted and dissected by Francis Bacon—of whose work a notable short horror film has already been made; in opera, from Mozart to Richard Rodney Bennett's shattering "Mines of Sulphur"; and even in pure music—the finale of Vaughan Williams fourth symphony and the disintegrating scherzo of Britten's "Sinfonia da Requiem," to take only two modern examples.

In drama the power of horror has been recognised from earliest times, and few horror stories have surpassed the climax of the *Oedipus* of Sophocles or the murder of Agamemnon in the *Oresteia*—"slow build-up" and all. The Greeks, also, knew the value of leaving the ultimate terror to the imagination, and their most fearful happenings took place off-stage. This may, as Stephenson and Debrix suggest in their book *The Cinema as Art* (Penguin, 1966) result partly from the fact that the wearing of the mask and cothurnus precluded violent action, but it is certainly also due to the instinct of great dramatists.

With the days of Roman decadence came the "bread and circuses," the latter foreshadowing the more sensational and sadistic types of modern Horror Films. Elizabethan and Jacobean drama "supped full of horrors." Shakespeare's Lavinia, entering "ravished, her hands cut off and her tongue cut out" and later writing "with her stumps," would find herself at home in many a Hammer epic. Webster surrounded his Duchess of Malfi with lunatics and murderers, and during the following years the stage was weltering in gore, with authors piling agony on agony, and body on body, in the best horror fashion. During the Age of Sensibility the demand seems to have declined somewhat (though in literature we have the Gothic School of Mrs. Radcliffe, and Walpole's gigantic magic helmet); but Victorian melodrama revelled in green lights and ghastly apparitions. Irving in *The Bells* raised a mediocre ghost-thriller to great art with a brilliant study of the effects of guilt on a tortured mind. Then the cinema arrived, and with it even greater power to harass the nerves of its audience.

For several reasons, film is a particularly suitable medium for the creation of horror. There is its ability to conjure up the fantastic with conviction, the power of the camera to penetrate beneath the surface of the apparently normal and secure, its capacity for approaching each individual spectator, or drawing that spectator into itself, by the use of close-up—and finally its hypnotic effect, a film being viewed in the dark and consisting of moving shapes against a light-reflecting background, the effect being stronger when viewed from slightly below, i.e., the stalls of a cinema.

From very early days this quality has been realised and exploited in the cinema. It is perhaps stretching a point to say that Méliès made use of it—his fantasies leaned rather towards the opposite poles of the screen, comedy and charm. But it is quite possible that the famous pistol-firing close-up at the end (or the beginning, from choice) of *The Great Train Robbery* sent much the same thrill of terror through the unsophisticated audiences of 1903 as those of today are presumed to receive from the latest vampirical metamorphosis or planetary Thing which leaps or creeps at them from the contemporary screen.

The apparently indestructible interest in the supernatural and fantastic Horror Film is an

ordinary phenomenon in an age which increasingly rejects religious beliefs and upholds the
materialistic values of science and technology. To
say that nobody takes such stories seriously is
begging the question. It is not wholly correct, and
if it were it would only increase the difficulty of
explaining their fascination. Nor is their continuing
profusion solely due to the fact that vampires,
ghosts and monsters are often extremely photo-
genic, and can also provide an easy excuse for
staging scenes of sadistic or erotic sensationalism.
It is, rather, as if, despite our protestations of the
triumph of commonsense over superstition, something very deep inside us is loth to bid farewell to
the ancient beliefs, the "old religions" of our less
enlightened but perhaps more imaginative ances-
tors.

*   *   *

Before embarking on our journey through the
history and development of the subject, a few
general comments on the treatment of horror in
the cinema may be useful. Just as a door half-open-
ing on to a sinister room can be more alarming
than one which reveals fully the terror lurking
within, so the unseen is often more frightening
than the seen. In her review of *The Innocents*
(1961), Penelope Houston remarked: "The key to
any ghost story is knowing when to stop, when to
suggest without statement." This may be applied
to almost any manifestation of horror. The most
chilling moment in the play version of *The Cat and
the Canary* is not the appearance of the claw-like
hand through the wall, nor the final emergence of
the "monster", but the curtain to the first act.
There, the heroine is left alone in the shadowy
room. A secret panel behind the sofa opens.
Nothing is seen. The girl, sensing menace, gasps and
runs from the room, slamming the door. From
behind a tall armchair, some little way from the
panel, a vague shape starts to rear itself up—but,
before anything definite appears, the curtain is
down, the house-lights are up. Imagination does
the rest. In the film versions this moment has been
lost.

Similarly, the revelation of the "frightful fiend"
too early or too closely, weakens the impact. An
interesting example of this is to be found by
comparing the two versions of the famous Wax
Museum film. In *The Mystery of the Wax Museum*
(1933) there is not a great deal of the horrific
(apart from the burning of the building) until close
to the climax of the story. The shock engendered
then, as the handsome, calm face of the museum

owner (Lionel Atwill) suddenly cracks and disin-
tegrates as the girl beats her hands on it in warding
off his attack, revealing it as a mere waxed covering
to the shrivelled skull beneath, is so strong as to
leave its impression on the memory after thirty
years. In *The House of Wax* (1952) the man's
features (more contrivedly repulsive but actually
less fearsome) are revealed quite early on, and the
creeping, black-hatted figure runs around through
the rest of the film. The result is that, after one
quite effective moment, not much else is left, and
the climax is fatally weakened—in addition to
being less strongly handled in itself. This later
version was first issued as a 3-D picture, and it is
interesting to note that this added a few very
artificial shocks, but little in the way of true terror.
It was later reissued "flat." The 1932 version, now
unavailable, remains much the superior.

On the same lines, Stephenson and Debrix say,
in *The Cinema as Art:* "The most fearful monster
is the one we never see, the worst torture one
whose details are withheld—we supply them to suit
our own case. Thus by suggestion the artist
can . . . deal with subjects which would be too
shocking . . ."

The trouble with many Horror Films is that they
promise too much. In example after example,
tension and suspense are worked up with admirable
ingenuity, effective minor shocks being injected en
route. If the film is to be finally satisfying,
however, the promise must be fulfilled—the ultimate climax exceed all that has gone before. An
elementary condition, it might be supposed, but
one that is only too often ignored. How many
horror climaxes must we all have seen, which have
either collapsed into bathos or toppled over into
absurdity. A good example is to be found in
Monster of Terror (1965)—pointlessly retitled from
the much more apt *House at the End of the World*,
presumably for publicity purposes. This is a minor
science-fiction film, but very competently made,
with some good atmospheric photography, neat
natural dialogue, and believable characters. That
played by Boris Karloff, in particular, a man who
comes into possession of a radio-active meteorite,
is a welcome change from the usual mad scientist
to a well-meaning, guilt-ridden and indeed pathetic
human being. The film mounts to a strong scene
showing the dreadful death of his maddened,
radiation-destroyed wife, who, hidden behind net
curtains in bed as her illness ravages her, is *never
fully seen.* Raging and disintegrating figures are of
course a commonplace of the Horror Film, but
now and again skill and reticence in treatment lifts
such sequences above the ordinary. This happens

here, and the result is truly horrifying. If only the skill and reticence could have been extended a little further, and the film have closed with the man's broken realisation of what his greed and ambition have led him to. But, alas, we have to bow to the conventional pattern, and so we are treated to the ludicrous spectacle of Karloff, the stone having apparently exploded in his face, tearing about the house (after being confined to a wheelchair until this moment) with his face and hands apparently turned into tin and glittering with trick photography—yet he is still able to see, hear and run up flights of stairs, attacking (for no good reason) his daughter, and finally, need it be said, sizzling to death on the floor and starting the inevitable conflagration. Horror dissolves into derisive laughter. A perfect example of "not knowing when to stop."

The most frightening climax to a period of tension may often be a true, or apparent, anticlimax. A menacing approaching shadow suddenly speaks and reveals itself as the gentle servant—a shock encounter turns out to be the way of escape. And if this apparent easing is suspected a moment later of being a snare and a mockery, the result can turn the screw even more tightly. A memorable example of this occurred in the original version of *The Old Dark House,* a most notable thriller directed by James Whale in 1932. Throughout the film, the visitors stranded in the House during a night of howling storm and rain have been warned by the occupants (themselves a strange and alarming enough collection) of the fearful madman who is kept locked and bolted in an upstairs room. In the midst of a scene of mounting uproar and excitement the door of this room is suddenly opened. Everyone shrinks back, waiting. We see a close-up of the banisters. Slowly down them creeps a hand. It stops, and for some moments this is all we see. Eventually the dreaded figure moves into view—a small, gentle, harmless-looking old man. The contrast between what we are led to expect and what we see is unforgettable. The general behaviour of the other occupants has been so extraordinary that we wonder what they are up to, imprisoning this poor creature. But—suddenly—we catch a glimpse of his expression when he thinks he is unwatched . . . a member of one audience fainted at this moment. Had the apparition turned out at first sight to be as fearful as she had been led to anticipate, she would probably have merely screamed herself back into laughter again.

Despite exceptions, comedy and horror do not as a rule combine comfortably. Always the comedy will tend to dissolve the horror itself. Comedy-

thrillers are legion, but a comedy-horror film is a contradiction in terms, unless it is unintentional. "Spoof" horror, such as *The Comedy of Terrors,* the somebody-or-other *Meets Frankenstein* series, or the Bob Hope version of *The Cat and the Canary,* come into another category. This does not, of course, preclude occasional relief. No suspense situation can be sustained overlong without easing. If it attempts to do so, the audience itself will break the strain by laughter. Even this relief, however, needs careful handling. Once the heat is on it must not be allowed to cool very noticeably until the final climax is passed.

On the other hand, beauty and horror can be strangely allied. Many demoniac Horror Films have settings and shots of memorable visual beauty. To mention at random three films widely separated in time—practically the whole of Dreyer's *Vampyr* (1931), the creation of the false Brigitte Helm in Lang's *Metropolis* (1926) and several scenes in Corman's *The Tomb of Ligeia* (1964). Numerous other examples will spring readily to mind.

The great majority of Horror Films are fantastical in setting, often remote in time and place. Thus our emotions also are engaged, as it were, from a distance. The nearer the surroundings and circumstances approach the norm, the deeper will the horror penetrate. A conventional film such as *The Haunted and the Hunted* (1964), good of its kind and with a strong immediate impact, soon merges in the memory with others similar to it, and the effect fades. A film such as Polanski's masterly *Repulsion,* however, of which there will be more to say later on, dealing with madness and terror in a dingy South Kensington flat, can haunt the mind for months.

Boris Karloff and Gloria Stuart in *The Old Dark House* (1932 version).

Almost any degree of horror will prove acceptable to an audience provided it appears to fit into the context and not to be gratuitously thrown in to satisfy their own presumed taste for violence. When a spectator of normal sensibility revolts it is invariably because the film seems to be indulging in beastliness for its own sake, to be *enjoying* cruelty. It is a mistaken idea, in the cinema at any rate (though not always, apparently, in the realm of pornographic or sadistic literature) that the lower the instincts appealed to, the wider the audience.

An argument often put forward is that the Horror Film sets a bad example. As already pointed out, however, the situations of the vast majority are so far removed from reality that this possibility is really remote. Many of the horrific events are as much a convention as the fights and gunplay in a Western. One would feel fairly safe in asserting that not a single werewolf or vampire stalks the streets of our cities as a result of an audience watching a monster film, not a single coven of witches has been formed following a visit to, say, *Witchcraft* (1964).

On the other hand, of course, it is improbable that the makers of, say, *The Horror of Party Beach* (1964) or *Plague of the Zombies* (1966) were particularly interested in achieving the ennobling and purifying catharsis of Aristotle, and a more legitimate criticism may be to inquire whether a surfeit of highly spiced, manipulated, improbable horrors may not blunt the sensibilities against the more subtle and deeper emotions where fear is mingled with pity, either in records of fact or in the genuinely tragic story film. This is a criticism which bears some weight. The point was put forward strongly some years ago in an article by Derek Hill attacking the Horror Film (*Sight and Sound* 1958/59).

It has been said that the test of a good thriller is whether one would want to see it again, when the attraction of an unsolved mystery would no longer apply. Obviously this is not an infallible test of the worth of a Horror Film. An erotic or sadistic scene may be watched again and again for reasons which have nothing to do with artistic merit. However, it may be taken as a general rule that any film worth seeing at all is worth seeing more than once—indeed, any "good" film both deserves and requires repeated viewings if it is to be properly appreciated, in the same way that a piece of music of any complexity cannot be assimilated in one hearing. Worthless horror films abound, but so do worthless romantic films, worthless crook films, worthless Westerns, worthless musicals, worthless documentaries, even (dare one say it?) worthless art-cinema offerings. In Horror Films, even among those which pretend to be nothing more and can only be placed in the first of our categories, may be found direction as exciting and original, acting as convincing and subtle, dialogue as vital and pointed (though admittedly this is generally the weakness of the *genre*), and settings as ingenious and beautiful, as those in any other branch of the cinema.

Horror has its place in the film, as in every other art, and is an integral part of some of the very greatest. It was described earlier as good coinage in the currency of the arts. Like all coinage, it can be debased—there is no need to hunt for examples. But even the commercial Horror Film itself, abused and degraded though it may often be, is a thriving country in the world of film, and at its best, made with integrity, artistry, enthusiasm and cinematic skill, is worthy of consideration and respect.

3. The Macabre in the Silent Cinema

Horror in the film only came into its full flowering after the advent of sound—the extra dimension apparently necessary for the full assault on our sensibilities. In addition, arbitrary and often unsuitable musical accompaniments, and especially the constant interruptions of the action by subtitles often fatally destroyed the atmosphere and slackened suspense.

Nevertheless, in the sphere of the macabre much imaginative work was produced. The determination to shock was demonstrated very early on. In 1893 a picture of the execution of Mary, Queen of Scots, though under one minute in length, contrived to show the actual decapitation, complete with blood-dripping head rolling in the dust. The first Frankenstein monster appeared in an Edison film of 1910, and the supernatural and fantastic formed a large part of the output of Georges Méliès. He is said to have discovered the magical powers of the movie camera by accident: when filming a scene in the streets of Paris the camera jammed, and had to be re-started a few moments later. When the resulting film was projected, it was discovered that a carriage had miraculously turned into a hearse. However, as indicated above, Méliès used his fantasy for comedy rather than horror.

Early Faust and Satan films abounded. Laclos lists twelve between 1896 and 1911 (in *Le Fantastique au Cinéma*). America produced a *Dr. Jekyll and Mr. Hyde* in 1913, with King Baggot in the title roles, and *A Village Vampire* in 1916. As a general rule, however, "vampire" in early American pictures indicated the *femme fatale* rather than the blood-sucker. Moments of horrific suspense were, of course, plentiful in the serials, which began as one-reelers by about 1914 and flourished into the Thirties, but these were thrillers rather than horror films, and outside the scope of this study. For a detailed examination of the American serial see *Continued Next Week* by Kalton Lahue (University of Oklahoma Press, 1964).

The first great horror school grew up in Germany and rose to its greatest heights just after the First World War, although some films—the first versions of *The Golem* and *The Student of Prague*, for instance—appeared in 1913 and 1914. A most detailed account of these German films is to be found in Siegfried Kracauer's book *From Caligari to Hitler* (Dennis Dobson, 1947), and though he deals primarily with the cinema of the period as an indication of the psychological stresses in Germany which led to the rise of Nazism, rather than its aesthetic and dramatic qualities, the work contains a vast amount of invaluable information for anyone interested in the subject. They are also fully discussed in Lotte Eisner's erudite and splendidly illustrated *The Haunted Screen*.

The film which really brought the German school into prominence was *The Cabinet of Dr. Caligari* (Wiene, 1919). So much has been written about this famous picture that it need not be discussed in great detail here. It was filmed entirely within the studio, in macabre, expressionist sets (apart from the brief prologue and epilogue in a strange garden), designed by three artists affiliated with the Berlin *Sturm* group. The story concerns a sinister doctor who displays a somnambulist (Cesare) at a fair in a small town, and who is afterwards accused of using this figure to commit a number of murders. The doctor and Cesare are made up in the same grotesque manner as the sets, but most of the other characters use only the somewhat heavy make-up customary in this early period. The story is recounted in the garden to a man by a person who represents himself as the hero who ultimately unmasks the Doctor, but an epilogue reveals that the young man is himself insane, the Doctor the head of the Institute to which the garden belongs, and the whole story has been seen through the distorted vision of the lunatic. The film ends on a note of ambiguous hope—the Doctor (whose expression even then does not really convince us of his true benevolence) saying that now the young man is exorcised

Werner Krauss in *The Cabinet of Dr. Caligari.*

and can be cured. This framing story was not in the original script, but was placed round it by the director Robert Wiene, to the intense anger of the original authors, Carl Mayer and Hans Janowitz. The settings were supposed to have been primarily due to lack of money, which forced the makers to remain in the studio and make use of whatever cheap materials they could find. Whatever the reason, the result is a *tour-de-force,* of unease perhaps rather than of horror, but a film whose effect can never be forgotten. In *Caligari* may be found, in rudimentary form, most of the basic ingredients of the horror film formulae of later years: the mad scientist and the monster (both inherent in the Doctor)—the "undead" and the zombie (the somnambulist who sleeps in a coffin-shaped box and automatically follows his master's commands)—the girl dragged around in white flowing draperies—the general feeling of isolation and claustrophobia.

The monster proper makes his first important appearance in *The Golem* (Galeen and Wegener, 1914, and a second more elaborate version in

1920), based on a medieval Jewish legend of a Rabbi who makes a statue of clay and imbues it with life. The figure serves satisfactorily as his maker's servant for a while, but later develops his own personality and runs amok—as only too many of his descendants were to do in after years. Later versions of this legend include one by the French director Julien Duvivier in 1936 and a Czech production in 1951. The 1920 *Golem* had great visual beauty, with its strange twisted buildings and crooked streets filled with steeple-hatted inhabitants, and there was a powerful performance by Paul Wegener. The similarity to the Frankenstein theme is obvious, with the significant difference that the man-made figure receives life by magical means in the earlier story, and by "scientific" means in the later. In both, the monster gets out of control, creates havoc, and is destroyed—not too finally in later films, so as to leave an excuse for sequels should the demand arise. In both themes there is a form of self-development in the monster over and above the gift of life—an awakening of personality or "soul". In the case of the Golem it is this which leads to destruction, when it falls in love with its master's daughter. In the first Frankenstein picture it is sparked off by a little girl—the only person who does not shrink in horror from it, and whom it unwittingly kills. This Frankenstein episode, a very touching one, is also foreshadowed in *The Golem,* and a still can be seen showing almost identically the same situation.

The earliest *Dracula* version of note also came from this German period, Murnau's *Nosferatu* (1921). This will be considered more fully in a separate chapter.

Paul Wegener was associated with the first *Student of Prague* (1913), a Faustian story of a young man who sells his soul (represented by his reflection in a mirror) to the devil in return for temporal advantages. This early film is unfortunately lost, but the story was remade in 1926 (directed by Galeen) with Conrad Veidt in the title role. The film, a visually beautiful one, combined the Faustian legend with Jekyll-and-Hyde moralisings.

In 1926 appeared another famous film dealing, in part, with the artificial creation of life. This was Fritz Lang's *Metropolis,* a vision of the future (foreshadowing another Horror Film ingredient, science fiction), with the mad scientist, or genius, Rudolf Klein-Rogge, making a metal cast of a woman and endowing it with life to become the evil replica of a Christian girl and wreak the usual destruction and havoc. The sequence of the "transference of being" from human to robot was one of unforgettable beauty, with its rays and waves of light sparkling and flowing round the unconscious girl in ever-increasing intensity. Its treatment of the situation may be taken as an epitomised contrast between these early fantasy pictures and similar scenes in the cruder type of Horror Film.

Another creation-of-life variant appears in *Alraune* (Galeen, 1928) where the customary scientist (Paul Wegener) uses artificial insemination to produce his customary ruinous creature—this time the daughter of a hanged criminal and a prostitute. (Eventually one cannot help wondering why these

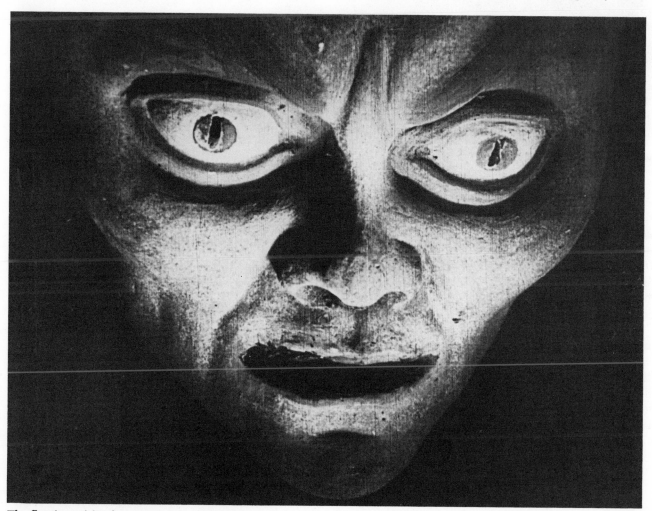

The floating spirit of Astaroth from *The Golem.*

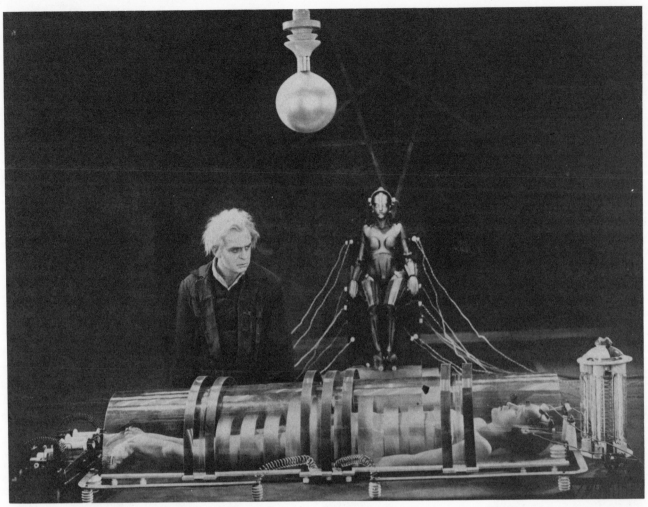

Rudolf Klein-Rogge and Brigitte Helm in *Metropolis.*

experimenters continue to take such unnecessary risks in their choice of subjects. Surely more care could have been taken in the choice of ancestry—and could not Frankenstein have started off with a *little* monster?) The great German star Brigitte Helm appeared in this role. She also played, most beautifully, the contrasting girls, real and artificial, in *Metropolis.*

Other notable films of the German fantastic period include *Waxworks* (directed by Paul Leni, whom we shall meet again in America)—a film in three episodes, in the last of which a young man has a nightmare in which he and his girl companion are relentlessly pursued among Caligari-like surroundings by a Jack-the-Ripper figure. Kracauer rates this episode as "one of the great achievements of film art." *Warning Shadows* (Arthur Robison, 1922) was a moral story of approaching disaster avoided by prophecy, hypnotism, hallucinations and nightmare—heavily but effectively done. In *The Hands of Orlac* the hands of a murderer were grafted on to Conrad Veidt. The film, however, in spite of being directed by Wiene, the maker of *Caligari,* was a failure which did not terrify. Veidt also appeared in a Jekyll-and-Hyde role in a Murnau film, *Der Januskopf* (English title, *Love's Mockery*) in 1920. This does not rival the Barrymore version. The man-made monster appeared again in a serial, *Homunculus* (1916), this time generated chemically.

In the realm of nightmare we may perhaps include Pabst's *Secrets of a Soul.* As an exposition of psychoanalysis the film appears crude and over-simplified, with a ridiculous ending showing the hitherto impotent husband, after a night's dreaming and a visit to a psychoanalyst, becoming (apparently instantaneously) the father of a bouncing boy. The central portion of the film, however, a long and detailed construction of the dream itself, is marvellously done, creating a real sense of the helpless horror of nightmare from the simplest means. A child's train, sprouting towers of paper, moving rods and bars, floating faces and figures,

The Devil at work in *Haxan (Witchcraft through the Ages)*.

and other images are accumulated and interwoven by ingenious camerawork into an unnerving phantasmagoria. The beauty of many of the compositions only serves to increase the feeling of uneasiness. Werner Krauss gives a noteworthy performance as the inhibited husband.

No other country approached Germany in the field of the macabre during this early period. From Sweden came a number of films which combined the supernatural with a somewhat heavy-handed mysticism, such as Victor Sjöström's *The Phantom Carriage* (1920) which came to collect the souls of sinners. Sjöström many years later was to play magnificently the leading part in a film which opens with one of the most terrifying nightmare sequences ever filmed—Ingmar Bergman's *Wild Strawberries*. In 1922 appeared the famous *Häxan* (Benjamin Christensen), with the director himself featured as a rumbustious Devil. It is a most exhilarating film, imaginative and original, and contains several scenes fully qualifying for our definition of horror. The film was reissued in 1968 with a sound-track (unnecessarily obtrusive) and a commentary based on the original titles and entertainingly declaimed by William Burroughs. As always, to see this old silent film in a "good" new print was a revelation, and in 1977 a British distributor enterprisingly released an even more faithful version. Despite the rather facile psycho-analysing of the less interesting modern sections (a very brief proportion of the whole), it dates remarkably little, and draws full and appreciative audiences whenever it is revived. Denmark produced one or two little-known fantasy films such as *The Isle of the Dead* (Gluckstadt, 1913) and *Spirits* (Madsen, 1914), but the most famous of all Danish horror films, Dreyer's *Vampyr,* had to await the coming of sound.

From France came an early waxworks film, *L'homme aux figures de cire* (1913), directed by

Maurice Tourneur, later to become well-known, and under-rated, in America. Abel Gance created a Caligari-like figure in Dr. Tube (*La folie du Docteur Tube,* 1915), a mad scientist who succeeded in breaking up light rays, with consequent deformation of the world. The film involved much use (according to some critics, abuse) of distorting lenses and other camera tricks. *Le systeme du Docteur Gourdon et du Professeur Plume* (1912) dealt with murder, madness and padded cells, and in the following year came *Balaoo* (Victorin Jasset), based on a series by Gaston Leroux, of which a notably macabre still shows a Hyde-like figure creeping upside down across the ceiling of a grim, bare room. Later, in 1928, came the first important adaptation of a story by Edgar Allan Poe, *La chute de la Maison Usher* (Jean Epstein). The Germanic influence was strong, with heavy shadows, symbolism, draperies and moving cameras, but the film had moments of visual beauty. It is interesting to note that Epstein's assistant on this film was Luis Buñuel. Buñuel's own first film, the surrealist *Un chien andalou,* made the same year, opened with a scene as horrifying as any seen before or since, in which a girl's eye is held open and cut across with a razor blade. The shot was put in deliberately to shock and alienate the audience. It certainly succeeded—thereafter they were prepared for anything.

No real horror films came from English studios during the silent period. Alfred Hitchcock's *The Lodger* dealt vaguely with a Jack-the-Ripper theme, but treated it in the style of a cosy thriller, creating a certain suspense but making no attempt to bring out the horror inherent in the subject. Even so, it was streets ahead of the average British thriller, and the light that was to burn so brightly, first in this country and later in America, gleamed through here and there.

It is to the United States that we must turn to trace the development of horror in the cinema after its German flowering in the early twenties. Curtis Harrington notes (in *Sight and Sound* April-June 1952) that it was not until the coming of sound ("and incidentally the stock market crash") that the fantastic horror film became a staple Hollywood commodity. This is broadly correct, but there were some notable examples of the macabre from quite early on in the silent period. In 1920 appeared the first important version of *Dr. Jekyll and Mr. Hyde,* directed by John S. Robertson. A previous one, graced with a happy ending revealing the whole thing to have been a dream, and located in New York, was, not surprisingly, of short life. As in all adaptations of

John Barrymore in the 1920 *Dr. Jekyll and Mr. Hyde.*

Stevenson's famous morality drama, liberties were taken with the story in the 1920 version also. Not only was Nita Naldi brought in as a seductive dancer, but Lord Henry was filched from Oscar Wilde's *The Picture of Dorian Gray,* thus anticipating the intermingling of monsters and vampires in later films. Much of the atmosphere, however, was retained, and John Barrymore's performance in the dual role was a *tour-de-force.* He accomplished the metamorphosis with a minimum of make-up in the early stages, relying on his extraordinary powers of facial distortion. He was the most successful of all the actors who have attempted the part, in the *Dr. Jekyll* side of the character, and the total impression is still, after so many years, unforgettable.

In 1925 Harry Hoyt directed *The Lost World,* based (with imported feminine interest) on Conan Doyle's story of a group of scientists exploring a jungle full of prehistoric monsters. The models and trick photography, though ingenious for their time, appear nowadays crude and unconvincing, and there are few people whom the film would frighten today. It was, nevertheless, the precursor of the great 1933 *King Kong,* and all that followed therefrom. In one respect, in fact, it scored over its successor, in which, conveniently but improbably, one species and one of only of each monster seemed to have survived on the island, to try their strength with Kong in turn like a series of variety acts. One of the most charming scenes in *The Lost World* was a group of baby prehistoric animals at play. Wallace Beery and Lewis Stone starred in this picture.

In the same year appeared one of the first American "mad scientist" pictures, Lon Chaney's *The Monster.* In it Chaney (the first authentic horror-film star) plays a demented doctor who tricks unwary motorists into car crashes from which they slide down a conveniently placed chute into his underground lair, there to become victims to his mania for vivisection. Eventually, needless to say, he is prevented in the nick of time from carving up the beautiful heroine whom he has secured (modestly but improbably covered from head to foot in butter muslin) to his operating trolley. The difference between the girl's appearance in this situation and her undoubted one had the film been made in the fifties is neatly symbolic of the trend of such films over the years. Chaney, in an effective but unusually simple make-up, played this part, not surprisingly, with his tongue firmly in his cheek—but the film did contain some quite chilling moments, notably the opening sequence of the looming headlights of a doomed car catching the deliberately planted reflecting mirrors, and swerving aside to crash.

Two years later Chaney was to star in a vampire film, *London after Midnight,* under one of the leading directors of early horror films, Tod Browning. Before this, however, he made one of the most memorable of all macabre silent films, *The Phantom of the Opera.* The story has been remade twice since, but Chaney's version is still unmatched.

It was directed by Rupert Julian—quite unre-

Lon Chaney, mask removed, in *The Phantom of the Opera.*

membered today except as the man who took over from Erich von Stroheim on *Merry-Go-Round* after the latter's dispute with Universal Studios. In *The Phantom of the Opera,* doubtless under Chaney's influence, Julian excelled. Numerous scenes remain etched in the memory—Chaney as Erik (the Phantom) gliding along the sewers of Paris, visible only as a breathing tube projecting from the murky waters until his hand emerged to drag down his victim; the chandelier swinging above the crowded opera house; above all, the moment when the Phantom is unmasked. Here, for once, reality (in Chaney's brilliant and ghastly make-up) matched imagination. He is seated playing the organ, his face mainly covered by a mask of gentle refinement. Unsuspected by him, the girl (Mary Philbin) creeps up softly behind and, unable to resist her curiosity in spite of his repeated warnings, whips off the mask. Instantly Chaney rears up to his full

height (seeming enormous) and the full horror of his appearance is revealed. For a moment nightmare becomes actual. It was an unforgettable moment, never again brought off so successfully until the cracking of Lionel Atwill's features in the 1933 *Wax Museum.* The story was, of course, nonsense, and the performances of Norman Kerry and Mary Philbin pedestrian, but Chaney towered over all. The film's appearance in Great Britain was delayed for some time as the result of an absurd scandal. By some means, the Universal publicity men contrived to have the cans containing the reels met at the landing dock and escorted on shore by a contingent of the army. This doubtless reprehensible but diverting piece of publicity so shocked Government and Army officials that they lost any little sense of humour they possessed. Instead of laughing the whole affair off, they confiscated the film, and avenged the "insult" by depriving the

Lon Chaney, with skull mask, in *The Phantom of the Opera.*

totally innocent British filmgoer of the pleasure of seeing it until a considerable period had elapsed. Undoubtedly, if illogically, this robbed the film of some of its initial impact.

In 1927 Chaney played the apparent vampire in *London after Midnight,* which Browning remade eight years later under the title *The Mark of the Vampire.* The first version contained too much "comedy relief" for the sinister elements to obtain their full effect, and in any case the whole thing turns out, in a weak ending, to have been a hoax. All the same, the silent version was directed with considerable panache, and Chaney's make-up was another triumph of the macabre. There was a notable shot of his black-clad, high-hatted figure gliding, half-creeping, along a deserted hotel corridor, and another effective one of the vampirical mist billowing beneath a closed door, then clearing to reveal his crouching figure—at first only the black circle of his hat, gradually lifting as he raises his head and draws to his feet. Chaney made a most effective vampire, set in a supposedly haunted theatre. All the above came from Universal Studios, whose name became closely linked with the silent and early sound horror film.

Finally we may recall at random a few effectively macabre moments in films not primarily of the horror school. From America, Arthur Edmund Carewe's chilling performance in an otherwise undistinguished *Trilby* (1923); the murder of Zasu Pitts in Stroheim's *Greed* (1923); the wind uncovering the murdered body in *The Wind* (Sjöström, 1928). From Russia, the famous Odessa steps sequence from *Battleship Potemkin* (Eisenstein, 1925), in particular the shots of the runaway pram and the terrible final glimpse of the blinded woman, her blood and her broken spectacles spattering her face. From Germany, scenes from such allegorical films as *Destiny* (Fritz Lang, 1921), the uneasy sense of lurking madness and anarchy beneath his thrillers *Dr. Mabuse, The Gambler* (1922) and *The Spy* (1928), the Caligari-like distortions of *The Tell-Tale Heart* (Klein, 1928). From France, preserved only in an eerie still, a film entitled *La proie* (*The Victim,* Monca, 1916), of which Nicole Vedrès comments in *Images du Cinéma Français:* ". . . a kind of intimate horror . . . obtained by very simple means. In the corridor of a hotel a man prepares to chloroform a beautiful woman. She has not seen him. She does not know him. His face is concealed beneath a loose black gauze. The image, however, is more terrifying than that of a man screaming as he faces his death."

We return finally to America for the most horrifying scene of all—the unforgettable moment in Griffith's *Broken Blossoms* (1919) where Lillian Gish, having shut herself in a tiny cupboard to escape from her persecutor (Donald Crisp), whirls round and round in wild panic as he beats against the door—a moment which, it is reported, reduced the hardboiled technicians on the set to white-faced, shaken silence. This brief sequence, shot partly from above, produces an overwhelming effect of claustrophobic terror and, as an example of the power of the silent film to horrify and unnerve, may fittingly conclude this short survey.

4. Dracula and Frankenstein

It is interesting to speculate on the reactions of the original writers of *Dracula* and *Frankenstein* could they see what has happened to their respective creations. Bram Stoker, who wrote *Dracula* as one among a number of similar macabre thrillers, would probably shrug his shoulders, and, man of the theatre as he was, welcome the stream of sequels and consequent royalties for which the Count has been responsible. Mary Wollstonecraft Shelley, the poet's second wife, who brought forth "Frankenstein" from the imagination of a girl of eighteen, while on holiday with her husband and Lord Byron in Switzerland, might have somewhat different feelings. Although conceived principally as a Gothic terror story, the fable of a man who took upon himself the highest power of God and was destroyed by his own presumption was also intended to point a moral—of which precious little remains in some of the later variations on her theme and characters.

Both tales, according to their authors, began as nightmares. Both have certainly caused plenty since. The two characters are the archetypes of fantastic horror film protagonists—the supernatural fiend, and the man-made monster. From one or other of ·them most of the smaller fry—wolfmen, zombies, "things" in general—descend, sometimes to very low depths indeed.

Dracula

Bram Stoker, the burly bearded business-manager for Sir Henry Irving, went to considerable trouble and research to obtain authenticity for his famous shocker. He investigated thoroughly the legéndary basis for the vampire. There was, as is now well known, a real-life Dracula. He was the son of Vlad Dracul, who belonged to an Order of Knighthood established by King Sigismund of Hungary in 1418—"The Order of the Dragon"—Dracul being the Romanian word for Dragon. It also means Devil. Dracula signifies "Son of

Dracul": son of the Dragon—or of the Devil . . .

Dracula himself was a Voivode (Ruling Prince) of Wallachia, a man of such cruelty that he was known, significantly, as Tepes (The Impaler). He was also, to be just, a man of great physical courage, a brilliant general who won the admiration of his countrymen for successfully defending the territory against the invading Turks—his impaling activities being directed against (or, more accurately, into) the bodies of his captives. He himself died in battle. There appears to be no evidence of his being described as a vampire during his lifetime, but his general character and behaviour (added to the fact that, having been converted to Roman Catholicism for political reasons, he was later excommunicated) rendered him eligible for such nomination in after years.** Stoker's book is somewhat turgidly written and, except for certain descriptive passage, may strike some modern readers as rather stodgy going. On its publication in 1896, however, it was something of a sensation. A dramatised version was given a single production to protect copyright, but this was really little more than a crudely adapted reading, and some thirty years were to pass before it leapt to fame in this form.

A famous film version was made in 1922 (silent, of course) by F.W. Murnau, later to be renowned for *The Last Laugh* and the very beautiful and moving *Sunrise* (1927). The adaptation was by Henrik Galeen. Until recently, *Nosferatu* (as it was called) was an exceedingly rare film, largely owing to copyright troubles which resulted in an order to

**The flourishing British "Dracula Society", founded by Bruce Wightman and Bernard Davies in 1973 and currently numbering over 300 members, has organised (among other activities including an annual Dracula Dinner) several vampiric tours of Transylvania, enthusiastically encouraged by the Romanian Ministry of Tourism. Visits were made to such ensanguined sites as Dracula's birthplace, Sighişoura (1431), the castle of Poenari erected by him around 1460, the Golden Crown, Bistrita, and the Borgo Pass—the locale of the Vampire's castle—and the island monastery of Snagov, where Vlad Dracula was buried (1476), and where—surely—"Count Dracula" rose from the tomb. (I am indebted to Bruce Wightman for the above particulars, and also for the details of the "real" Dracula.)

Max Schreck in *Nosferatu.*

destroy all prints. Luckily, this was avoided. The film makes use of many camera tricks which, commonplace today, were at that time excitingly novel. To show the phantom coach jerking along in eerie fashion Murnau and his cameraman, Fritz Arno Wagner, used a one-turn-one-picture device. To give his woods and skies an uncanny, ghastly appearance he had them printed in negative. The film combines almost equally the magnificent and the absurd. There is some beautiful exterior work, and much creaking melodrama. Germanic mystic moralising is imposed on the story, but otherwise it follows the original fairly closely. It ends abruptly, however, on Dracula's first encounter with the heroine. At considerable risk to herself, she agrees to seduce him into remaining too long with her before engorging: he is caught by the sun's rays, and melts into thin air before he can do much harm to her. Earlier, he has been responsible for horrors enough. In Kracauer's phrase, he is made to appear "an incarnation of pestilence. Wherever he emerges, rats swarm out and people fall dead." Though exaggerated, Max Schreck's make-up (he was a music-hall artiste) is a fine example of Gothic grotesque. Standing on the prow of the sailing ship, he resembles a combination of a vulture and the Flying Dutchman. The full script of this famous old film is included in Lotte Eisner's book on F.W. Murnau.

Two years after *Nosferatu,* the famous stage version opened, almost unnoticed, on tour at Derby. The adapter was Hamilton Deane, and it was from this dramatisation that the Tod Browning film was directly taken—or, to be exact, from a slightly different one on which Deane collaborated with the American writer John F. Balderston. Hamilton Deane was to be associated with Dracula for years, but never appeared in a film. Three years after the opening the play came to the West End, receiving some of the worst press notices and best

box-office receipts for years, and a film version was inevitable.

As stated, this was directed by Tod Browning. It was hoped that Lon Chaney would play the part, but his death prevented this. The Hungarian actor Bela Lugosi eventually took it on—and continued playing it in various guises until his own death in 1956.

Browning retained the modernised setting in which the play had been placed, an error which proved more destructive of atmosphere in the film than in the play, which remained enclosed in one house and an outbuilding.

It is difficult, on re-viewing the film nowadays, to see it through the eyes of the early Thirties. The dialogue, even by former standards, is deadeningly slow, and long stretches never break away from the confines of the stage. Much of the camerawork is uninspired and static, though there is one travelling shot, through the Doctor's sanatorium grounds, which is remarkable for those days of enclosed booths. The sea journey to Whitby promises much, but then cuts straight to the finding of the dead crew. Almost every climax, in fact, is cut before it reaches its peak. Even leaving things to the

Hamilton Deane, author of the original stage version of *Dracula.*

imagination can be overdone. The final destruction of Dracula is handled with such reticence that one is unsure of what is happening at all. The epilogue, showing the actor who played the professor (Edward van Sloan) as himself standing in front of a portion of blank screen and warning the audience that there are such things as vampires, does not come off because the audience does not realise that they are supposed to be looking at someone in a cinema talking directly to them. It worked in the theatre because the curtain had fallen and risen again to show the cast in the familiar line-up.

Nevertheless, even when much of the film is written off, enough remains of a kind of macabre poetry to leave a stronger impression in the memory than many slicker examples since. The whole opening sequence is splendid. The young agent arriving in the little mid-European village as the sun sets, the frightened inhabitants shutting themselves up as the light thickens, the clattering old cab, the first sight of the gaunt coachman who takes over for the final part of the journey, the misty ruined castle, the rats and dust, the Count and his three wraith-like concubines grouped on the wide stairs, all this is highly atmospheric, and magnificently photographed by Karl Freund. It is with the start of the Count's dialogue that the magic fails. Even in the rest of the film there are effective moments—the Count's "invisibility" in a silver box, the un-dead Lucy wandering spectre-like in the shadows, the dark arches of Dracula's Hampstead cellar, even the very unlikely London of swirling fogs. The mistiest parts are, in fact, the best; when the lights go up interest goes down. Bela Lugosi was a rather solid vampire, and most of his "shock" appearances consisted in having to stand perfectly still so as to make sure that the spots focussed correctly on his eyes to give them the necessary glare—even so, one of them missed by inches. However, he at least invested the character with formidable dignity and stalked about the West End in his cloak and top-hat with ghastly relish. Dwight Frye was weak in his opening scenes as the agent, but went mad nicely, and Edward van Sloan almost managed to persuade us to believe in vampires—but not quite. For all its weakness the film had Gothic grandeur.

Its success was immediate. Two years later the Count was accorded the signal honour, roughly equivalent at the time to a presentation at Court, of appearing in a Mickey Mouse cartoon. In the next dozen years Dracula appeared in five more films, only the first of which, Dracula's Daughter (1936), had any connection with Bram Stoker, being adapted from his story "Dracula's Guest."

Each sequel was worse than the one before. In 1943 Robert Siodmak (who in 1945 was to direct The Spiral Staircase, a notable essay in claustrophobic terror), was responsible for Son of Dracula. According to him it "had its moments," but they apparently did not add up to very much. Eventually the degradation of the Count was complete, and he appeared in Abbott and Costello Meet Frankenstein.

After that there was a pause. Then in 1957 American-International released a film entitled Blood of Dracula, and in 1958 United Artists issued The Return of Dracula. In neither did the Count appear. In the first, a schoolgirl develops a thirst for blood after a somewhat unusual experiment by her chemistry teacher, and runs mildly amok. In the second, a character named Bellac (played by Francis Lederer) comes to America for the customary purpose and is duly thwarted. Both were spurious "cashings-in" on the great Name.

The real, and apparently everlasting, new lease of life came with the first of the Hammer series, Dracula, directed in 1958 by Terence Fisher, following the considerable financial success of his previous film for the same company, The Curse of Frankenstein. The scenario, by Jimmy Sangster, went back in principle to Bram Stoker's original, but made considerable changes in detail, including a radical alteration in the character of Dracula himself, who lost most of his magical powers such as being able to disappear at will, pass through walls, etc. He retained, however, doubtless with a view to future Hammer box-office receipts, his longevity and powers of resuscitation. Christopher Lee had the advantage over Lugosi of extra height and a generally less solid appearance, and by appearing more normal in his non-vampirical moments, gave his horrific activities an added bite. It is a pity, however, that Fisher's usual determination to be horrid at all costs was allowed such free rein. Any suggestion of dark Gothic mystery—the saving grace of the old version—was sacrificed to an orgy of blood-letting, stake-driving and general mayhem. Where originally the horrors were passed over with such restraint as at times to become unintelligible, here they were dwelt on so lovingly that, paradoxically, the feeling of fear was dissipated, and become either boredom or glee according to temperament. Colour also turned out to be a positive disadvantage. Black and white, or grey, is the stuff for Dracula. More sensibly, the period was put back rather than forward, but unfortunately was far from convincing, particularly in the dialogue. All this admitted, there was much technical brilliance—the final disintegration of Dracula, for

Bela Lugosi as *Dracula.*

instance—and some of the settings were first-rate[1]. Christopher Lee, tall, handsome, with an imposing personality, was to become the Dracula *par excellence,* overshadowing Lugosi both in appearance and in acting ability; but the old Hungarian, who died in unhappy circumstances in 1956, will always retain a warm corner in the hearts of those who remember him as the first screen Count.

Fisher's next Dracula film for Hammer, *The Brides of Dracula,* did not introduce the Count himself, but dealt with a Transylvanian nobleman who had picked up the same unpleasant habits through dissolute living. It was very much a routine picture of its kind, made with the usual Hammer splashes of colour and décor, redeemed by one or two good macabre performances.

[1] Note without comment. When the film was shown in Birmingham an exhibition to recruit blood transfusion donors was planned to be linked to the publicity. The Midland Regional Blood Transfusion Service announced its approval. Forty-one people volunteered to become donors before shocked complaints put an end to the scheme. Some person's life may since have been saved by the gift of one of those forty-one volunteers.

The same director's *Dracula—Prince of Darkness* (1965) followed the same paths—effective, often beautiful, settings, technical competence, Christopher Lee's imposing presence, the period superficially suggested but constantly betrayed by anachronistic dialogue, a nasty dwelling on the repulsive—for instance, in the scene of the revivification of Dracula. The ending, as expected, left the way open for a sequel, which duly arrived (in 1968) as *Dracula Has Risen from the Grave.* The situation is the usual one of frightened villagers, suspicious looks and silences greeting the stranger (a Catholic priest), sinister neighbouring castle, etc., but the film, directed by Freddie Francis, recovered something of the old lost panache. Both opening (bloody body suspended from churchbell clapper) and closing (the Count symbolically impaled on an enormous cross) are grandly grisly, and one or two scenes, such as the long trek of the white-draperied girl following the Count across the countryside, have the true touch of macabre

Christopher Lee in *Dracula Has Risen from the Grave.*

beauty. Interesting also is the emphasis on the sexual basis of vampirism—the victim welcoming the bloodsucker almost as a lover.

Understandably exhausted, Lee remained quietly impaled on his cross for a couple of years or so. Meanwhile, however, the Count made a trip to America to appear, in the person of Alex D'Arcy, in *Blood of Dracula's Castle,* masquerading under the unexciting name of Count Townsend and bringing with him an unlikely wife, Paula Raymond. The story, concerning a young couple who visit an old castle which the man has inherited, unaware of what is lurking in the cellar coffins, is an uneasy mixture of parody and seriousness. The best thing in it is John Carradine's sinister butler. (Carradine has played Dracula himself: in 1966 in a silly affair called *Billy the Kid vs. Dracula* and much earlier, in 1945, in both *House of Frankenstein* and *House of Dracula*—of equally little worth.)

In 1970 Lee's definitive Count was revived (having been reduced to a phial of dried blood) by Peter Sasdy. The film, *Taste the Blood of Dracula,* is a moderately feeble effort, most of the attention being paid to the repressive and perverted activities of a totally unrepresentative Victorian family, with the Count, much reduced, figuratively, in stature, involving himself in the goings-on of a totally unbelievable group of costumed characters, with little eventual satisfaction either for himself or for us. For compensatory titillation the sexual aspect of vampirism is emphasised further, and the film is handsomely mounted: but the strain of what-shall-we-do-with-him-next was becoming woefully apparent.

As if to make up for his two years rest on the cross, Lee's Count made a second film appearance in 1970, in *The Scars of Dracula,* back again with his faithful and remarkably long-suffering peasants. It is interesting to note that the moment in this generally unmemorable film which aroused most comment is when Dracula crawls bat-like (or lizard-like) along his castle wall. This famous peculiarity of the Count's has been strangely neglected in the films—where it would have been so easy to present. It appears in the Prologue in the script of Hamilton Deane's stage play but was never, so far as I know, attempted by him—though when I was a member of his touring Company one of the publicity posters strikingly depicted it.

Though the film was not shown in Britain until three years later, it was in this hat-trick year that Lee also worked in a project that had long been attractive to him. Surfeited with stories that strayed ever further from Stoker's original—and the

Christopher Lee in *Taste the Blood of Dracula*.

further the feebler—he had wanted, before leaving the part finally, to play the Count in a truly representative version. It looked as though the chance had come when Harry Alan Towers produced a film *(Count Dracula—El Conde Dracula),* directed by Jesús Franco, which openly stated its intention of paying the author this long deferred compliment. It is thus particularly unfortunate that the result should have fallen so far below these good intentions. The Babelian confusion of tongues (it was a Spanish/West German/Italian/Lichtensteinian brew), the flat, uninspired direction, the omissions from and distortions to the text despite the high resolve, the general tattiness and at times ludicrously unconvincing *décor*—all these resulted in a dire disappointment. The film is, in fact, a ghastly bore. So abysmally slow is the action in some parts that when I first viewed the film, through a movieola, I thought, watching one interminable silent scene focussed on the mad Renfield, that the machine had gone wrong, and tried speeding things up—until the sound of a voice squeaking several octaves too high revealed my error. One thing stands out high among the wreckage—Lee's dignified, intelligent, convincing portrayal; old and heavily moustached to begin with, recovering youthful vigour with each pint of blood. It has been suggested that the film failed financially because the public would not accept a moustached "Lee-Dracula"; but this is probably to underrate the public's intelligence. Given Lee's skill, experience and knowledge of the character and the book, a really definitive and *accurate* Dracula might have resulted. It was a great opportunity missed.

Lee made two further Dracula films—*Dracula AD 1972* (1972) and *The Satanic Rites of Dracula*

The female vampire at work: Anoushka Hempel in *Scars of Dracula*.

Christopher Lee's other self: *Scars of Dracula.*

(1973): the latter title substituted, mercifully, for *Dracula is Dead and Well and Living in London.* The first is set in Chelsea among the trendies of the period. The second presents the Count as an industrial millionaire involved with black magic, a plague virus and world domination. Both play havoc with the probabilities, and both decline to dusty death.

A very strange affair, of which details are scarce, emerged from an American studio in 1970, entitled *Guess What Happened to Count Dracula.* One never would! Apparently he went to Hollywood, grew tired of his girlfriend (charmingly named Vamp), made a sort of Faustian deal with an out-of-work actor for a new girlfriend (Angelica), clashed with a rival vampire (Imp), and finished up, after ruining the out-of-work actor, in happy eternity with his Angelica.

Countess Dracula (1971) is quite an effective shocker, with Ingrid Pitt giving a bravura performance as an ageing Countess (based on the real

Sixteenth-century Elizabeth Bathory) who finds that virgin blood taken internally is an effective rejuvenator; but it has no right whatever to the use of the Count's name as a box-office lure. The only reference is in the closing shot, when a group of village women, watching the villainess being led away to her just deserts, mutter at us from the screen: "Countess Dracula—Countess Dracula . . . " A specious bit of name-dropping if ever there was one.

Dracula versus Frankenstein (or, if preferred, *El hombre que vino de ummo*), turned up in 1969, a piece of sci-fi-horror nonsense in which Things from Another World attempt to use various renowned monsters to take control of the world: a Spanish/West German/Italian dubbed monstrosity with the unfortunate Michael Rennie caught in the middle of it.

Jack Palance may seem an unexpected choice for the Count, but is rather surprisingly successful in a 1974 *Dracula* set in period and retaining the

Ingrid Pitt as Elizabeth Bathory before rejuvenation, in *Countess Dracula*.

names of such characters as appear from the original. Otherwise, by courtesy of Richard Matheson, scriptwriter, it is far from Bram. Matheson, however, who is among the most famous and skilful of all screen horror writers, almost excuses his liberties by the interest he arouses in his own treatment of the story. Dracula is presented with unusual sympathy, given historical motivation for much of his irregularities, and generally presented as a character as well as a menace. The film was originally made for American television, but was shown in Britain on the cinema screen.

It was probably inevitable that Andy Warhol (as presenter) and Paul Morrissey (as director) would feel impelled to "have a go" at Dracula, as they had already done at Frankenstein's monster. The Count, who has engaged a manservant named Anton, visits Italy in search of virgin's blood, and there goes through much the usual series of events, but treated in the schoolboyish anything-to-shock-you manner which might be expected, with scenes such as the Count graphically vomiting up non-virginal blood, and a prolonged climactic body-axing sequence. The film contains one surprise—whatever is Vittorio De Sica doing in this farrago?

Countess Dracula, after her rejuvenating draught of virgin blood.

Victim prepared but vampire thwarted: Jack Palance as *Dracula*.

A black vampire launched on his career by the old Count himself suggests intriguing possibilities—but alas, *Blacula* and *Scream, Blacula, Scream* follow well-trodden paths—only the colouring is changed. The first opens in 1815 with an African potentate trying to persuade Dracula to help end the slave trade—a somewhat optimistic hope, one might think. Instead, the Count—as we all knew he would—turns the African and his wife into vampires themselves. The rest, with a few variations, is depressingly predictable.

At the time of writing it seems that the Count is surely drained dry. A rest for a few years—without the painful impairments and other hazards he has undergone for so many years—might enable the film-makers to inject new blood into him, with revitalising results.

Frankenstein

In the same way that he was the real starting-point of the Dracula saga on stage and screen, so Hamilton Deane had a considerable share in setting Frankenstein and his monster off on their equally chequered career. Though a one-reeler was produced by Edison in 1910 (with Charles Ogle), and another little-known version was made in 1915 (with Percy Standing) it was not until after Deane's stage version (in which he himself played the monster) that the famous Universal picture was created.

*   *   *

The stage play, bloodthirstily adapted by a gentle little grey-haired lady called Peggy Webling, did not repeat the material success of *Dracula*, but was in many ways a better piece of work. It was set in the correct period, and aimed at being more than a mere thriller. Deane's performance was masterly by any standards. He brought out to the full the pity as well as the terror of the tormented creature—a dimension increasingly lost sight of as the American series degenerated from James Whale's fine first conception to mere sensationalism and final burlesque.

Whale was an Englishman who worked during his early years in the British theatre. He first became known in connection with R.C. Sheriff's *Journey's End*, and left for Hollywood to direct the film version. *Frankenstein* followed in 1931, and the first Count Frankenstein (Colin Clive) had played a leading part in the former picture. Whale's *Frankenstein* stands up to the test of time considerably better than Browning's *Dracula*, in spite of a similar error in bringing the period up to date, the same stiff dullness in the "normal" scenes and characters, and some unbelievable junketings by extremely unconvincing mid-European peasants.

Colin Clive has some good moments of high melodrama, and, with his drawn, tormented face, really does manage to convey something of the driven, possessed mania of the creator, speaking lines such as "That body is not dead; it has never lived!" with a fine apocalyptic fervour.

Hamilton Deane as *Frankenstein's* monster in his stage production (written by Peggy Webling) at the Little Theatre, London, 1930.

Three film faces of *Frankenstein's* monster: Charles Ogle (1910) (above), Karloff (page 38), Christopher Lee (page 39).

The film opens with low-angle shots of grave-stones in a louring dusk, a scene often repeated but rarely bettered. Frankenstein's experiments take place in an extremely high tower, an imposing set of which the camera makes the most with a variety of angled and tracking shots. The familiar apparatus is all around, but electrodes and transformers rather than test-tubes and retorts. The actual bestowing of life, in a raging storm, is thrillingly done, reminiscent in its beauty of the electric sparks and rings of *Metropolis*. At the height of the storm the trestle bearing the creature is slowly raised an immense height to an opening in the tower roof, remaining there viewed from below while the lightning glares and the storm thunders. As it is lowered the elements quieten as if their purpose was accomplished. By this treatment Whale generates a feeling of something larger than man-making-monster, as if a lifeless being had been offered up to Nature, and received the highest of all her gifts. As the trestle comes to ground, the inert hand gives its first quiver of life.

The first sight of Karloff, despite its over-familiarity nowadays, still manages to shock. His gaunt features and dark-socketed eyes have a true charnel-house appearance which is missing not only from subsequent monsters but from his own later fuller-faced recreations. More remarkable is the

sympathy he creates beneath all the familiar trappings of horror. It is, indeed, more than sympathy—a tragic sense of human potentiality wasted, destroyed by a lack of understanding which leads so quickly to panic and disaster. Almost his first movement is to lift his clumsy mis-shapen hands in slow wonder towards the light pouring in from the roof where he received life. At once, symbolically, Frankenstein closes the shutter, and a few minutes later the other light—that of burning fire—starts the trail of destruction. The reactions of the watchers, Frankenstein's revulsion, his companions' disbelieving wonder, a general sense of barely controlled panic, all these are wonderfully conveyed, and indeed the whole sequence is as powerful now as thirty-five years ago.

The film never regains equal heights after the abysmal plunge into the inanities of the wedding preparations and the rest of the village nonsense, but one or two further episodes deserve mention. The scene of the drowning of the little girl was cut on the original release, a piece of senseless censorship if ever there was one. The monster, lost, hated and raging, comes upon the small child by a lakeside. She is the only being not to shrink from him with loathing, and asks him to play with her. They throw flowers into the water, watching them float. Expecting her to float as beautifully as the flowers, the monster picks her up and throws her in among them. The girl drowns and the monster, half-understanding, staggers away. The scene, which could have been so sentimental and embarrassing, is handled with such restraint by Whale, and played with such sympathy by Karloff, that no falsity mars it. Karloff's final departure, wringing his hands in an agony of dawning comprehension, is as moving a moment as any on the screen. Whale had the subtlety to choose an *ugly* little girl (with, alas, an even uglier accent), which added pathos to the episode. It is, in reality, the climax of the film, and all the more effective in that we are not invited to watch the child's death struggles, water bubbling from her lips, eyes glazing, and all the rest of the latter-day stock-in-trade. The censoring of the last part of the scene, whereby the audience is not even aware of what the monster does to the girl, merely invites far more lurid imaginings than the truth when the dead body is discovered. The father's progress, stony-faced, through the dancing villagers, with the small body in his arms, was also impressively handled.

The ultimate tracking down of the monster took place among mountain passes and ridges patently studio-made, but so atmospherically lit and composed that this was not difficult to forgive. The

Boris Karloff (1931).

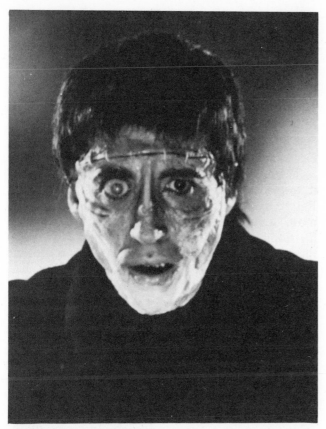
Christopher Lee (1957).

new character, a Doctor whose hobby is keeping little people in large jam-jars (played with splendid relish by Ernest Thesiger), insists that Frankenstein should provide his monster—who, to our not very great astonishment, escaped from the burning windmill—with a mate. He does so, and she proves a far more attractive creature than his own insipid choice. The film, which contains several scenes of even greater power than the earlier film, reaches its climax in Elsa Lanchester's amazing performance. Her appearance, despite its cold inhumanity and the visible scars where she had been sewn together, is strikingly beautiful, with more than a slight resemblance to the famous head of Queen Nefertiti. With her frizzed, up-drawn, white streaked hair, her enormous flashing eyes, her quick darting movements, she is like some sparkling personification of electricity—Electra herself.

The third picture, the last in which Karloff appeared as the monster, was *The Son of Frankenstein* (1939), directed by Rowland V. Lee. We have now moved on a generation, but the monster is still there, ready for reincarnation. The film had its moments, notably a nice chilling performance by Bela Lugosi as a murderer who was hanged but survived, broken-necked, to wreak his vengeance.

torch-lit groups of converging and diverging search-parties, the baying dogs and distant summonses, the confrontation of Frankenstein with his creation, the final conflagration in the windmill—for once a justified and not merely convenient way of removing the villain—all these still remain exciting cinema. But the great quality which Whale brought to *Frankenstein* was dignity. A dignity of treatment; a respect, not only for the "normal" people, not only for the monster, but for the whole inherent significance of his subject. Despite its many weaknesses, there is in this early *Frankenstein* a largeness of purpose, a hint of the grandeur of mysteries beyond our knowledge.

Three years later, in 1935, James Whale also directed the first of the many sequels, *The Bride of Frankenstein*. The fact that Frankenstein himself had a bride, and was also to make one for his creature, is probably largely responsible for the confusion which has persisted ever since as to whether the name refers to man or monster. In the stage version the creature was always spoken to as "Frankenstein" because of the necessity of developing a play through dialogue. One could hardly, without grave discourtesy address even a synthetic being to his face as "Monster," or "Thing." Already Mary Shelley has been left far behind. A

Elsa Lanchester as the monster's mate in *The Bride of Frankenstein*.

Thereafter James Whale's great original joined Dracula on the sad path to the Abbott and Costello travesty.

As in the case of Dracula, and actually anticipating the vampire by a year, a new Frankenstein series was launched from the Hammer studios. *The Curse of Frankenstein* (1957) was the first, directed by Terence Fisher. It was an immense commercial success. The story was set in roughly the correct period, but convincing historical atmosphere is not to be engendered merely by dressing up actors in whiskers and stocks. Apart from settings and photography, which were effective, the film was unremarkable. Christopher Lee, obviously hampered by an extremely uncomfortable make-up (different, for copyright reasons, from the original Karloff one) managed to infuse pathos, if not menace, into the monster, but script and dialogue were weak, and once again over-indulgence in sensationalism defeated its own purpose. Peter Cushing, a most sympathetic and subtle player, started on his long series of failed experiments as Frankenstein.

With *The Revenge of Frankenstein* the sad story continues. Frankenstein now calls himself Dr. Stein, and at the end of the film reappears from hiding as Victor Frank. So little connection with the original in either fact or spirit remains that there seems little point, apart from publicity value, in retaining the title name at all. In the same year Boris Karloff appeared in an American film, *Frankenstein 1970,* playing a descendant of the original Baron. It was a feeble affair, making no attempt at a convincing futuristic world—in fact, just one more hack shocker.

In *The Evil of Frankenstein* (1964) the monster, played by Kiwi Kingston, returned more or less to the original Karloff make-up but the resemblance was merely superficial. The rest was routine.

In *Frankenstein Created Woman* (1966), the indestructible Baron has a second shot at creating a female, but it is a sad come-down from his first attempt. Though he is now after souls as well as bodies, it is a minor piece of work since he has merely to resuscitate an already more or less complete corpse. Admittedly a good deal of grafting is called for to insert the soul of her wrongly executed lover into the girl's body and at the same time to cure her lameness. It all goes wrong once again, however; the girl runs amok and finally kills herself, and Frankenstein realises that yet another experiment has bitten the dust. Will the man *never* bring anything off successfully? Not, at any rate, in *Frankenstein Must Be Destroyed* (1969), where he cannot even manage a simple

brain transplant without provoking his usual cataclysm of madness, murders and burning buildings. What makes the feebleness of this effort the more disappointing is that a germ of a serious and important theme appears briefly in the genuinely moving scene between the pathetic transplantee and his horrified wife. The film, however, contains one memorable moment, when a gentleman expresses his (and our) astonishment at finding the Baron *still* in residence.

The Seventies opened with Hammer still hard at it monster-making. In *Horror of Frankenstein* Ralph Bates took over (as "Viktor") but with no more success scientifically, and a good deal less histrionically. This was the fault of the script rather than the actor, who was required to turn the man into a trendily sex-obsessed fumbler. The monster he produced (David Prowse) was about worthy of him.

Canada, Italy and America all entered the creature-creating stakes, with *Frankenstein on Campus* (1969, seen in Britain 1971), *Lady Frankenstein* (1971) and *Blood of Frankenstein* (1970) respectively, the Italian effort featuring Joseph Cotten. The best that can be said of any of them is that all concerned get their just deserts, though taking a tedious time to do so. In terms of the abysmal, first place must go to *Blood of Franken-*

Further monsters:
David Prowse in *The Horror of Frankenstein.*

40

stein, which brings in Dracula and a mad Zombie and degrades everyone involved.

With *Frankenstein and the Monster from Hell* (1973), we return to Hammer, and Peter Cushing's latest effort to date to bring at least one "scientific" project to a successful conclusion. Organ transplantation seems to have taken over from complete assemblages, but otherwise the train of events moves along depressingly familiar rails. For a change, however, the monster is torn to pieces by lunatics. As always, Peter Cushing plays his part with dignity and integrity, bringing to the film a touch of quality which it otherwise sadly lacks.

Two very different parodies must be mentioned, but need not long detain us. *Flesh for Frankenstein* (1973), an Italian/French "English version". production from Warhol and Morrissey had its puerility originally accentuated by 3-D, but looked as nasty flat. *Young Frankenstein* (1974), with the always likeable Gene Wilder as the Baron's grandson, has some quite witty and some hilarious moments, but seems oddly unsure of itself, and finishes up on the whole rather less laughable

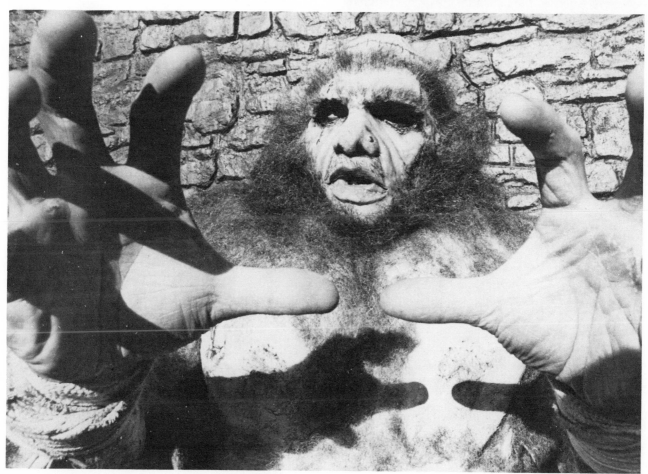

And also in *Frankenstein and the Monster from Hell.*

(though also less tedious) than some of the "serious" versions. Mel Brooks directed.

Finally—*Frankenstein—The True Story*—labelled a British film (1973, directed by Jack Smight), but in fact a condensation into some two hours of a television film of more than twice as long made for America. Boldly claiming to be a return to the original, it is, of course, nothing of the sort. Neither characters, nor incidents, nor settings, nor purpose approximate to Mary Shelley's classic horror/morality. Prestige is written large over all: script by Christopher Isherwood and Don Bachardy; cast graced by such members of the illustrious Pantheon as Sir John Gielgud, Sir Ralph Richardson, Mr. James Mason, Miss Margaret Leighton.

With such claims the film was bound to come up against a certain amount of prejudged criticism. It is very probable that the truncation of the film badly upset the balance of the story: better perhaps to have shown it fully, in two parts. In its present form it is oddly disproportionate, moving erratically from overlong scenes to jerky, apparently cut ones. Even so, there are striking sequences—such as the ballroom episode, culminating in a "synthetic" girl's head being torn off her neck before the understandably astonished dancers—a moment so powerfully handled that even the audience's shock-laughter is muted. There is also some fine art and special effects work (by Wilfrid Shingleton and Roy Whybrow), and a striking, if overlong, climax among the icefloes. Perhaps the most original touch was that of making the "creature" a handsome young man whose flesh gradually deteriorates into foulness. This basic idea has, of course, been used before, and an obvious resemblance to *The Picture of Dorian Gray* has been generally remarked on by critics; but the dreadful situation in which the unhappy, disintegrating being (played with great sympathy by Michael Sarrazin) finds itself, gives a depth of pathos to the story rarely witnessed since Boris Karloff first raised his heavy hands towards the light.

*   *   *

Reviewing in the mind's eye the whole series of Frankenstein films, in every single case of which the man-made creature runs amok and brings death and destruction to all and sundry (and particularly to mid-European peasants), one is left obsessed by a fundamental query. *Why* does the Baron—or his associate—always make the monster so LARGE—and so MUSCULAR? Why not a weak-kneed monster, just to begin with at any rate, on whom the creator could practise methods of control, and even perhaps teach a modicum of civilised behaviour? One cannot but feel that, with appalling catastrophe following appalling catastrophe, anyone who goes stubbornly on putting together these great lumbering super-muscular menaces is culpably stupid and deserves all he gets. He should also be severely reprimanded for all the trouble he causes to others—particularly mid-European peasants.

5. Three Early Sound Horror Classics

At about the same time as Browning's *Dracula* the Dane Carl Dreyer produced and directed his film *Vampyr* (English title *The Strange Adventures of David Gray*), dealing with a similar subject but in so vastly different a style as to make any comparisons between them pointless. This strange, unique film is the supreme example of horror sensed rather than seen, evil suggested rather than exposed. The story (very freely adapted from Sheridan Le Fanu) concerns a young man, David Gray, who comes to spend a night in a lonely inn. The location is vague but has a somewhat Swiss or Austrian (or Transylvanian?) character. In the middle of the night—a weird, non-dark, creeping night—a stranger slips into his room and gives him a parcel, telling him to open it should the stranger die. The following day David Gray visits a *château*, after a strange interlude in a white building full of flickering shadows and odd, briefly glimpsed characters, and a meeting with a doctor and an apparently pleasant old lady. Everything is misty, shifting, uncertain. In the *château* he meets the owner, who turns out to be the man who has left him the package, and also his two daughters, one of whom is suffering from a strange wasting illness. Also about the place are two servants. Shortly afterwards the owner is mysteriously shot dead. Gray opens the parcel and uncovers a book on vampires and how to destroy them. Meanwhile we have learnt that the old lady is herself a vampire and responsible, it seems—with the doctor's connivance—for the illness of the elder daughter, Léonie. Odd, indefinite encounters take place between the younger girl and David Gray. Later, Léonie is lured out into the woods and again attacked. The young man offers his blood for transfusion. By now, however, Léonie herself is becoming infected with vampirism. As if in some way the donation of his blood somehow links him with her, he sees himself, in a dream, screwed down in a coffin and carried out to be buried alive. He awakes from this

nightmare and, with the aid of one of the servants, opens the old lady's coffin and drives the customary stake through her heart. The doctor is, somewhat arbitrarily, trapped in a cage in a mill and drowned in white flour, leaving David and the younger daughter, Gisèle, to drift away in a boat through a misty sunshine.

No outline of the vague, deliberately confused story (never clearly defined) can convey anything of the extraordinary atmosphere engendered by the film. The conventional trappings of horror are not displayed, except in one or two incidents such as the squeaky screwing down of the coffin, the older girl's attack on her sister, and one or two shots of individuals such as the doctor. All else is done by hints and suggestions. Shadows have apparently no solid counterparts; weird unexplained sounds are heard, such as barking dogs and crying children where none exist; characters appear and disappear without reason or motive; at any moment, one feels, buildings and persons are liable to dissolve into mist. Only evil itself is real—and that is invisible. In the dream sequence the camera becomes briefly objective. We look up with David Gray's eyes from the coffin, through a little glass window, as the lid is screwed down and the old vampire woman stares fixedly down at us—we are carried out staring up at the passing trees.

Herman Melville in *Moby Dick* speaks of the horror of whiteness. Whiteness is one of the results of loss of blood, and Dreyer makes full use of it in his film on the blood-sucking vampire. White buildings, white mist, the terrible death of the doctor, drowning in white flour. *Vampyr* is a pale film.

In his monograph on Dreyer (British Film Institute, 1950), Ebbe Neergaard gives some interesting details of the making of the film. No sets were built. The inn was a real inn, the *château* a deserted castle specially hired (the film was made in France), the building with the dancing shadows

A pale film—*Vampyr*.

Sybille Schmitz in *Vampyr*.

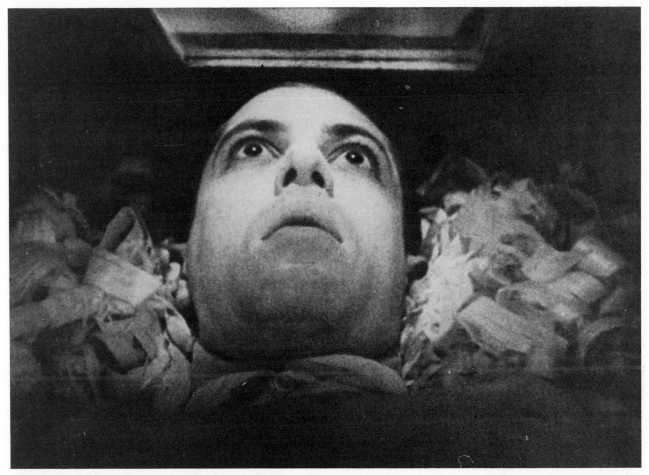

Vampyr: **David Gray (Julian West) inside the coffin.**

a derelict ice-factory. The discovery of a plaster works decided the ending of the story. Originally the doctor was to have sunk in a morass, until one day Dreyer came across his white dust-covered building, and in a moment of inspiration altered his first plan. On such small happenings may the manner of our death depend. It was, perhaps, owing to this sudden change that the doctor's death—however effective in itself—seem arbitrarily contrived.

Vampyr has been both over-praised and over-attacked. On the one hand, its inadequacies have been treated as merits, on the other, its story has been accused (by Paul Rotha) of obscure mysticism, its photography of meretriciousness. Rotha, indeed, regards it as "very much of a museum piece" *(The Film Till Now).* Its great failing, apparently, was to have been applauded by the intelligentsia.

It is, however, no more obscure than many an accepted poem (which it somewhat resembles) or piece of music, and its so-called mysticism need trouble nobody anxious to enjoy the film as an essay in the vague macabre. Where it does fail is in

the extreme poorness of most of the performances. Only one character, Léonie, was played by a professional actress, all the others being chosen by Dreyer, according to Neergaard, for their "mental resemblance." It is a pity this mental accord could not have been translated into action. Non-actors and non-acting in fictional films is often, of course, successful (though not, I venture to suggest, as often as is sometimes claimed), but in examples such as this, where strong and sustained emotion need portraying, and where long uninterrupted scenes preclude the possibility of quick cutting to conceal deficiencies, the skill of the professional is essential. David Gray himself (played by Julian West, otherwise Baron Nicolas de Gunzburg, significantly the backer of the film) is, though a pleasant-looking young man, particularly weak, and his hamming and lack of self-discipline are mainly responsible for the derision with which some parts of the film are apt to be received nowadays.

The loss suffered by the film from this lack of professional skill is pointed by the one big scene where the protagonist *is* a professional—Léonie's

45

attack on her sister. Despite our present-day over-familiarity with the snarling appearance of the vampirical pointed teeth, the strength of Sybille Schmitz is sufficient to send the authentic shiver along the spine.

Rotha is to some extent correct in labelling the film as a museum piece, but it is, after all, in museums that items of value are kept, and despite its weaknesses *Vampyr,* with its white, diffused, shifting mystery and its brooding sense of unseen malevolence, is undoubtedly a film worthy of such preservation. It was over eleven years before Dreyer made another film (the grimly beautiful *Day of Wrath* (1943), which has affinities with *Vampyr*), and the loss of creative activity during this long period can only be deplored by any lover of the cinema.

*

Rouben Mamoulian's is not a name which springs naturally to the mind as a director of horror films. In his early years in Hollywood he was remarkable rather for his pioneer work in releasing the sound camera from its subservience to "canned theatre" (ironically, he came to the cinema as an already renowned theatre director), and for the freshness and beauty of his imagery and shot composition. However, his one essay in the *genre, Dr. Jekyll and Mr. Hyde* (1932), is not only the most horrific but also much the best of the various versions of Stevenson's over-adapted classic. Unfortunately the copy occasionally shown nowadays, in the National Film Theatre or on television, is a mangled one. The opening sequence, and a very important, if brief, moment later on when a cat kills a bird singing in a tree, are both cut. We should, I suppose, be grateful for the chance to see even an imperfect version of a rare masterpiece, but such vandalism is wholly deplorable.

The well-known story is inevitably but not outrageously embellished, the atmosphere of time and place is caught sufficiently well not to jolt our

Fredric March in Mamoulian's *Dr. Jekyll and Mr. Hyde.*

Fredric March transformed as Hyde in *Dr. Jekyll and Mr. Hyde.*

suspension of disbelief, and where extravagances occur (it is doubtful whether Dr. Jekyll would have had a full-size organ in his house or if he had, whether he would have got far into his fortissimo Bach fugues without neighbourly protests), they are used to such good effect that they are easy to forgive.

For its period the film is extremely venturesome technically, both in the mobility of the camera and the imaginative use of sound. During most of the opening sequence the subjective camera was used. Though not of course by any means the first use of such a device (one need only cite Murnau's *The Last Laugh* or the ordeal of David Gray in his coffin in *Vampyr* as random examples), it is doubtful if it had been used for so extended a sequence hitherto—at any rate with such success. The film opens to the sound of a Bach fugue on the organ. The opening shot is a close-up of the music and Jekyll's (our) hands on the keyboard. The devoted manservant (a part beautifully played by Edgar Norton) brings hat and cloak, handing them direct to the camera. We walk through our house to the mirror in the hall—briefly glance at ourselves as we put on our hat—we leave the house, preceded by the figure of the servant as he opens

the door, climb shakily into the carriage, are joltily driven along, the coachman's back looming blackly ahead of us, and so through the jostling students into the Hall.

There the camera does a complete revolution and, snap on the first spoken word—"Gentlemen!" cuts to the back of the auditorium, looking down on the Doctor himself. It is a beautifully neat shift from the subjective to the objective viewpoint. Whether this long sequence has the effect (which Mamoulian has said he wanted) of drawing us into Jekyll's brain, is open to question, but undoubtedly it most effectively increases the tension and curiosity to see from outside the man who we know is later to turn into a monster before our eyes.

Mamoulian's gift for beautifully lit and composed camerawork is frequently in evidence, notably in this opening sequence in Jekyll's house, and also later in the same setting when, assured of his engagement to Muriel Carew, he runs to the organ and pours out his exultation in music. Such a scene could easily topple over into the ridiculous, but Mamoulian manages to create such a joyous radiance in a succession of brief shots (particularly telling is a large close-up of the wrinkled, devoted, smiling face of the old servant), that we are wholly attracted into sharing it. There are few occasions when sheer happiness has been so successfully and yet so simply captured on the screen.

Anyone watching *Dr. Jekyll and Mr. Hyde* is, of course, waiting for "the change." Even by today's standards, Mamoulian's contrivance is masterly. The camera, becoming briefly subjective again, slowly approaches a mirror on the Doctor's laboratory. The potion is drunk, to the expected, but discreetly restrained, choking and gasping. Then, with no cuts, no dissolves, the transformation begins. Lines and shadows etch themselves into Jekyll's face. In an interview in 1961 *(Sight and Sound)*, Mamoulian said he had never disclosed how this was done, and never would. It is clearly an extremely ingenious use of lighting. An explanation I have read (I must confess ignorance of its authenticity but it is at least very possible) is that these first lines and shadows were painted beforehand on Fredric March's face, in red. The preliminary scene in the mirror was shot with red filters over the lights, thus killing the shadows. At the appropriate moment the filters were removed, and the lines and shadings appeared—as simply as that.*

*Meeting Rouben Mamoulian some time after these words appeared in the previous edition of this book, I challenged him on this point. His comment was: "No comment."

Almost immediately the camera turns from the mirror and starts to revolve—slowly at first then with increasing speed until it is spinning round the room and everything becomes a blur. Simultaneously the famous sound effects begin. Mamoulian's own heartbeats, a struck gong with the moment of impact cut off and the vibrations reversed, light frequencies photographed on to the soundtrack. For all the ingenious noises which have been created in films since, it is doubtful if this effect has ever been surpassed in hypnotic menace. An extraordinary sense of claustrophobic muffledness was felt, as if indeed our ears had been stuffed with cotton wool so that we heard the thumps of our own heart, the singing in our own brain. Gradually the rotary movement slows down, the sound quietens. The camera stops, not looking into the mirror. We are looking at the laboratory—just as it was—nothing, apparently changed. But we ourselves? There is no sound, except for Jekyll's (our) laboured breathing. Slowly the camera approaches the mirror. It is a magnificent build-up, and it speaks well for March's make-up and performance that the first revelation of Hyde is not a disappointment.

The subsequent changes (throughout the film the suspense of not knowing just *when* the changes may occur is extremely cleverly sustained) are equally well managed. Aware that no repeat can equal the full effect of the first transformation, Mamoulian makes no attempt to do so. All the others are much briefer, or appear to be, except possibly the first change back to Jekyll. One very effective transformation takes place in evening light in the park. Jekyll, on his way to an important dinner at his fiancée's house, and a little early, sits down beneath a tree to watch a nightingale—in fact to quote Keats at it, "Thou wast not made for death, immortal bird . . ." A cat creeps along the bough, and, amid Jekyll's horrified protests, slaughters the bird. Despite his revulsion, the sight of cruelty breaks through his weakened defences—a close-up of his hands shows them becoming mis-shapen, brutal and coarse—and Hyde is in power again. An unlucky cut in the Danish copy deleted the cat's appearance (and, as far as I can remember, the Keats also), so that Hyde's triumph appeared to be arbitrary and unmotivated. As his hunched figure lopes across the shadowy park, growing smaller and smaller towards the top left corner of the screen, a diagonal "wipe", sloping towards that corner, reveals Muriel and her family anxiously and indignantly wondering a young Jekyll's non-arrival—a most effective use of this now outmoded device. Each successive

change is made to reveal a further deterioration in Hyde's character and the final mask of horror which appears when he is at last cornered in his laboratory is anything but an anti-climax. The first "contra-transformation" from Hyde to Jekyll in the office of his horrified friend is also admirably approached and achieved.

The various scenes of Hyde's misdeeds are satisfyingly garish and rowdy, but his brutalities are treated with restraint and at no time is there a feeling of cruelty enjoyed or displayed for its own sake. Notable is the murder of the prostitute he has drawn into his power, "Champagne Ivy" (Miriam Hopkins in a brave if not wholly successful attempt at a pathetic cockney slut). Hyde forces the girl to sing to him. We hear, but do not see her. Then suddenly he bends over her, also disappearing out of camera. The song ceases abruptly. There is a long silence, while the camera rests motionless on a florid bedpost carving. Then, slowly, Hyde rises into view. The deed is accomplished.

Fredric March's performance, in both parts, is masterly. Despite being hidden behind increasingly heavy make-up his Hyde never becomes merely a figure of horror, but manages to show glimpses of the tortured Jekyll behind the fiend, and as Jekyll he conveys not only the charming and upright exterior, but also the relentless pride, the curiosity of Adam, the *hubris* which drags him to his downfall. As Hyde, too, his leapings and jerky, grimacing movements suggest the atavistic return to ape-ish animalism once the restraints of human nature are removed.

The film has its absurdities. Hyde's later appearances, however effective as shock, would surely have led to his apprehension even in the foggy streets of late Victorian London, if not to his immurement in the zoological gardens. There are one or two misjudgments of timing and reactions which today appeal too strongly to the sense of the ridiculous. On the whole, however, this is a noteworthy horror classic, not least because in addition to shocking it elicits our sympathy—thanks to the performances of March, Miriam Hopkins and in particular Edgar Norton.

*

In 1930 Tod Browning had started the Hollywood horror cycle of the early thirties and launched Count Dracula on his astonishing and unforeseeable career. Two years later he made a film which has ever since remained (and undoubtedly always will remain) unique of its kind—*Freaks*. The story is simple. Cleopatra, a fine,

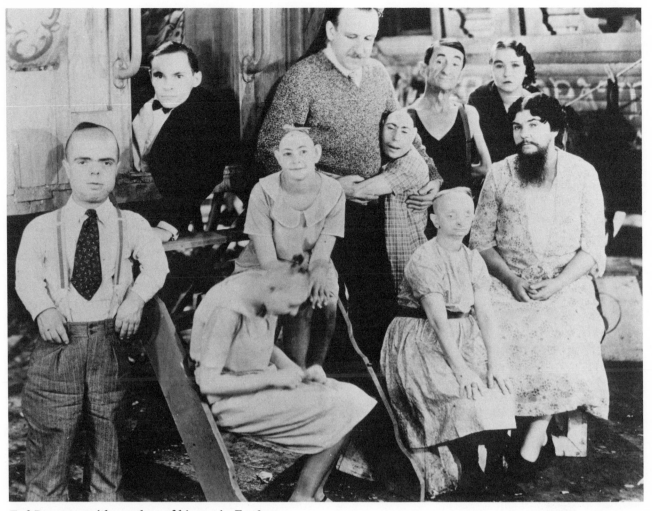

Tod Browning with members of his cast in *Freaks*.

handsome young woman, is a trapeze artiste in a small and rather grubby circus which relies mainly for its attraction on a collection of human oddities—midgets, "pin-heads," Siamese twins, a bearded lady among others. Much the same sort of attraction, in fact, which the later and ever more lurid horror films set out to exploit. Hans, a midget, is engaged to a girl of his kind, Frieda, but is drawn towards Cleopatra. That Browning has avoided making such a desire appear perverted, and has in fact throughout commanded our sympathy and understanding, is a measure of the sensitivity with which he handles so delicate a situation. Cleopatra, in reality the lover of the strong man Hercules, plays Hans along for a while as a cruelly amusing joke—until she discovers that he has financial prospects. Thereupon, with the connivance of Hercules, she plans to marry Hans and then to poison him and obtain the money. At the wedding ceremony, however, she is unable to conceal her abhorrence and revulsion. With a kind

of horrible and reckless glee she taunts and humiliates Hans before the others. They at last realise the truth and band together to protect him and revenge themselves. Their method is appalling. Throughout the film Browning stresses the solidarity among the band of freaks—an attack on one is an attack on all.

In this extraordinary film Browning has turned the popular convention of horror topsy-turvy. It is the ordinary, the apparently normal, the beautiful which horrify—the monstrous and distorted which compel our respect, our sympathy, ultimately our affection. The visible beauty conceals the unseen evil, the visible horror is the real goodness. As is well known, Browning used real circus freaks for the film. He also showed his cunning in selecting the Russian-bearded lady's baby, with a pin-head lady's new dress and her pathetic pride, with other homely incidents of their wandering life. Even the skill with which they overcome their various disabilities is played down and demonstrated quite

49

casually, in order to break down the sense of strangeness.

All this, of course, is building up the atmosphere and frame of mind for the horrifying climax, when strangeness and terror do take over and we are made to realise just what power the apparently helpless and handicapped can command when united for a common and unswerving purpose. Leading up to this is the long wedding banquet scene, the real turning point of the film. On either side of the long table the freaks joke, laugh and celebrate. At the head sit Cleopatra and Hans. The party grows rowdier—weird songs are chanted celebrating their mutual acceptance. In subtle touches, emphasising the differences rather than (as hitherto) the resemblances between the freaks and the "normal"—that is, presumably, ourselves— a hint of nightmare and menace is introduced. Cleopatra is less and less able, even in her own interests, to conceal her loathing and repugnance. She becomes increasingly insulting to her little bridegroom, eventually carrying him about the room on her splendid shoulders, parading him in front of the now angered and disillusioned company.

Thereafter the horror mounts quickly. All the infamous plans of Cleopatra and Hercules are spied on by secret eyes. Figures scuttle away under circus caravans, dodge behind wheels—always watching. Eventually, in a night of storm and mud, the freaks attack. The nerves of the plotters give way, they try frantically to escape, running to and fro in a blind screaming panic. Everything is confusion—a dark, wild, pelting downpour, slithering mud, scurrying figures, knives, wheels, shapeless objects of terror.

The sequence ends indefinitely. We do not know the outcome. An epilogue shows the circus at a much later date, on a bright day, bustling with spectators. Slowly the camera approaches a small enclosed pit, climbs the canvas wall, and tips to look down on what is inside.

The ending has been criticised as anti-climactic, unconvincing, a trick of make-up—but though later one may wonder just how the freaks managed to reduce the beautiful woman to so fearful and truncated an object without killing her, at the moment the effect is truly shattering. Here was a case where suggestion alone would not have sufficed. Justice had to be *seen* to have been done, and the sight revealed that it was indeed a terrible one. Even in these over-monstrous days, even when one has previously seen the still (a mistake, surely, to have thus anticipated the sight), it is not easy to forget the slow movement of the camera down towards that crouching, limbless, faintly moving figure, clawed, and covered with feathers.

Freaks was banned in this country until 1963, and certain aspects of it—the stilted dialogue, the style of some of the acting—have been somewhat unfairly criticised by the standards of today. (How will these standards appear in 1966?). On the whole, however, it is acknowledged to be a remarkable work. Amidst the flood of horror films offering monsters of every kind—one after another endeavouring to outdo its predecessors in dreadfulness—it is strange to see a film made thirty years previously hinting that normal people gaping at monstrosity may in fact be the more monstrous.

The film was a financial failure, and Browning never again achieved similar heights of macabre originality. He made a few unimportant films. *Mark of the Vampire* (1935) was a mere tracing of *Dracula,* and *The Devil Doll* equally unmemorable. His last film was *Miracles for Sale* (1939). Thereafter he retired, dying in 1962 at the age of eighty.

One interesting speculation remains: what would our reaction to *Freaks* have been had Browning used, for his circus creatures, made-up "normal" actors and actresses?

6. Val Lewton and the Forties Cycle

Val (Vladimir) Lewton was born in Yalta in 1904 and died in America in 1951. He was at one time a script editor and a writer. When RKO in 1942 decided to take a chance on a series of inexpensive macabre pictures, Lewton was engaged as producer. Following the totally unexpected success of the first film, *The Cat People,* he built up a considerable reputation as a producer of highly atmospheric and imaginative "B" pictures, mainly in the fantasy school. He was described in his obituary as a "producer of high-grade, low-budget movies," and more than most producers, as against directors, he has left his own mark on any film for which he was responsible. His costume films *(The Body Snatcher, Bedlam)* were notable for attention to period and for giving the viewer the "feel" of the times. His contemporary thrillers were written, directed, edited and photographed with an imaginative dignity and feeling for the medium which have stood the test of time remarkably well.

The idea for *The Cat People* grew from the title. Someone at a party suggested to Jacques Tourneur that he should make a film called The Cat People. Tourneur passed the idea on to Lewton who decided to invent a folklore of women who developed into cats. The whole concept was approached from an angle then entirely new in the commercial thriller. The people and events concerned should be made believable and understandable—and horrors should be suggested rather than revealed. Tourneur remarks: ". . . anything which was really horrible was never shown. Whenever the panther was shown I made a little shadow . . . people were horrified but didn't know whether they had seen the panther or not." The result was a highly atmospheric, intelligent and dignified film. Simone Simon wonderfully suggests the feline nature beneath the baby-face exterior. There are four main climaxes when the cat-woman attacks: the first following a pursuit along shadowy empty streets, the second in a deserted swimming-pool,

the third in a large darkened office, the fourth in her own flat where she kills the psychiatrist who has been treating her. Together they might be taken as a series of variations on the theme of shadows. The hackneyed scene of an isolated figure hearing following footsteps in lonely streets has rarely been rendered more eerily, and the subtly lit changes of expression in the girl's face as her panther part takes over prior to the last killing is in the same imaginative vein. Most striking of all is the echoing, water-dripping swimming-pool, with the grotesquely foreshortened figure of the frightened victim as she treads water in the centre of it, surrounded by vaguely menacing sounds and reflected shadows.

I Walked with a Zombie (1943) was the second film of Tourneur and Lewton, preferred by the former to almost all his other films on account of its poetry. The climactic scene, a lonely walk by two women through cane fields, is notable for its use of sound—native drums—to inspire increasing terror.

The Leopard Man (1943) is somewhat weakened by a flat *dénouement,* and the fact that the leopard man is not nearly so credible as the cat woman. However, there is a fine atmospheric sequence near the beginning, as we follow a frightened young girl's journey through the dark to purchase groceries, the tracking and attack by the animal, and her death outside a closed door as her frantic mother tries to open the way to safety. Once again the Lewton-Tourneur use of shadow excels, and there is a stunning shot of the glaring-eyed beast. The chanting procession of "monks" at the end is ruthlessly dragged in, but once there it is put to good use. Sounds throughout effectively heighten tension, notably the dancer's clicking castanets and the leopard-like, throaty cough of a suddenly halting car.

The Curse of the Cat People (1944), an indirect sequel, is as much a melodramatic study of a child's loneliness as a conventional horror story. The child, a six-year-old girl, keeps herself company with the ghost of her dead formerly insane mother (Simone Simon, from the earlier film). Part of the fascination, as James Agee points out, lies in the uncertainty as to whether it is all part of the introverted little girl's imagination—a somewhat overworked approached nowadays, but seldom treated more effectively.

Other memorable Lewton productions include the two costume pieces *The Body Snatcher* (1945) and *Bedlam* (1946), both starring Boris Karloff. James Agee regrets Lewton's interest in costume pictures, but at least the atmosphere of early-Victorian Edinburgh is reasonably convincing, aided by bravura performances by Henry Daniell as an ex-pupil of the notorious Dr. Knox, and Karloff as a smoothly sinister but entirely credible follower in the footsteps of Burke and Hare. The final ride

with the corpse in a rickety chaise is a splendidly macabre climax: and there is one excellent long-shot—reminiscent of the great days of Germanic fantasy—where the street-singer meets her death, the girl and the following clip-clopping cab being slowly swallowed up beneath the shadowy archway, the camera remaining on the darkness until moments later the girl's song is abruptly cut off.

Bedlam was the final film in the Lewton horror series, based on the eighth picture of Hogarth's *Rake's Progress.* As in *The Body Snatcher,* the period atmosphere gives an impression of at least acceptable accuracy, particularly in the smaller details. The horrors of the lunatics' plight are comparatively mild, and their behaviour—particularly that of the motionless, staring girl who makes one sudden movement to stab the villainous keeper and then returns to her cataleptic trance—would probably not impress an expert in mental illness.

Christine Gordon, Frances Dee and Darby Jones in *I Walked with a Zombie.*

Boris Karloff, Bela Lugosi and Henry Daniell in *The Body Snatcher*.

However, the overall sense of the horror of the old system is strongly conveyed. There is a really chilling moment at the end of the film when Karloff, presumably dead, is bricked up in the wall by the inmates, and at the very last moment, unseen by any of them, stirs and opens his eyes. This brief understated shot is more gruesome than any moment of agonised yelling and banging on stone walls would have been. There follows a nicely ironical close when the life-respecting Quaker, who has noticed the new brickwork, decides not to point this out to the authorities (and thereby unknowingly rescue the imprisoned man), in order to spare the lunatics from punishment. Lewton made one or two more pictures after *Bedlam,* but this was his last horror film. His death, at the early age of forty-six, was a considerable loss to the cinema.

7. British Horror, 1957-1966

British cinema made a late entry into the field of the macabre. It is difficult to recollect anything in the *genre* during the silent period, nor indeed, except for *Dead of Night* (see Chapter 8), in the early years of sound. It was 1957, when *The Curse of Frankenstein* put Hammer Films on the map, which opened the floodgates—never since closed.

The term "Hammer Horror" has become a title known throughout the world of film. Their productions have received extravagant praise from devotees, and equally extravagant abuse from the critical *élite*. They have also made fortunes. The lurid publicity with which some of them have been launched has, understandably, roused violent reactions against them—sometimes justifiably. Much rubbish has emanated from their studios to take up valuable screen time. Many very well-known artistes have lent them the prestige of their presence, and the high quality of much of their camerawork and settings have been an example to more highly esteemed film-makers.

Hammer is a development of Exclusive Films, which was producing at Bray, on the upper reaches of the Thames, shortly after the Second World War. It had been responsible for films of various types before the resounding success of *The Curse of Frankenstein*, but the only one which really comes into the horror-sci-fi category is the first Quatermass film, *The Quatermass Xperiment* (1955, directed by Val Guest) based on Nigel Kneale's television serial. A second Quatermass *(Quatermass II)* appeared in 1957, and a third, *Quatermass and the Pit* (directed by Roy Ward Baker) in 1967. All were concerned with the efforts of alien beings to take over the human race. In the last of the three they had been whiling away the intervening aeons under a London tube railway—probably the Northern Line, where they could rest for long periods undisturbed by any passing train. The first starred Richard Wordsworth, giving a notable performance of a man

slowly turning into a sort of minced vegetable.

The 1959 Terence Fisher directed Christopher Lee in a re-make of the famous 1932 Karloff vehicle, *The Mummy*, Lee being remarkably successful in conveying suffering beneath yet another all-enveloping, wretchedly uncomfortable make-up.

The following year Fisher made *The Two Faces of Dr. Jekyll*—a "version" of Stevenson's story so far removed from the original as to make the author wonder what his name is doing on the credits at all. The idea of making the good Jekyll a gruff, unapproachable, bewiskered man, and representing evil in Hyde as smooth, smiling and outwardly charming, was ingenious and interesting psychologically; but the script was so feeble and the motivation so cheapened that dullness conquered all. As a critic indicated, if a classic is to be tampered with, it should at least be done with wit and competence.

1960 was, indeed, a notable year for the indefatigable Terence Fisher. From Jekyll he turned to Dracula *(The Brides of . . .)*, then, after a glance at Robin Hood *(Sword of Sherwood Forest)* and *The Stranglers of Bombay*, launched Hammer into lycanthropy with *The Curse of the Werewolf*, memorable for an impressive performance from the comparatively unknown Oliver Reed, both as himself and in a fine make-up (by Roy Ashton).

Taste of Fear (1961) was considerably less pretentious and considerably more satisfactory, with an excellent performance from Ann Todd. Derivative in parts from *Les Diaboliques,* but with little of the atmosphere of that Grand Guignol epic, the film nevertheless had some nice moments of eeriness and suspense, and Seth Holt, the director, made fresh use of well-worn but still effective thriller *clichés.*

An unusual production of the same year was *The Damned,* made by Joseph Losey. The story is an odd mixture of science fiction (radio-active

QP.12

Quatermass and the Pit: **the third film in the Quatermass
series.**

children kept in a cliff cave by a scientist who
hopes they will survive nuclear war and repopulate
the world) and motorcycle gang thriller. Unfortunately an attempt is made to point up the story as
a sort of parable on modern evils, with the result
that it falls between three stools, and the original's
impact is weakened. On a lower level, however,
there are effective moments of menace: the slow
progress of a protectively-clothed figure through
the children's quarters; the cold, withdrawn
strangeness of the children themselves (the cold
being due to literal cold-bloodedness); and the final
sequences, the escaping children being hustled back
to their cave but with their damage done, the curt
unemotional shooting of the sculptress, the pursuit
of the fleeing gang leader by helicopters, the young
couple drifting out to sea doomed to die of
radio-activity. All this is grippingly done. Losey
also manages to invest unlikely surroundings, such
as cliffs burning white with sunshine, and quietly

sparkling seascapes, with a threatening quality as
real as any conjured up in a dark, curtain-fluttering
passage.

In 1962 Terence Fisher directed a remake of
The Phantom of the Opera, with Herbert Lom.
Perhaps he was still feeling the exhausting effects
of his marathon at the beginning of the decade, for
the film was remarkably tame. In 1964 he made
The Earth Dies Screaming—possibly one of the
silliest and most exaggerated titles in the *genre.*
Fisher is probably the best known and most
prolific Hammer director. The film, a minor
example of his work, is mentioned here as it seems
to epitomise his virtues and his failings—apart from
his worst excesses of sensationalism. The opening is
quite impressive. An American test pilot arrives at a
small hotel in an English village. There is no sign of
life anywhere, indeed; there are signs of death—
people lying motionless where they have suddenly
fallen. The pilot's attitude indicates he has seen

Escape of the radio-active children in Joseph Losey's *The Damned.*

similar sights on his journey. From a radio in the deserted hotel he can obtain only a metallic whine. Other people arrive—a middle-aged couple, a young man and his wife, who is pregnant. All other human beings seem mysteriously to have died. Suddenly into the empty village square two figures come plodding stiffly and heavily along in protective armour. They appear to ignore the little group. The older woman calls after them for an explanation, then, somewhat indignant at their impassive progress, runs after one of them and catches his arm. He turns—and reveals no face, merely a steel dome of batteries and dials. The woman is killed by a built-in reflex from the robot. All this is done with a fine feeling for growing tension. Even though the turning figure has been so often exploited before, and we know we shall probably see some sort of monstrous thing, the sight of the blind steel "face" affords a shock. The suspense is well maintained through further developments, up to the point where the woman's "body" rises from the bed on which it has been laid, and reveals

herself as a "zombie." Apparently her mind has been stolen—and also her eyes. Thereafter absurdity runs riot, other zombies appear, and soon the screen is filled with them, all tottering around and peering through cupboards and doors in close-ups which only too clearly reveal the white blobs of make-up pasted over their eyes. When later on our old friend Dennis Price (another former survivor) staggers in in the same unhappy condition, the collapse is complete. The film is harmless enough (not even an X-certificate in Britain, forsooth), but laughable. A glimpse of one zombie can be nasty, a dozen at close range are just fun. But the fun was unintentional—the result of the determination to pile sensation on sensation at all costs. What makes this the more regrettable is that the scenes involving the birth of the young wife's baby are sensitively and even movingly handled, and seem to indicate an aspect of Fisher's ability which is seldom displayed. Terence Fisher's films are seen by a vast public, and his influence should not be underestimated. In 1962 the French periodical "Midi-Minuit Fantastique" devoted its entire first

56

number to the director and his films. According to an interview reported in *Gothique,* Terence Fisher prefers that his films should be called macabre rather than horrific. "Horror has become almost a derogatory word suggesting the sensationally worse side of the cinema. I always use my camera to show things, particularly unpleasant things, happening by implication." The number of "Midi-Minuit Fantastique" cited above has an article on erotic and sadistic scenes, followed by a list, headed Psychopathologia Sexualis, of his work. The list, two pages long, includes: orgies, exhibitionism, "singular amorous tendencies" (sub-headings: incest, love for inferior beings), fetichism, bestiality, necrophilia, sexual desires of the dead for the living, sadism (ten sub-headings), masochism, homosexuality. Implication par excellence!

Fanatic (1965), directed by Silvio Narizzano, introduced Tallulah Bankhead to Hammer Films. Here we are away from the world of monsters and radio-active children and entering the darker world of human aberrations. For the first three-quarters of the film, script and dialogue are on a high level, intelligent and plausible, and shot through with a nice streak of sardonic humour. As Mrs. Trefoile, a woman combining religious mania with an obsessive devotion to her dead son, and declining rapidly from oddness to insanity, Tallulah Bankhead gives a performance of gleeful relish, obviously enjoying herself hugely but at the same time creating a formidable and frightening figure. Stefanie Powers is quite exceptional as the girl who pays the old woman a courtesy visit, having been engaged briefly to her son, then finds that she is looked upon as being actually and irretrievably married to him and expected to stay in the grim old house for ever. Her early scenes are played with a refreshing tartness—a slightly impatient but good-humoured acceptance of her hostess's foibles. This makes her

a more human figure than the majority of passage-roaming heroines, and greatly increases the effectiveness of the subsequent descent through growing puzzlement to degradation and terror. The interminable Bible readings at table, the austere rooms, the dreary meals, the blank frames from which all mirrors have been removed, the equivocal attitudes of the strange servants, the dim-lit greenhouse and enclosed house (all this early part of the film leaves an impression of an imprisoning greenness)—such things build up a growing sense of oppression surrounding the girl, and the first outbreak of overt violence, when she is forcibly prevented from trying to leave, is almost a relief. Some old clichés of attempted escape, such as notes fluttering down from windows towards the wrong person, are given nice little extra twists, and the one episode of "horror violence" involving a pair of scissors is nasty enough to shock anyone, yet is not treated with repelling relish, and is necessary to the development of the plot. The claustrophobic misery of the girl's physical and mental degeneration as she is imprisoned in her little attic room is convincingly suggested, and the whole screen seems imbued with a suffocating sense of impending madness. Unfortunately, the film itself goes mad towards the end, with draped altars to dead sons in cellars, gaudy and totally sourceless lights flickering over the scene, Mrs. Trefoile first murdering her servants and running around all bloody-fingered and then being murdered herself by her housekeeper. What was an improbable, but at least consistent thriller becomes a complete absurdity. It is almost as if the last part of the film had been tacked on by another hand—undoubtedly a severed one.

In the same year another great name, Bette Davis, appeared in *The Nanny,* directed by Seth Holt—more of a suspense than a horror film, but with at least two eminently macabre scenes: the first showing Miss Davis as Nanny watching a woman dying of a heart attack (an unnervingly realistic performance by Jill Bennett), refusing to give her the necessary medicine and regaling her instead with the story of her own tragedy; the second a series of cleverly timed cuts showing alternative hallucinatory and actual shots, from Nanny's viewpoint, of the happy little girl playing in her bath and the dreadful truth of the small drowned body. The film seems uncertain of its direction—it could have been a serious study of a pathological case—but at least it holds together in its own convention, besides giving Bette Davis a chance of showing she can be as effective in restraint as in the full flood of her other recent excursions into mania.

Stefanie Powers and Tallulah Bankhead find something nasty in the sink: a scene from *Fanatic.*

With *The Plague of the Zombies* (1966), directed by John Gilling, we are back with the monsters again, but the film is noteworthy for two sequences—a frightening picture of unruly young fox-hunters on the rampage, and a really horrific dream experienced by one of the characters, of the dead rising again, groping their way out of their graves, all photographed in a hellish green glow.

The same director's *The Reptile* (1966) is another above-average monster film, a tale of Eastern black magic about a white girl who has been cursed and as a consequence turns periodically into a snake, sloughs off her skin, and sinks her fangs into various unfortunate people who then turn black in the face and die foaming. Panic, understandably enough, spreads through the village where she lives with her cold and mysterious father (splendidly played by Noel Willman), until the mystery is solved by the brother of one of the victims. Jacqueline Pearce as the snake-girl, though generally masked in a serpent's head so unconvincing that at close quarters one can almost smell the *papier-mâché,* contrives to engage our sympathy to an extent unusual in such films. Three scenes are particularly effective, a few moments showing the girl's reactions to some sinuous oriental music, her first, half-seen attack from a dark doorway, and some nasty serpentine writhings under a blanket by the hot basement fire where she hibernates. Colour and settings were very pleasant. A small-scale film which demonstrated what can be done with the most conventional horror fantasy by restrained treatment and sympathetic characterisation.

One more Hammer Film should be mentioned, *Rasputin, The Mad Monk* (1965), director Don Sharp. The subtitle is significant. No wisp of Old Russian atmosphere is engendered. Typical Hammer horrors, attempted rape, mutilated hands, vitriolic attacks, are brought, or dragged, in. History is ruthlessly distorted—the true situation in the country which brought Rasputin to power and held him there is never made clear. The Tsar is not even seen. The final killing of Rasputin alone follows reasonably closely the account given by Prince Yussupoff, but this is practically a Hammer story anyway. The film deserves mention because of Christopher Lee's powerful performance in the name part. Lee is an actor of considerable presence. He has appeared in a long list of films, but is best known for his many Hammer monsters. He claims, undoubtedly correctly, to be the only screen actor to have portrayed Dracula, Frankenstein's creature, Fu Manchu, a Mummy, *and* (surely surprised to find himself in such company) Sherlock Holmes! To all he brings a strong personality and impressive appearance—the straighter roles showing that he need not depend on a grotesque make-up for results. His Rasputin was a *tour-de-force* which dwarfed the rest of the film and made one wish to see him portray the "monk" in a more serious and worthwhile treatment of the period.

*

How much influence Hammer has had over the past ten years cannot be estimated, but one or two non-Hammer Hammer-types may be briefly noted. *Witchcraft* (1964), produced by Lippert Films and directed by Don Sharp, was remarkable for an unusually convincing atmosphere of brooding evil and a bravura performance from Marie Ney. The opening scenes of bulldozers digging up a cemetery as part of a building project, photographed in a kind of thick grey light, and the first sounds and sight of the witch disturbed from her long rest in the grave, are splendidly menacing—in particular the slow upward movement of the camera along the dark shroud to the dark, beautiful, threatening face. Her later visitations are equally well managed, and the whole film is pleasantly old-fashioned in appearance.

Dr. Terror's House of Horrors (1964)—another idiotically titled film—is a sort of compendium of horror types, five short stories offering a sample of the five most common themes: werewolf, voodoo,

Jacqueline Pearce as the snake lady in *The Reptile,* with Jennifer Daniel.

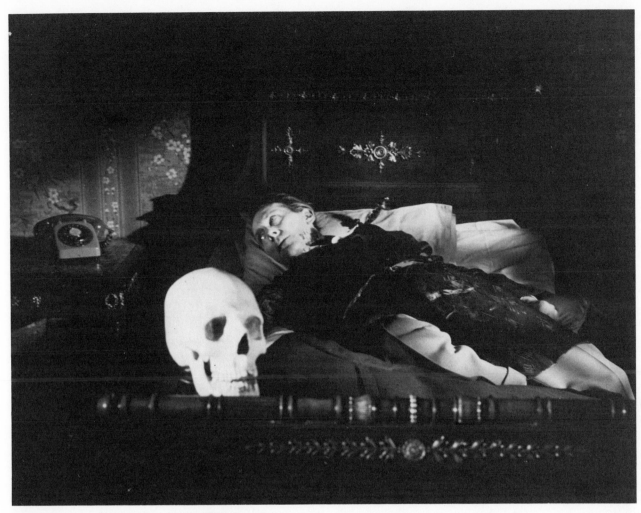

Peter Cushing and title object in *The Skull*.

vampire, crawling hand, murderous greenery. The stories are linked together by a mysterious doctor in a railway carriage who tells the other occupants—five men—their fortunes. The end in each case is death. The actual stories are commonplace enough (Christopher Lee's battle with a wandering hand, and the taut, ironical little vampire tale come off best), but the introductory and intermediary scenes are handled with considerable imagination: the dingy railway carriage, the grubby, ambiguous doctor, the black glass windows, the rattle and shake of the train, the five increasingly anxious men—Lee holding out to the last against being drawn into the business. The ending, with the five men alighting at a strange, deserted station and meeting the doctor (who had disappeared)—now approaching them along the darkened platform and revealing instead of his former unshaven cheeks the smooth skull of Death—is genuinely macabre. The film was directed by Freddie Francis.

In 1965 the same director made two contrasting

horror films, both commendable examples of their type. *The Skull*, dealing with the evil wrought through the medium of the skull of our old friend de Sade, is a good ghost story, honest enough to remain supernatural and not seek to explain some of the minor happenings. The wildly swinging pendants and tilting pictures as the skull moves around the house on its nefarious business are splendidly eerie, and some fine atmospheric (and beautiful) sets add much to the general effect. A notable sequence is that in which the Professor (Peter Cushing) sits reading in his mask-and-trophy cluttered room before dropping off into a nightmare—photographed from a whole series of different angles, each one emphasising some particular facet of his collection and occult interests. The nightmare itself does not come up to this preliminary, perhaps because it is in colours so pleasant to look at that it never becomes frightening. The terror of finding oneself in a completely strange house *after* waking up does not have the strong

59

impact it should. The floating skull wobbles a bit and is rather obviously suspended—it is better at sudden leaps than protracted peripateticism.

For the most part, however, once it escapes from its Wardour Street costume opening, this is a very satisfying piece of macabre. There is a nicely sardonic ending when the detective, asked whether the mystifying murders could be explained by the supernatural, remarks smugly "Not in this day and age"—the scene being shot from behind the eye-sockets of the grimly watching skull.

Francis's other film, *The Psychopath* (scenario by Robert Bloch, author of *Psycho*—and also of *The Skull*) has not the flair and neatness of the former, but is also above the average of its kind. It is a mixture of mystery and horror, moving from one to the other in slow, increasingly sinister progression. This gradual darkening from what appears to be a mysterious but "reasonable" murder to madness and terror is in the true spirit of the *genre*.

Our last three films in this short survey are of larger scale and less fantastic. It is rather difficult to understand the howls of execration with which Michael Powell's *Peeping Tom* (1959) was greeted in some quarters. Admittedly it deals with perversion—admittedly it takes a theme of perversion and uses it as a basis for a commercial shocker. At least, however, this film makes no plea for tolerance of perversion—it does not suggest that perverted instincts are humorous or perhaps even rather admirable. It does on the other hand ask for, and command, sympathy for the unfortunate victim of a sadistic father. Its considerable success on this score is largely due to the performance of Carl Boehm, and Powell's sensitive direction of his scenes with the girl, Anna Massey. In addition, except for the last few minutes (the least effective, incidentally) the film treats its horrific scenes with extreme restraint—at any rate in the version shown in Britain. Apparently more lurid scenes were inserted for tougher customers elsewhere. In the English edition the three murders are hardly seen. The third one, which one might expect to form a climax, is never shown at all—we merely see the murderer entering the shop where it occurs, and leaving it a little later. And this film was made at a time when numerous others—not only horrors, but even "respectable" ones—were weltering in blood, killings, beatings-up and various questionable activities, with gleeful relish. Only in the final suicide (and perhaps in the unnecessary episode of the deformed model) does the film seem to descend to sensationalism—and even this loses its effect (admittedly unintentionally) because it

looks singularly unconvincing.

Technically the film is brilliantly done. The atmosphere fails in only one respect: the feeling that the young man's house is the actual one of his frightful childhood is never convincingly conveyed. It is difficult to pin down the reason for this failure of communication, but it does rob the film of one dimension of horror.

A criticism which has more weight than many directed against the film is one which has been applied to Ian Fleming for his Bond books (and to Elgar for his "Salut d'Amour"!), namely that Powell is wasting on a commercial trifle a talent which can produce work of more lasting merit. Even this view, however, is open to question. In a perceptive article in "Motion" (February 1963) Ian Johnson (who describes it as "a sad and beautiful film") points out the many layers of meaning which can be read into it. The constant thrusting on our attention of the camera—every kind of camera—raises the question: "Who is the *voyeur*. Is it Mark?" (the young man) "or is it us, the cinema audience?" Or even the readers of this book? "One might feel a little uneasy over Mark's dark room cum projection room," writes Johnson, "for, filled with all his atrocious documents, doesn't it represent the secret place for all our own secret, dark, perverted thoughts?"

Powell himself plays the father who records (for "scientific" purposes) his small son's fear, fear which he actually induces for this very end. The film is really a penetrating comment on probing of all kinds—whether in the name of "science," "a free press," "social necessity," "good of the soul," "religion," or less high-sounding but more honest reasons. The fact that the film itself probes serves to strengthen its point. Perhaps, after all, the howls of execration are difficult to justify, rather than difficult to understand. We are all sensitive when our raw spots are touched.

The Collector (1965), directed by the American William Wyler, tells the story of a repressed and psychopathic young bank clerk who wins a fortune on the football pools, buys a lonely country house, kidnaps a suburban young girl on whom he has had his eye, and imprisons her there in a comfortably prepared cellar, much as he pins down his collection of butterflies. It is an uneven film, flawed by the miscasting of the clerk (Terence Stamp) who, though giving a good and often sympathetic performance, in the early stages at any rate, would surely in real life have had no need to go to such lengths to satisfy his requirements. The underlying threat of insanity is, however, kept admirably alive. The girl's attempted escape and her attack on her

Samantha Eggar in *The Collector:*
Frightened.

kidnapper are ferociously effective, particularly in contrast to her character hitherto. His frenzied drive to hospital to have his wounded head attended to, the car careering and swaying dizzily to a dangerous stop, his blind staggering run to the hospital, all thoughts of his captive forgotten, are also horribly gripping. So too, in a different tempo, is the girl's ghastly death in the freezing, fireless room.

Bunny Lake is Missing (1965), directed by Otto Preminger, starts off as an intriguing if implausible mystery story. A young woman comes to London from America in order to live with her brother, bringing with her a four-year-old illegitimate daughter. She leaves the child in a nursery school, from which, on the very first morning, it disappears. When she goes to collect it, no one seems to know anything about it, and the child's very existence is doubted. We ourselves have never seen

Hitting back.

her. An inspector who is called in also has his doubts. Eventually, after much twisting and turning, it transpires that the brother has kidnapped the child with intent to murder her. His reason—a pathological (but not incestuous) affection for his sister which cause him to fear the child might come between them. He has really mentally never left the nursery where they used to play together. From then on the film mounts to an impressive climax of horror. The moment of the girl's realisation of her brother's manic possessiveness, taking place in a sinister, lamplit dolls' hospital, is familiar in substance but well contrived and photographed. The final wild chases in a large walled suburban garden, developing from grotesque parodies of children's games as the girl distractedly tries to keep his mind away from his murderous intentions, through some beautifully timed shock effects in a greenhouse, and culminating in a whirling, shouting climax on a swing, build up to a most satisfying pitch of horror. A picture of the three of them, the child's tiny figure between the frantic girl and the mad yet pathetic brother, dancing round a trampoline singing a nursery rhyme, is as prickling a moment as any in the category.

8. Two British Classics

Britain's first significant entry into the sphere of the supernatural is still one of the most notable; a film which retains much of its power and originality after twenty years. *Dead of Night* was produced by Michael Balcon at Ealing in 1945, shortly before those studios became renowned for the famous comedy series. The film consists of five stories of the supernatural (the inexplicable is perhaps a better description), and a linking story as strange and ingenious as any of the others. Four directors shared in its creation, each taking one or more of the episodes.

Michael Redgrave in *Dead of Night*.

The linking story, directed by Basil Dearden, concerns Walter Craig, an architect, who is summoned down to a house called Pilgrim's Farm by a prospective client whom he does not know. On arrival he experiences strongly the feeling that he has been to the place before. He is taken into the house (with the details of which he is oddly cognizant) and introduced by his host to a group of people. These also are familiar, though none of them appear to know him. After somewhat constrained greetings he tells them that he has met them all, and the house, and the situation, in a recurring dream. He explains how this dream always starts quietly and pleasantly—as at the present moment—but after a certain small incident invariably begins to darken into ghastly nightmare, culminating in horror—a horror of his own creation—from which he wakes up sweating with fear. He never (a point to be noted) remembers his dream for more than a few moments after waking, until the next time it occurs. The pleasant, friendly group are understandably both intrigued and incredulous. They tease him gently, but as time passes they find that he is strangely capable of foretelling certain small events, such as the arrival of a dark young woman, and the unexpected sudden departure of a young girl who had proposed to stay for the evening. He then describes the incident which will mark the turning point of his dream—the breaking of a pair of glasses belonging to one of the party, a psychiatrist. Increasingly fascinated, the party one by one reveal that each has at some time undergone an "inexplicable" experience. The narration of these make up the body of the film.

In due course the psychiatrist, who has been taking a somewhat sceptical attitude, breaks his glasses. A little later this man, Dr. van Straaten, is left alone with Craig. Anxious to help, he asks Craig what is this dreadful thing he does in his dream. Craig explains that he is overcome by an overpowering desire to kill someone—a man almost unknown to him, one who has never done him any harm, in fact only wishes him well. As he speaks, he moves quietly behind the Doctor, and suddenly strangles him. Everything then becomes confused. All the members of the party, and also the characters from their stories, appear chasing and jeering at the distraught Craig who, trying in desperate panic to escape, even finds himself in the other houses, until at last he manages to wake himself up, sweating and shaking, in his own bed, after another recurrence of the dream. Weak but thankful, he relaxes. But what has wakened him is the telephone. It is a stranger, Mr. Foley. Could Craig come down to his house, Pilgrim's Farm, on a matter of business? Craig, the dream already faded, agrees. We leave him arriving at the house, in precisely the same shot as the film began . . .

Basil Dearden also directed the first of the episodes, the shortest and one of the best. It tells of a racing driver, convalescing after a crash, who receives a "supernatural" warning not to travel from the hospital on a certain bus the following day. The sense of eeriness is most beautifully caught in this little cameo—the sudden ceasing of the bedside clock's friendly tick, and the changed position of the hands—the peculiarly unnerving feeling of chaos, of time gone mad, when the sick man flings open the window curtains to reveal bright day when it should be night (this reversal of the more conventional horror of dark where there should be light is also used with terrifying effect in *Repulsion,* above a closed door)—the black plumed hearse motionless on the white empty street—the swift plunge of the camera on to the driver's upturned face—"Just room for one inside, sir." A moment after the invalid has returned, shaken, to bed, the clock ticks again. He looks up, to find friendly moonlight and street lamps outside. But it was no dream, and the curtains which were closed are now still apart. The following morning, when the bus drives up to take him from the hospital, the conductor, of course, is the man on the hearse. "Just room for one inside, sir." Horrified, he refuses, and a minute or two later watches the bus plunge over a bridge into the river.

The second story, of a young girl who sees the ghost of Francis Kent, the little boy murdered by his sister Constance, in a forgotten room during a children's fancy-dress party, is much less satisfactory. It was probably a mistake to make use of a real and famous murder case, and certainly a mistake to leave the climactic revelation solely to a hurried verbal explanation by the hostess, whom we had never seen before. At the very least we needed to see the room as it now appeared, not merely to be told that everything had happened long ago. Cavalcanti, who directed this episode seemingly with little interest, was also responsible for the finest of all, the last.

The third concerns an old mirror given by a girl to her *fiancé.* When using it, he soon finds himself looking, not into the actual modern apartment behind him, but into a strange, old-fashioned room. This Victorian bedroom which should not be there but is, enclosed by the ornate mirror frame, with its burning log fire, and its four-poster bed cunningly angled so that we are never quite sure whether it has an occupant or not, has a really sinister quality in its quiet, determined presence. The mirror had originally belonged to a man of evil temper who had strangled his wife before it. The climax, when the new owner feels impelled to do the same but is saved by her smashing the glass at the last moment, is predictable, but directed with a nice sense of the macabre by Robert Hamer. Before the young man attacks her, the girl has never been visible in the mirror. Her sudden first appearance, struggling for her life, gives us the necessary shock.

Charles Crichton directed the following episode, a farce involving Basil Radford and Naunton Wayne. Fairly amusing in itself, it is a complete error of judgment in its present position, destructive of the atmosphere so carefully built up, a totally unnecessary interpolation of "comic relief." Some feeble attempt is made to excuse its inclusion. "You told it to help me," says Craig to his host, whose story it is, but it is not at all clear how it helped, or why.

However, the film rises to its greatest heights in the next and final story (Cavalcanti), told by the sceptical psychiatrist. He has attempted to rationalise each story as it was told, and has been floored each time by the one following. Now he himself produces the finest of all, the tale of a ventriloquist's "possession" by his dummy. The relationship of ventriloquist and dummy has been used before and since (*The Great Gabbo, Devil Doll*), but never with such horrific power. Michael Redgrave's performance has a nervous intensity which rises to a shattering climax as he attacks the doll in his cell; and earlier moments, when for instance we are given the first intimations that the dummy is speaking his own lines and not his master's, are equally, if more quietly, unnerving. The last shot—the camera slowly approaching the hospital bed, the gaunt, stricken figure slowly turning his head, struggling to speak, producing only the high inhuman voice of the dummy— anticipates another famous closing passage equal in horror, the ending of *Psycho.*

The linking story is handled with a skill apt to be overshadowed by the more flamboyant episodes. The gradual encroachment of strangeness and menace upon the complete normality of the opening party indicated by the growing distortion of viewing angles, the slow fading of day to dusk—so much easier in the theatre than the film—these are still impressive today. After the killing of the Doctor, when the horror is come upon us, all reality vanishes. Dominated, ingeniously, by the innocent fancy-dressed children from the party scene, the terror of nightmare is created in a wild swirl of distorted staircases and passages, the camera swinging and twisting about as Craig himself does in his efforts to waken up.

The subtlest touch of the film, however, is a momentary shot almost at the very end. We finally leave Craig in exactly the position that we first found him—arriving at Foley's house in his car. *Dead of Night,* then, like Joyce's *Finnegans Wake,* is circular—it will go on for ever, ninety per cent dream, ten per cent awake. So, but for this one shot, it might appear. Before leaving his house, however, Craig has been speaking to Foley on the telephone. As he speaks, we see—for just a few frames—Foley himself, at his house, on the other end of the telephone. That shot tells us the truth. The film throughout has been seen from Craig's viewpoint. Even the stories, where he was not present, are seen as told to him. Now, suddenly, *we* see Foley. Craig has not met him. The dream has faded. He does not know what Foley and his house look like. Now, we see Foley. He really is there, waiting. This tiny shot is the most frightening in the film, for through it the dream becomes reality. This time, it is really happening. There will be no waking relief for Craig. This time, he drives to his doom. In no other medium but the film could the situation be so briefly yet devastatingly made clear. This is ghost-story telling with a vengeance!

*

In spite of its sometimes tortuous style Henry James's *The Turn of the Screw* is possibly the best story of haunting in the language.

The plot itself is much less involved than the writing. A governess who had lived, as she herself describes it, a "small, smothered life" is engaged by a remote and disinterested guardian uncle to look after two young children. They live in a large country mansion and are at present being cared for by a housekeeper, Mrs. Grose. At first the governess, whose simple heart has already been stirred by her distant employer, is enchanted with her new life. Very soon, however, she senses that all is not well. An indefinable sense of evil permeates the lovely setting. There appear to be people around the place of whom she knows nothing. The children behave oddly. There is much whispering in corners—a slyness she cannot pin down, a secrecy, an unnatural and unpleasant precociousness. From the housekeeper she hears about two former servants, a man Quint, and her own predecessor, Miss Jessel, both now dead. Quint, she learns, had been thoroughly vile, and Miss Jessel under his influence. She becomes more and more convinced that the spirits of the dead couple haunt the place, and actually use the bodies of the two children for their own evil purposes. She resolves to save the innocents, as the figures become clearer and the menace draws closer. But her fight for their preservation fails. The girl collapses in hysteria and is taken away by the now indignant housekeeper. The boy, left alone with her, after a violent emotional scene as she tries to exorcise him, dies in her arms. The mystery is unsolved.

The American playwright William Archibald tackled the formidable task of adapting James's elusive, shadowy and ambiguous work for the stage. He called his play *The Innocents.* It was a brave attempt, though suffering from three inevitable drawbacks: the constant scene drops (five in the first act) destroyed the delicate atmosphere; the huge gap between audience and setting dwarfed the characters, living and dead, and consequently minimised their predicament; and it was difficult for two young children, however admirably cast, to sustain the necessary emotional level through lengthy performances.

In 1961 Jack Clayton directed a film version adapted from Archibald's play by the author and Truman Capote. None of the above problems faced him, and in addition he brought to the making of the picture a sensitivity and feeling for the subject which resulted in a highly successful work.

Two main decisions, interrelated, have to be made by anyone dramatising James's story. The first is, should the "ghosts" be visible, the second, what is our attitude towards the governess? Both Archibald and Clayton show us the ghosts, and thus indicate their opinion of the governess's state of mind. The American critic Edmund Wilson suggested some time ago that the whole story of wicked spirits might be a mere figment in the mind of a sexually frustrated spinster, that in fact she and not they were responsible for the haunting of the children. The book is, in fact, a psychiatric case history. This is an amiable and cleverly reasoned academic argument, but does not really hold water. It is doubtful, to start with, whether such a girl would be capable, even a few years later, of writing so detached and sophisticated an account of the affair, in so cool and literary a style. Quite apart from this, in the manuscript itself (which presumably we are intended to take as true, for otherwise there is no story), there are definite pointers indicating that the ghosts are ghosts, and the children possessed by them. In his play, there is never any doubt that Archibald is treating the ghosts as existing in their own right and not as mere figments in Miss Giddens's imagination, and that we are seeing them through her eyes. When Quint appears we see him, and we see her, from apart in the auditorium. In the film, admittedly, the camera is used to a certain extent subjectively but not so as to identify us wholly with Miss Giddens, or to detach us from the objective reality of her surroundings. The result is to convince us that we are sharing an actual experience, rather than undergoing an imaginary one in isolation. A comparison with *Repulsion* is interesting. Here we really do "experience" things which are not happening. The girl's interior world of terror is becoming imposed on her external world. We are shut in alone with her and share the deterioration of her mind. Her ending, too, is consistent with this—complete collapse, no book of carefully composed memoirs a few years later.

The Innocents opens and closes in darkness. Behind the credit titles we see vaguely a close-up of clasped beseeching hands the meaning of which is not clear until at the very end those same hands clasp the dead boy, and then are slowly withdrawn.

In a prelude Miss Giddens is seen being interviewed by the uncle. This is, I think, a pity. He is better left as a distant, imagined figure—in the book, her manuscript does not start until her arrival at Bly. The dialogue, too, in this opening scene is none too happy. ("Do you have an imagination?"). Once we reach Bly, however, the

Flora, housekeeper and governess: Pamela Franklin, Megs Jenkins and Deborah Kerr in *The Innocents*.

Is there a figure across the lake? Pamela Franklin and Deborah Kerr in *The Innocents*.

film rarely loses its grip until the terrifying conclusion. The settings (photographed at Sheffield Park in Sussex, by Freddie Francis) are unfailingly lovely. It is exactly this visual beauty that gives an added dimension to the horrors to come.

The first sight of Quint, seen through a blinding haze of sunshine on the top of the old tower, is marvellously done. Miss Giddens is picking flowers in the beautiful garden. All around are the sounds of summer, somewhere in the distance the little girl Flora is singing (an old tune we shall remember uncomfortably later in the film). Suddenly she comes upon a broken, leering statue. A black insect creeps obscenely out of its mouth. Suddenly every sound has ceased, except the loathsome buzzing of—what, a bluebottle, perhaps? Then she looks up at the tower. A moment later, with the breaking of

the spell, the summer sounds return. Throughout the entire film sound is used with considerable imagination. Horror, in fact, is conveyed as much through the ear as through the eye.

There is one long sequence in which Miss Giddens walks through the darkened house with a candle. Nothing is seen, except one brief, ambiguous shadow, but she is accompanied and surrounded by little chuckles and whisperings which gradually grow in intensity to a cacophony of mocking voices. An old device, perhaps, but rarely used with better effect. The sequence finishes with a shot from directly above the distracted girl as she whirls round in panic trying to locate the source of the evil din. The shot oddly recalls the one already referred to from *Broken Blossoms* where Lillian Gish is shut in the closet, and it conveys much the same sense of claustrophobic terror. Miss Giddens

Dawning horror: Deborah Kerr in *The Innocents*.

is enclosed by walls of sound.

Unexpectedly, the appearances of the unhappy Miss Jessel are more unnerving than those of Quint. The first glimpse of her, far away across the reedy lake, is so indefinite that we cannot be absolutely sure whether she is really there or whether it is a trick of bushes and shadows. The next time we see her there; however, she is clear enough, and that much nearer to us. It is difficult to convey in words the feeling of unease engendered by the sight of the black-gowned, motionless, unhappy figure in the midst of the flowers and reeds. At the end of the scene, after Flora has been led shrieking away, Miss Giddens turns slowly back, and we await the relief of finding the figure no longer there—but are denied it. Miss Jessel's other appearance is in the schoolroom—a small, low-roofed attic containing a little dais for Miss Giddens's desk in an arched window. The governess, collecting together her books preparatory to leaving, hears once again the sinister buzzing. She looks up, and before her, only a few feet away now, filling the small space with her dark figure, is the weeping, haggard ghost . . . ("I could almost find it in my heart to pity her," Miss Giddens has said in effect earlier, "if what she is doing were not so wicked.") Here we are given a clue. Miss Jessel disappears, not dissolving before our eyes, but vanishing while the camera is turned momentarily elsewhere. On the school slate over which she has been crying is a drop of water. Fallen from some flowers? Anyway, it is real enough, Miss Giddens dips her finger in it. But can a ghost weep real tears?

It is a mistake, I think, that we, and Miss Giddens, are allowed to see a photograph of Quint. His menace is the more strongly felt when his physical appearance is left vague. Of course, it affords grounds for the argument that Miss Giddens may have, at least partially, imagined things. One of the strongest points she puts to Mrs. Grose in the book was how, if she had "made it up," she could have given so accurate a description of the visitants.

The former relationship between Quint and Miss Jessel is made out to have been more explicitly sexual than appears from the book—e.g. Mrs. Grose's line: "Rooms—used by daylight as if they were dark woods." The point is stressed in the famous scene of Miles's goodnight kiss which so shakes Miss Giddens—and us—with its precocious passion.

The final sequence, Miles's outburst and death, is true horror. Jack Clayton has coaxed an almost unbelievably convincing performance out of the young Martin Stephens. Particularly macabre is the scene where, cleverly lit and photographed so that his face looks like a dark, bloated mask of evil, he screams out appalling abuse at the governess in his high, innocent, child's voice.

Deborah Kerr, looking much too attractive for us ever to consider she need have remained a sex-frustrated governess, gives a beautifully understanding performance. The Mrs. Grose of the film (an earthy portrayal by Megs Jenkins) is markedly less sympathetic towards Miss Giddens, particularly towards the end.

Clayton has been criticised for making use of old tricks of suspense such as billowing curtains, faces pressed to windows, ticking clocks, shock cuts and the rest. It is not the fact that such effects have been used in the past and will be used in the future that matters, however, but how they are used in the present. Here they are handled superbly, and it is difficult to imagine a better film version of the famous ghost story.

9. A French Classic

In early 1943 the enormous and totally unexpected success of a fantastic thriller *The Cat People* (director Jacques Tourneur, producer Val Lewton), set in motion the horror cycle—perhaps spiral would be a more suitable word—which has gone on expanding ever since and still shows no sign of contraction. During the same year Henri-Georges Clouzot made a film dealing in horror of a subtler kind—the degeneration of a community. Its title was *Le corbeau*, and the echoes of the scandal it stirred up are still not forgotten. The film was seized upon with delight by the occupying Germans, retitled *A Little Town in France*, and exhibited as an example of the depravity of French provincial life. After the Liberation, the picture was indignantly banned by the military censorship, and is even now regarded with disfavour in certain quarters.

Clouzot was born in 1907 (and died at the age of seventy) and after sounding out one or two careers was suddenly forced to earn a quick living by the financial collapse of his parents. He became secretary to a singer, thus making an acquaintance with the world of show business. He soon turned to films, first as cutter, then script adaptor. He went to Berlin, worked with Anatole Litvak and others on French dialogue (and absorbed a German approach which is evident in his own films), and eventually became an assistant director. Then, tragically, illness struck him, and for five years he was in a sanatorium. On recovering he once again turned to script writing, and to the rebuilding of his interrupted career. After further frustration caused by the outbreak of the war, he eventually directed his first film, *L'assassin habite au 21* in 1942. *Le corbeau* followed in the next year.

In 1947 he made *Quai des Orfèvres*, an unusually realistic and uncompromising police film, and the following year the notorious *Manon*, with its closing scene of the little band of Jews arriving in Palestine and being slaughtered by Arabs, and the final burial (severely curtailed in England) of Manon's body in the sand. 1953 saw what is probably his most famous production, *Le salaire de la peur*. This story of four men driving lorries loaded with nitro-glycerine across Central America for use in blowing up a burning oil-well is primarily an exercise in suspense—a long-drawn agony of slow tension—but at least two sequences (the hauling of Jo's oil-drenched body from the pool, and the final scene of Mario's death) touch the deeper nerve.

Les diaboliques appeared in 1955. In *Le salaire de la peur* and *Le corbeau* horror is an incidental ingredient. In *Les diaboliques* it is almost the entire recipe. As seems inevitable with Clouzot, *Les diaboliques* was received with praise and condemnation in about equal, and sometimes extravagant, proportions. Comments ranged from "his most brilliant film," "surprise ending brilliantly concealed," "a masterly thriller," to "basic absurdity of plot" and "vulgar, nasty and French"—the last adjective presumably, but ill-manneredly, meant as derogatory. One critic, astonishingly, finds in it something in common with Stroheim's *Greed*. Paul Dehn could hardly find words strong enough to express his praise. "Guignol at its grandest. Clouzot handles this bloodcurdling material in the one way guaranteed to make it horrifically effective, i.e., by *rejecting* every melodramatic artifice . . . and photographing his story head-on—at human eye-level—as though he were making a newsreel. The result is, in its ghastly way an even more shattering triumph than the same director's *Le salaire de la peur*."

The setting, brilliantly suggested, is a seedy public school for boys in a French provincial town—ugly, decaying buildings, bumbling, browbeaten ushers, stale and unappetising meals, shrill, loutish, pathetic and probably corrupt pupils, dead leaves, stagnant water, schoolbooks smelling of mildew. The story, taken from the novel *Celle qui n'était plus*, by Boileau and Narcejac, concerns the murder of the sadistic brute of a headmaster,

Three scenes from *Les Diaboliques:*
Simone Signoret and laundry basket.

Simone Signoret, Véra Clouzot and laundry basket.

Michel Delasalle. The school and the capital necessary to run it belong to his wife Christina, a pale, cowed, fragile young woman with a weak heart. The teaching staff consists of two male nonentities and Nicole Horner, handsome, strong, forceful, who has been his mistress almost from the day she arrived. He has, however, treated her as badly as his wife, and the two young women have been driven into an alliance against him. At the opening of the film Nicole is wearing dark glasses to conceal the bruised eye he has given her. Together they work out an elaborate plan to rid themselves of their common tormentor. Luring him away from the school to her cheap lodging house, they induce him to drink some doctored whiskey—and drown him in a bath. The body is later wrapped in a nylon tablecloth, packed into a laundry basket, taken back to the school, and at dark tipped into the grimy water of the school swimming pool.

The entire murder sequence is a clumsy, stumbling, panting scene of horror: the lugging of the heavy, uncannily resistant body to the bath, the bubbling immersion, the dark-soaked lounge suit,

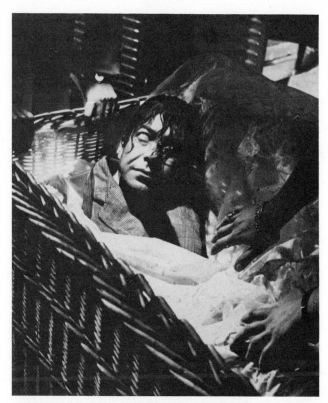
Laundry basket and contents: Paul Meurisse.

the horrible buoyancy, the desperate inspiration (Nicole's) of placing a heavy ornament on its chest to keep it submerged, a shot (which is intended for a purpose to print itself on the mind's eye—and succeeds) of the staring, upturned eyes in the flabby, dead face under the water. It is all ghastly, and all done without any hint of the sadistic revelling in violent death which makes many routine films so repellent. In some degree it resembles the killing in Hitchcock's *Torn Curtain,* in which he has stated his intention of showing just how difficult it is to deprive a man of his life. It is, when one considers it, a more salutary, a fundamentally less indecent method of presentation than the balletic deaths in a Western or the techni-colored glamourised slayings in historical or roman-tic "epics," where murder appears as simple or aesthetically satisfying. Killing is a difficult and filthy business, Clouzot and Hitchcock say, and should appear as such.

The loading of the creaking, pliant wicker basket on the van, the journey through the countryside, the water starting to ooze out of the nylon tablecloth wrapping, the ungainly dragging of the thing to the edge of the pool in the dark of night—all this is done with such power, as coldly and factually as if (to quote Paul Dehn) we are watching a newsreel, that we are made to feel—perhaps reprehensibly—a corresponding load off our minds as the heavy body splashes at last into

the water, and the lightened basket is tipped back.

So far the horror, however fearful, is at any rate of the earth earthy. But now another dimension is reached. For when, shortly after, the pool is drained (the slow emptying, watched in anguished expectation from a window by the women, is another brilliantly timed suspense scene), no corpse is there. Soon other mysterious events occur. Michel's suit is returned, newly pressed, from the cleaners; a school-group photograph taken after the death shows a shadowy face, strangely like his, gazing out from a window in the background. Is he, in fact, dead? But we saw his body tipped into the pool. An unidentified dead man is found. The pair go to the morgue, but it is not Michel. A scruffy, dubious ex-policeman brow-beats them into letting him attempt to solve the mystery. Eventually Nicole's nerve gives, and she departs. Christine's health also has given way, and she has to retire to her bed. She is now alone in the dingy, rambling, ill-lit school—alone, that is, except for an odd visit from the Inspector, whose manner is far from bedside. The climactic sequence, with the frightened woman, in her white nightdress, wandering through the dark passages, makes bril-liant use of every means of tautening the nerves. A typewriter taps behind a half-open door, but the room is empty. A hat and gloves on a table assume terrifying significance. A light flickers. Water pours from a tap. A hand, in a glove, turns a knob, moves along a banister. Her nerve breaks. She runs for sanctuary—to her own bathroom—but finds no sanctuary there; finds, indeed, the ultimate horror which kills her. Before her in the bath—exactly as in the shot we could not forget earlier in the film—is Michel's body. The shock finally destroys her weakened heart. With a long, strangled moan, sliding slowly down the white-tiled wall, she dies. It is one of the truly horrific moments in the cinema, paling the most elaborate *papier-mâché* monster into significance.

What follows is the famous, or notorious, double twist. Whether or not it does what it has been accused of doing, and makes nonsense of the human relationships which have so far been built up (I think one must admit that to a certain extent it does), it is highly effective as a shock surprise, and this is its main purpose. Clouzot was not, after all, setting out to study the interaction of human characters (though they have more individuality and depth than may be found in many a more pretentious and "serious" film), but to raise our hackles. And raise them he undeniably does. The field may be limited, but in it Clouzot has accomplished, in the words of Arthur Knight, "film-making of breath-taking virtuosity."

10. Hitchcock and Psycho

With the possible exception of *The Birds* (1963), *Psycho* (1960) is the only Alfred Hitchcock film which qualifies for entry into the category of horror. In many others, however, there are moments when the atmosphere of suspense or excitement may suddenly darken, when chaos appears to take command, when we find ourselves looking down into the pit. It is interesting to note that as often as not these are moments selected as exemplifying "typical Hitchcock": the "knife" episode in his first sound film, *Blackmail* (1929), horrible not so much for the distorted voice but for the muting away of other voices as we are drawn into the girl murderer's secret, closed, panicking mind; the moment in *The Lady Vanishes* when Margaret Lockwood, thinking she has at last found the

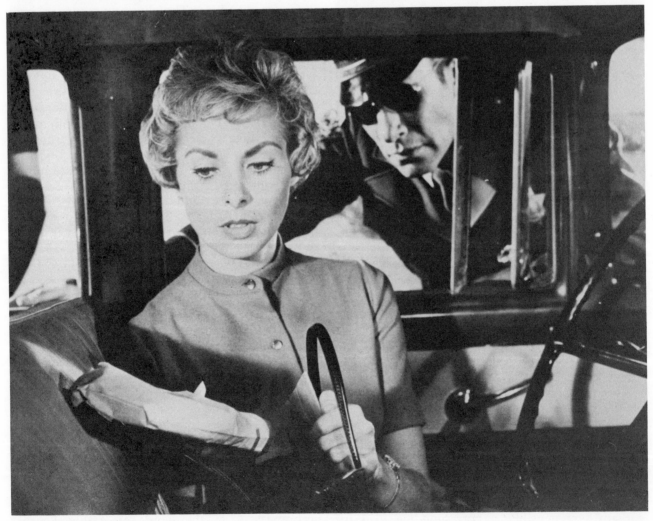

Janet Leigh in *Psycho*.

"The old dark house" in *Psycho*.

missing old lady in the railway compartment, cries out in relief, "Miss Froy!"—and the hard, grim, strange face of the young German woman rises slowly into view beneath what has appeared to be a familiar hat. There is the organ note which goes on for too long in *The Secret Agent* (1936); the distant aeroplane sowing fertiliser where no crops are, in *North by Northwest* (1959)—Hitchcock well knows that the horror of a bright empty space can equal that of the dark enclosed room; the carousel out of control in *Strangers on a Train*. In *Rear Window* (1954) there is the sudden close-up of the murderer's face in the binoculars realising that he is being seen, and the extinguishing of the strip of light under the door which indicates that he is outside the room in which James Stewart is imprisoned by his broken leg. In *The Birds*, there is the silent gathering of the crows behind the girl waiting outside the school, and, perhaps the most horrid moment in the entire film—the appearance of one little sparrow beneath the chimney and the heroine's warning "Mitch—look . . . !"

To these may be added two instances from *Torn Curtain* (1966): the curiously unnerving stopped camera shots of the dancing ballerina, like an evil bird of prey, recognising the hunted couple in the audience (less effective, for some reason, on a second viewing), and the dreadful, struggling, inefficient killing of the Russian security man. "I wanted to show just how difficult it is to kill a man," said Hitchcock, and in this sequence, one of the most gruesome in all his work, murder is represented as the clumsy, obscene thing it is. The happy laughter with which the scene has been received by certain audiences is perhaps the most horrifying touch of all. Did Hitchcock in his cunning foresee this, one wonders, bringing the famous "transference of guilt" theme to its ultimate development, by transferring right out of the screen to those people themselves?

All these, however, are episodes. *Psycho* is horror entire. The scenario is adapted by Joseph Stefano from a novel by Robert Bloch. Marion Crane, a secretary, is reduced to sordid, hurried lunch time love-making because her lover cannot afford to marry her. An over-rich client of the firm, a thoroughly unpleasant boaster, brings forty thousand dollars to the office in the course of

Anthony Perkins in *Psycho*.

business and Marion is entrusted with banking it. Yielding to a sudden temptation, she decides to run off with it, join her lover, Sam Loomis, and get married. The very thoughtlessness of the act, coupled with the boasting fool to whom it belongs, helps to retain our sympathy. How on earth did she ever think she could get away with it? Pleading a supposed headache, she drives away in her car with the cash. After an unnerving encounter with a police officer on the lonely highway she exchanges her car for another—so obviously in a panic that the garage-man's suspicions are aroused, and continues on her flight. As night falls and rain starts to pour down she loses her way, and eventually arrives at a dingy, isolated motel. Its owner, Norman Bates, offers her a meal and talks to her in a room filled with the louring shapes of stuffed birds. His hobby, he explains. (It is interesting to consider the recurrence of bird images in later Hitchcock films; even in *Torn Curtain* the vulture-like aspect of the dancer recognising the runaways has been noted.) In the course of their conversation, Marion makes up her mind finally to do what she has already half decided—return the money and face the music. That night, while taking a shower, she is ferociously murdered—by a figure resembling Norman's description of his mentally unbalanced mother. Norman comes in, cleans up the dreadful

results, and buries Marion, wrapped in the shower curtain, and her car in a bog near the motel. The car, after a harrowing moment of hesitancy, sinks down into the mud with apparent finality.

Marion, however, has a sister who becomes worried about her disappearance. A private investigator, Arbogast, arrives at the motel, and is not satisfied about Norman. He enters the gaunt, Victorian frame house beside the motel on his way to speak to Mrs. Bates, and he, too, is stabbed to death. Now, however Sam Loomis also arrives on the scene. Together with the sister, Lila, he comes to see the Bates motel. Lila, alone, enters the old house and searches it from top to bottom, discovering disturbing evidence. Finally she enters the cellar, where earlier on we have seen Norman carrying the chattering, protesting but apparently helpless Mrs. Bates. There she encounters nightmare and imminent death, but is saved by the appearance of Sam. At this interval of time it is probably giving away no secrets to divulge that the psychopath is Norman himself, who had disinterred his mother's corpse, mummified it, and kept it in the house as his companion. A psychologist "explains" the case in terms of obsessive mother-possessiveness leading to infantilism, sexual inhibition and mania, and we are left with a final shot of Norman seated wrapped in a blanket against the cell wall, motionless, now finally "possessed."

A very great deal has been written about this most horrific of thrillers. It is not the intention here to go again over ground already well covered, but rather to consider briefly Hitchcock's method of manipulating his audience and leading them, willing victims, from apparent security, through unease, to final terror.

The film starts in heat and sunshine—a high travelling shot (taken from a helicopter) moving over the mid-Western town, and eventually entering a shaded room. Here we find Marion and Sam in torrid embrace at the end of one of their hurried meetings. The scene is too long. Apart from its plot necessity as a means of showing the motivation for Marion's theft, however (which could be equally well indicated if they had been sitting over a cup of coffee in the lounge), it has a deeper purpose—discernible by hindsight on a second viewing—in its depiction of normal, healthy "sex" as a contrast to the fearful results of repression and perverted instincts later on.

All the sequences leading to Marion's absconding with the money are fairly light in tone—promising excitement and suspense, but not hinting at anything much darker. The first shadow is cast as Marion is held up by traffic lights on her way out

74

of the town. Suddenly her boss crosses the road in front of her. Just as she starts off again we see his face through the windscreen, turned round to her in sharp astonishment. It is difficult to convey in words the disquieting effect of this brief moment. Hitchcock well knows the shock which can be created by sudden realisation in a staring face. (The dancer in *Torn Curtain,* the murderer in *Rear Window.*) Apart from being the first flaw in Marion's hasty plans, it is also the first tiny slit in the cosy cover of our security.

The quick change from the bustling, crowded streets to the deserted, wide countryside (again the open space) is another. The car, stationary and silent, which had seemed so powerful and secure in the enclosed city, now looks exposed and vulnerable. Inside it Marion sleeps. A police officer, the only moving figure in the wide expanse, looks in, and down, at her. He wears large dark glasses. He questions her, not exactly suspiciously, but a little too slowly, too heavily. A perfectly ordinary policeman, no doubt—and perfectly normal in wearing dark glasses to ward off the blinding light of the white expanse. But the whole encounter is slightly off-beat. An easy explanation would be that we are seeing it through Marion's eyes; but Hitchcock is subtler than that. We are sharing Marion's anxiety, but we are seeing it through our own eyes, sharing her emotions with our own in an ingenious softening-up process for the terror which is to come. The episode leads to nothing. Once she is in her new car and away the policeman (leaning glass-masked on the bonnet of his car across the road from the garage), passes out of Marion's life—the few hours of it that are left. But not out of our minds.

Her long drive to darkness and death continues, with marvellous shots of the gradual decline of the day—particularly the hour when the dusk is falling and it is both too early and too late for the lamps to be lit. Throughout all this section the atmosphere is enormously helped by Bernard Herrmann's music—with an undertone of monotonous rocking phrases somewhat like the tuneless chant a frightened child might sing to reassure itself in the dark, but the very reverse of comforting. As she at last turns into the courtyard of the motel, past the little entrance sign, half blinded by the pouring rain, the ground has been prepared for us better than, at a first viewing, we can know. At the very least, two visits to the film are necessary for a full appreciation of the skill displayed in this long, important opening.

The ensuing scenes with Norman Bates, surprisingly, lower the tension. This is, of course, deliberate, in preparation for the shock to come. From Marion's arrival until the moment when Norman removes the picture from the spyhole (how is it that Hitchcock endows even a small hole in a wall with a sinister existence of its own!), we are permitted, in a small measure, to relax—at least unless we have seen the film before. Once again, on subsequent visits, the ingenuity with which hints are dropped and details accumulated becomes apparent.

Marion, having lightened her soul by her decision to confess and seek absolution for her crime, prepares for sleep. She goes to take a shower. Naked under running water, as defenceless and close to rebirth as a human being can get, she finds fury and death. Hitchcock has told how this "murder under the shower" took an entire week to film. It lasts a few seconds—the English version was apparently slightly cut—and it is, quite simply, terrifying. After the film has been seen once it is difficult to think back and decide how much in the brief build-up seems sinister because one knows what is to happen. Everything in that bathroom seems premonitory of horror. The shower curtain-rings rattle a warning. The shower-spray itself—large in close-up, a looming metallic circle against the white tiles—takes on an extraordinary personality of its own, a bland, godlike indifference, obediently pouring out the water which not only cleanses Marion's body and spirit, but also drowns the sound of the approaching murderer and thus deprives her of any possible chance (small though it may be) of defending herself.

The actual murder is shown as a flurry of quick, stabbing confused shots to the sound of distorted screaming bird cries. It horrifies, but strangely does not disgust. From the first immobilising sight of the dark shadow through the plastic curtains to the final close-up we are caught and held, hypnotised, at the mercy of a few feet of film. But there is no revelling. It is at one and the same time the most brutal, and yet the cleanest, of killings. The white shining bath, the running water which so easily cleans and renews itself, the absence of sticky, bloodstained clothing all account for this—as does the austere black-and-white photography. *Psycho* in colour is inconceivable. The sequence ends with a stupefying shot as the camera spirals up and away from an enormous close-up of an eye. Everything dies away and only exhaustion is left—an odd peacefulness, almost like the aftermath of a mystical experience—and the ritual cleansing to follow.

Nothing in the remainder of the film approaches this sequence in horror, though there is plenty of nightmare to come: the killing of the detective (on a landing shot from high above, the camera hurtling down a full flight of stairs as it follows his fall)—Lila's approaching the old house, a subjective travelling shot, strangely foreboding—her confrontation with the mummified body, twisting suddenly round on the rocking chair, wildly swinging shadeless light, bird-shrieks, threatening knife—and of course the famous final shot of Norman on the prison bench. As the camera slowly approaches his hooded unmoving figure, shawled and shabby-black against the wall, we hear his [his mother's] thin voice protesting how harmless he (she) is—wouldn't hurt a fly (one is actually walking unharmed within reach). In the split second before he fades from sight the dreadful sunken corpse-face appears superimposed on his own. In the best tradition of horror the sight is gone before we clearly realise it has been there, and we are watching under the end-titles the symbolic return to light and sanity in the raising of the car—and Marion—and the stolen money—from the swamp.

The story line follows Bloch's novel fairly closely, except for the transposition of the opening and the characterisation of Norman, who originally was a pink, plump, balding man with rimless glasses. The book, however, is crudely and luridly written. Hitchcock and Stefano have skilfully raised the film script above this rather squalid level and—aided by the personality and performance of Anthony Perkins—have elicited a certain sympathy for the wretched Norman. It is this hint of the tragic flaw, together with the soberness and penetration with which the darker recesses of the human mind are examined (apart from the facile "psycho-analytical" explanation), that lift *Psycho* far out of the framework of sensationalism in which its bare story is moulded.

Criticism, as in the case of *Les diaboliques* and also later in that of *Repulsion*, was widely divergent. *Psycho* may be admired or detested—it cannot be just written off as a black joke. Robin Wood goes so far as to call it one of the key works of our age.*

Hitchcock is said to have been perturbed by the fact that audiences took his film seriously. But Hitchcock himself is not always to be taken seriously . . . when giving interviews.

*In *Hitchcock's Films* (London/New York, 1965).

11. Roger Corman and Edgar Allan Poe

Roger Corman's position is a somewhat ambiguous one. An enormous amount has been written about him, particularly in the last five years or so, and yet he remains something of a mystery. His output is prodigious, but not one of his films was press-shown in Britain until *The Fall of the House of Usher* (1960). He became the hero (or victim) of a horror-cult, but was—and often still is—treated with patronising condescension by many critics and film pundits. Although he directed his first film as late as 1955, accurate details of his work are sometimes difficult to obtain, even the unconquerable "Monthly Film Bulletin" of the British Film Institute being forced to confess to a few minor defeats.

Corman was born in Detroit in 1926, educated at Stanford University, and also spent one term at Oxford. After serving in the Navy during the Second World War, he started work as a bell boy with Twentieth Century-Fox, going on from there to story analysis.

He has himself produced almost all the films he has directed so far, and numerous others besides. Figures vary from different sources, but the number of his productions in the past twelve years must be around sixty to seventy, of which he has directed well over forty. Many of these were low-budget quickies, varying in subject from Westerns (*Five Guns West* (1955), *Gunslinger* (1956)), to science-fiction (*It Conquered the World, Not of this Earth,* both 1956). In 1959 came a reasonably successful science-horror, *The Wasp Woman,* telling the story of a glamorous cosmetics-firm owner who, realising that her fading beauty is affecting both her private and business life, uses a preparation of wasps' enzymes to restore her youth, with predictable results. This fantasy, somewhat resembling the basis of Roald Dahl's terrifying story

"Royal Jelly," was treated with considerable horrific flair.

*

It is, however, on the series of Edgar Allan Poe films that Corman's reputation thus far rests. The first, *The Fall of the House of Usher,* though cheaply made and (apart from the inimitable Vincent Price) stickily acted, was redeemed by its comparative restraint, its welcome period accuracy, its essential fidelity—despite elaboration—to the story, and Floyd Crosby's first-rate camera-work. The impression given was of a resourceful use of somewhat inadequate material. There was also a refreshing sense of humour which was *not* indulged in to the detriment of the horror. ("See to the crypt, will you?", says Roderick Usher to his ancient manservant after a coffin has upset its unpleasant contents on the floor.) Corman's early attitude towards Poe seems to combine affectionate amusement with genuine respect—not unsuited to a writer described by a contemporary as being "three-fifths genius and two-fifths fudge." At least Corman preserves on the screen, even in his less successful translations, the strange dark beauty that pervades and often illuminates his uneven author's work. It is perhaps significant that as the cycle progresses the tendency to "send up" the originals lessens, until in *The Tomb of Ligeia* it is conspicuous by its absence.

The Pit and the Pendulum (1961) was made by much the same team. With budgets still obviously restricted, it suffered from repetition and has a rather laboured touch. Poe's gruesome story was merely tacked on to provide a grisly climax to a scenario by Richard Matheson. Once again performances did little to help, although there was the advantage of the presence of Barbara Steele, arch-heroine of horror, and, of course, Vincent Price.

The Premature Burial (1961) shows little advance, the mixture being much as before. On the credit side is more atmospheric photography by Floyd Crosby. There are also several imaginative scenes, notably one where the hero dreams he is being buried alive—the start of which, with a black screen and only the sounds of loud heartbeats audible, awakens an odd memory of Jekyll's first change to Hyde in Mamoulian's masterpiece. Ray Milland, an excellent actor in many roles, did not here make up for the loss of Vincent Price.

Tales of Terror (1962) consisted of three short Poe stories, "Morella," "The Black Cat" (in which was cleverly incorporated "The Cask of Amontillado"), and "The Facts of the Case of M. Valdemar." Here Corman evidently had the advantage of a more generous budget, and certainly a better cast including, besides Mr. Price, Basil Rathbone and Peter Lorre. With less screentime to fill per story, Richard Matheson was able to present more con-

centrated, less padded versions, and the result was a noteworthy anthology.

In *The Haunted Palace* (1963), the Poe contribution was combined with H. P. Lovecraft's "Charles Dexter Ward." Corman has stated that he took Lovecraft's story and transposed it into the universe of Poe. The director very rightly refused to allow the distributors to omit Lovecraft's name from the credits, as the result was a much more closely knit and interesting story than some of the earlier, padded-out instances. The production once again showed signs of straitened economy, but Corman demonstrated anew his skill in finding beauty in the conventional misty landscapes, huge baroque rooms, unending stone-flagged passages and the rest of the stock-in-trade. The basis of the story is the worship of old gods resulting in the birth of a race of semi-monsters, and the atmosphere of brooding evil, ancient superstitions and dabblings in things better left alone is admirably caught. Some of the "mutants"—it is difficult to avoid use of the anachronistic word—are quite frightening at a first glance, particularly a little girl,

Hazel Court in *The Masque of the Red Death.*

78

Vincent Price with Jane Asher in *The Masque of the Red Death*.

but the effect is weakened by bringing them too close. A face which is half blank, eyeless skin does not horrify when the patch could so obviously be removed with ease. The chief monster, however, to which Vincent Price, possessed by his evil ancestor, prepares to offer up his wife, is hardly glimpsed and much more formidable—in spite of the theatrical colourings in which he spends his days. The chief merit of the film, however, is in the subtlety with which Corman and Price (who play's both parts) suggest the change of personality as Charles Dexter Ward's form is gradually taken over by the wicked forebear, Curwen. Corman's handling of this theme foreshadows its splendid flowering in *The Tomb of Ligeia.*

The ambiguous ending, where Charles, apparently once more back in his own body after the customary holocaust, is seen to look, after all, more like Curwen than himself (and his wife even starts to resemble Curwen's evil mistress) is brought off with a beautifully light, sardonic touch—never insisted on, but delicately hinted in the final shot to cause the requisite shiver.

Through all these films run flashes of imaginative power and originality which, one feels, required only favourable circumstances to fan them into full flame. With his first British film, *The Masque of the Red Death* (1964), Corman apparently found them. This story of the devil-worshipping Prince Prospero in medieval Italy abducting an innocent young village girl, Francesca, into his castle and trying to interest her in his diabolical practices while the plague rages outside, is treated with a combination of beauty and horror which results in a fine piece of *cinéma Gothique.* The magnificent settings, in which the camera seems to take an active delight in recording and passing on to us the loveliness of brilliant colours against grey stone, provide a bizarre contrasting background to the corruption, perversion and self-degradation of the castle's inhabitants. The physical details of torture and violent death are nowhere dwelt on—except perhaps in one or two brief dungeon scenes—but their proximity haunts the entire action.

Sequences such as Francesca's first discovery of

the Satanic goings-on may follow a familiar pattern—midnight awakening, mysterious echoing voices, slow wandering through enormous rooms, Bluebeardish opening of the forbidden door, shock confrontation, hectic screaming retreat—but they have seldom been done with such stunning effect. In particular her progress through a series of small contrastingly coloured rooms is remarkable. Much use is made of these through the film, and the result is extraordinarily beautiful.

The one touch of "Hammer horror"—the stringing up to a chandelier and burning alive of an evil Duke who has been inveigled into donning an ape's skin for the Masque—is sufficiently prepared for in its motivation (a gentle dwarf avenging the Duke's maltreatment of his tiny dancing partner) to avoid the charge of mere sensationalism. Even so, it seems incomprehensible that a Censor (in Britain) should pass this more or less extraneous horror scene, and yet expunge almost the whole of the black magic which has so important a bearing on the plot. Example-following seems unlikely in either case, and of the two, a little Satanic cavorting at midnight would be less reprehensible.

The film is full of subtleties. A fine scene with a falcon, when Prospero uses it to demonstrate the inevitability of cruel death in nature, is followed later by the killing of his mistress by the bird—an episode which equals Hitchcock's great film. The attack is led up to by a shot from behind a clock, the enormous blade-shaped pendulum of which, swinging across the camera, recalls—surely with intention—Poe's famous instrument of torture from another tale.

Corman has stated that he intended to show that neither evil nor good is the victor, and that the phrase which sums up the film's viewpoint is the Red Death's: "Each man makes his own heaven and his own hell." This ambiguity pervades the film. The gentle dwarf is responsible for the Duke's dreadful death; the tiny, childlike Esmeralda speaks with a husky, sexy voice (not her own); Francesca, the only wholly "good" character, is so colourless that one actually begins to long for a glimpse of the old Eve; Prospero kills and tortures with relish, yet treats Francesca with gentleness, and spares, for no personal reason, a little girl from the general slaughter of the villagers. This shifting uncertainty of values adds to the sense of unease, and thus of horror, which the film generates so powerfully.

The Masque itself, somewhat tame in its earlier stages, works up to a truly epic climax as Death spreads his red mark over the dancers. Prospero's final confrontation with the hooded figure, first in the tiny scarlet chamber and then in the huge central hall, culminates in a fine shock. We have seen so many skulls, shrivelled mummies and suchlike exposed by discarded masks that we are prepared for anything except what Prospero discovers—that Death has his own face.

From this moment until the end all naturalism is transcended. Prospero's death is led up to through a wild scurry of deliberately balletic movement among the plague-stricken dancers, and the final sequence shows, not the conventional reunion of young lovers, but a gathering in grey mist of other "Deaths" to report progress. The Red Death, discovered playing cards with the little girl, is joined by a yellow death and others of varying shades. After declaring the results of their passing, they move slowly off together. The scene, of considerable poetry and grandeur in itself, serves also to indicate that the Red Death is only one messenger among many others. Behind them all stands . . .?

The Red Death's final mysterious reference to an entirely unknown "old man in the village" among the half-dozen who escaped the plague is a wonderfully imaginative moment.

Vincent Price gives a fine bravura performance, never permitting his sardonic asides to tip over into burlesque, and the dialogue almost throughout is acceptable.

The second of Corman's British Poe films, *The Tomb of Ligeia,* has been regarded in some critical quarters as a falling off from its predecessor. Admittedly the epic sense of grandeur and doom may be missing, and the story reverts to the worn grooves of wax effigies in coffins, ghostly visitations and climactic holocausts, but the story is treated with seriousness and imagination, and taken on its own without irrelevant comparisons, as it should be, *Ligeia* shows that Corman's increase in stature with *The Masque* may be no freak growth.

Poe's enclosed story of a drug-soaked man who is haunted by his dead wife until he imagines her taking possession of his living one has inevitably been broadened out, and it is now post-mortem hypnotism which sets the ghostly ball rolling. Corman has brought his treatment of the transference of personality theme to its ultimate development here, both in the main case of the two wives Ligeia and Rowena (a "double" by Elizabeth Shepherd), and in a subsidiary example wherein the bemused husband Verden Fell (or Verdenfell according to an interview with Corman) becomes unable to recall by day what he has done by night.

The exterior signs of the feminine duplication—

Rowena's blonde-haired English sporting type, the black-tressed, white-faced Ligeia—supplement and reinforce the changes of character. Hair is a dominating symbol through the film. One of the most disturbing moments is when blonde Rowena discovers black hair in the brush which no one but herself uses. The climax of a terrifying dream sequence shows Rowena, after struggling frantically against the sluggishness of nightmare to escape from some unimaginable evil, seeing her husband and running to him in relief: he takes her in his arms, but suddenly his dark-clad figure is the long black hair of Ligeia who is embracing the panic-stricken girl. Nothing is overtly stated about Ligeia, which somehow makes her sinister presence the more inescapable. A black cat, which appears to be a sort of "familiar," makes vicious attacks on Rowena, in one marvellously eerie sequence luring her to the top of a tower by creeping ahead of her with Verden Fell's dark glasses dangling from its mouth.

The increasing strength of Ligeia's influence overcomes Rowena's personality until in the end it is difficult to know which is which. Eventually Rowena, horrified at seeing in a mirror that her

John Westbrook and Vincent Price in *The Tomb of Ligeia.*

Elizabeth Shepherd at the flaming climax of *The Tomb of Ligeia.*

hair has turned black and she is now Ligeia's counterpart, smashes the glass in a frenzy—and finds that it leads to a hidden part of the house. (A reminder of Cocteau's use of the mirrors to the underworld, in *Orphée*). The final quarter-of-an-hour has been criticised as too confused to follow, and certainly the metamorphoses occur with such rapidity that one is not sure which girl is which at any given moment. This, however, is merely the ultimate development of the theme, and it all makes for a splendid ending. If there must be a holocaust, this is at least a magnificent one. Verden Fell perishes with Ligeia (or is it?), and Rowena (or is it?) is rescued by her young lover. But, as a critic neatly commented, one doesn't give a penny for his chances of a happy future with a girl who only *looks* like Rowena.

The settings (Colin Southcott) are beautifully contrasted. The cool greys of the ruined abbey (according to one authority Glastonbury, but to Corman himself an old abbey in Norfolk), the yellows and blues in the huge shadowy house, and the reds and greens of the hunting scenes interplay with and reinforce each other in a kind of colour counterpoint.

12. Polanski and Repulsion

Monsters and vampires, man-made creatures and ghosts, mob cruelty and murderers, these are the stock ingredients of horror, and most of them have been handled on occasion with sufficient imagination to lift the result above the category of mere sensationalism. All such terrors, however, are seen from a distance, approaching us from outside ourselves. Our own feet rest on firm ground. Even the psychopathic killer of *Psycho* is treated from the viewpoint of his victims or pursuers, and his deeds are framed in the conventions of a mystery-thriller. But when the mind is the actual stuff of horror, when madness and collapse are presented from inside, rather than viewed from without, then the solid ground itself shifts and crumbles, and we do indeed find ourselves looking into the bottomless pit. This is the fearful theme of *Repulsion*, described by one critic as the most terrifying film ever made. In a most perceptive article, Kenneth Tynan states that Carol, the girl in *Repulsion* "has much in common with Tony Perkins in *Psycho*, but he [Polanski] goes deeper than *Psycho* by presenting a double murder from the killer's instead of the victim's point of view." Nor is there any attempt at a glib psychoanalytical explanation at the end. The film has been criticised for this (though in actual fact a broad hint is provided in the very last shot), but it is just the irrationality of much mental breakdown such as Carol's which gives an added "turn of the screw."

Roman Polanski, the director, was born in Paris of Polish parents in 1933. Both parents were put into a concentration camp by the Nazis—his father survived. After making several shorts, and achieving wide recognition with his first feature, *Knife in the Water*, Polanski met Gene Gutowski in 1964.

One result of this collaboration was *Repulsion*. Polanski has stated: "What interested me in making it is the study of a girl's disintegration; withdrawal turning to violence. I'm concerned with *showing* something—exposing a little bit of human behaviour that society likes to keep hidden because then

everyone can pretend it doesn't exist. But it does exist, and by lifting the curtain on the forbidden subject, I think one liberates it from this secrecy and shame." Thus pity is allied to terror and, as another critic has put it: "Polanski makes his fair murderess seem authentically tragic, herself the most pitiable victim of the evil she does."

Carol is a Belgian girl living in a somewhat dreary South Kensington flat with her sister Helen. Both girls are working, though Helen's job seems uncertain, and most of her time is taken up by an affair with a married man, Michael. Carol herself works in a beauty salon as a manicurist. Although apparently capable enough at her job, she is strangely withdrawn and moody. She treats with cool indifference her pleasant boy-friend, an extremely patient young man named Colin. She obviously resents Michael's presence in the flat, particularly his carelessness in leaving such things as his razor and toothbrush around in the bathroom. In all this, however, her attitude is in no way aggressive or deliberate—it is more a sort of helpless unhappiness. In the middle of an oppressive heat-wave Helen and Michael, despite a plea from Carol not to be left alone, go off for a holiday in Italy. In her loneliness (through the film Carol's essential loneliness is marvellously suggested) her mind starts to disintegrate. She begins to have hallucinations—of crumbling walls and strangers in the flat. After an incident at her work she is sent home. She shuts herself up finally in the flat, wandering aimlessly around in her nightgown. An abusive 'phone call (from Michael's wife, meant for Helen) further upsets her balance. The hallucinations become more terrifying. When Colin comes to see what is wrong and, worried and exasperated beyond bearing, breaks open the front door, she kills him with the utmost violence and hides the body in the bath. Later the landlord, a coarse boor, also forces his way into the flat, which she has feebly barricaded, and, misled by her appearance and manner, starts to make approaches to her. In

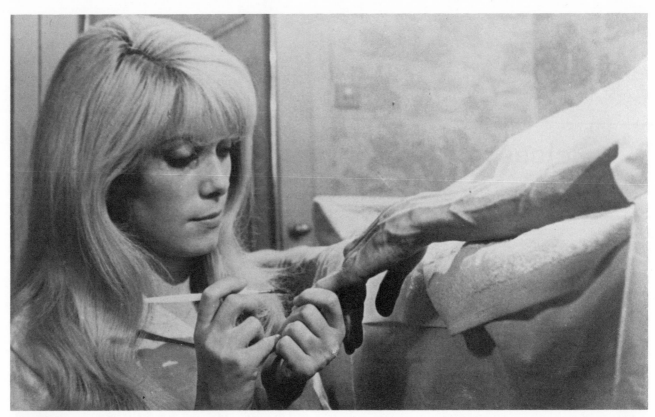

Repulsion:
Catherine Deneuve in the opening scene.

Yvonne Furneaux, as Helen, leaves her sister alone in the
flat.

wild panic and revulsion she slashes him to death with Michael's razor, and attempts to hide his body also. Rapidly the last shreds of sanity give way, and when Helen and Michael come back they find the flat a horrifying shambles, and Carol lying motionless and silent under a bed.

On the bare framework of this horror story Polanski has constructed a film of such complexity and subtlety that an entire book could be written about it. Here we must be content with a brief glance at some of the salient points. The film opens in darkness. We are, in fact, in Carol's mind almost literally, for as the camera draws back the darkness reveals itself as the pupil of her eye. On this enormous close-up the titles are imposed, accompanied by a single long-held note of music and monotonously alternating drumbeats, *pp*. As the titles finish the camera withdraws further to frame her face, sad, still and abstracted. Dressed in a white overall, she sits holding the hand of a woman who is lying, a bulky mound, on a raised couch. In the background are trolleys of instruments. It could be a hospital—but is in fact the beauty salon where Carol works, with the other girls, like vestal

A disintegrating mind.

Catherine Deneuve, as Carol, studies her distorted reflection.

Lining up a shot with Catherine Deneuve in Polanski's *Repulsion.*

virgins in a temple devoted to the sacred rites of artificial youth. A sharp protest from the inert, mud-masked woman jerks Carol out of her reverie. Later we accompany her, for the first of several important occasions, as she wanders absently through the South Kensington streets on her way to lunch. She passes a group of street workmen. One of them calls out some mild impertinence, which she ignores. The incident is not dwelt on, the words barely distinguishable, but the camera turns back for a brief moment to his face and his sweaty, vest-clad torso. Her boy-friend joins her and finds her aloof, shrinking back from his touch on her hair. After an odd conversation about rabbit for supper they part—he lingering to watch, a little wistfully, her colleague Bridget's affectionate leave-taking of her own boy-friend. Arrived home after work, Carol watches, equally wistfully, young nuns playing some childish game in an adjacent convent. The convent bell tolls. She carefully washes her feet, and removes with fastidious

distaste the razor and toothbrush from her glass. She wanders to the kitchen and, after a short exchange with Helen when she is told to mind her own business concerning Michael, remarks that a crack in the kitchen wall needs mending. Michael unexpectedly takes Helen out to dinner, leaving Carol alone in the flat, and the rabbit, prepared but uncooked, in the refrigerator. She wanders idly around the place, passing a family group on the sideboard, on which the camera momentarily pauses. It starts to approach it, but before the details become very clear the scene fades. Later that night, lying wakeful in the heat on her school-girlish bed, Carol gazes up at the wardrobe set against an unused door and the strangely foreboding shapes of suitcases and tennis rackets piled on top. An old-fashioned fireplace yawns blackly. The window curtains move gently and her bedside clock ticks. The convent bell tolls at midnight. Attracted and repelled, she listens to the chuckles and moans of physical enjoyment from her sister's room. As it reaches a climax and dies away, she buries her head in her pillows. Slowly the camera moves back from the quiet room.

This opening section has been described in some detail because every incident has its place in the development of Carol's breakdown. The rabbit, removed from storage and decaying in the heat, resembles a monstrous embryo, the bell triggers off her most violent hallucinations and heralds the second murder, the workman becomes her imaginary rapist, the unused door behind the dark wardrobe lights up, and opens to admit horror, the tiny crack in the kitchen develops into the breaking up of the flat's walls, the family group contains the hint as to Carol's secret, and becomes the last shot of the film, the little clock ticks thunderously in the otherwise dead silence of her nightmares.

Early in the film there is a long-held motionless shot of the full extent of the flat. Nothing happens, except an occasional glimpse of Helen making breakfast through the half-open kitchen door. This lengthy contemplation is very important, for seldom has an ordinary setting been given such significance. It is, indeed, a central character, and by the end we feel we have lived in it ourselves. Though by no means uncomfortable, it is as depressing as any living place which is not a home. Through it we can visualise the whole house full of solitary, rootless flat-dwellers—personalised in the glimpses of the woman opposite taking her dog down in the lift for "walkies," and keeping the door on the chain to refuse use of the telephone at the time of the tragedy, which, incidentally, she precipitates by causing Colin to shut Carol's front door behind him to prevent her from watching them. The flat, shut-off and solitary, reflects Carol's own withdrawn and lonely state, and eventually shares, literally, in her disintegration. By an inspired use of the distorting lens the sitting-room is made to become a vast cavern, the white-tiled bathroom a huge, dim, grey space with a tiny distant washbasin. All sense of proportion is lost. Huge cracks suddenly split the walls of the rooms, and those in the passage grow soft so that her hands sink into them—and later other hands reach through them to grab at her. A pendant in its plaster decoration swoops down at her as she lies in her bed. Finally the ceiling itself crumbles and dissolves into the pouring rain through which Helen and Michael drive up on their return from holiday.

All the hallucinations are handled with terrifying power. The first one of all, a momentary glimpse of a man's figure seen in a swinging wardrobe mirror, takes the breath away. The first time the light appears above the unused door Carol by a tremendous effort controls her imagination and when she looks up again, restful darkness has returned. The next time, however, there is no escape, and our horror equals hers as the door is pushed against the wardrobe. It is not happening to the heroine of a film; it is happening to us.

Throughout Polanski invites us to share, and thus to understand, Carol's repulsion. Even the clients in the beauty salon are gross, greedy, useless women, waited on by young girls with the ugly appurtenances of artificial beautification, their talk of either food, themselves or—scathingly—of men.

Polanski also comments ironically on our own attitude towards horror. Michael shrinks back horrified from the dreadful sight of Colin's body in the bath—but then leans forward for a further slow look. Carol picks up Michael's soiled vest in utter disgust, but cannot resist holding it to her face. She flings it away from her, but later it is in her room, and later still, as her mind goes, she is seen pathetically ironing it—with an unconnected iron. There is also an extraordinary moment towards the close of the film as Michael, refusing to wait for the ambulance, insists on carrying Carol out of the flat. On his way he pauses, gazing down at her face with its open, unseeing eyes. It is a quite unfathomable look, and one of the most disquieting moments of the whole film.

Some of the symbolism is fairly obvious—such as the postcard of the Leaning Tower of Pisa, and the playing nuns—but much of it is subtle and apt. There are two neat cuts from the flat to the beauty salon: one from the crumpled sheets of Helen's and Michael's bed to the girl's smooth white overall; the second from the wrinkled, ageing potatoes to the equally raddled face of Madame Denise. In the second the effect is increased by Madame's voice momentarily anticipating the visual cut. Left in the flat alone, Carol sees her reflection in a polished kettle, leaning forward so that her face is distorted by the curve. Returned from work, she slowly peels a glove off her hot fingers, as if removing not only the gross outer world, but a layer of her consciousness. After unexpectedly coming across Michael stripped to the waist as he shaves, she is seen crouched on the bed, absently wiping one hand across her nightgown. Lying alone in bed, just after Helen and Michael go, she moves her finger idly over the wall by her side, encounters a tiny crevice in the wallpaper and draws back sharply.

The scene with the landlord, which could so easily have been heavily melodramatic, is full of subtle touches. Having forced his way in, he comes across her standing just inside the sitting-room doorway, looking upwards and sideways at him rather like a child who is anxious to conceal a broken ornament. "Where is Miss Ledoux?" he asks her. She replies, "I am Miss Ledoux." But her tone is ambiguous, ending almost as a query. Is she, indeed, Miss Ledoux any longer? At what stage of mental collapse does personality cease to exist? Having handed him the money he has come to collect (and refused to allow him to let in the light to see it), she speaks only one word more: "Brussels," in answer to a question about where the family photograph was taken. Slouching listlessly on the sofa she watches, not his face, but his hands as they move in front of her—as a cat looks at a pointing finger rather than the object indicated. Only once does she look up at his face, raising her own in a most pathetic gesture when he asks if she is ill. Otherwise her abstraction is apparently complete—even his horrified exclamations at the general mess leave her unmoved—but when she is momentarily out of the room, she picks up the razor from the floor.

The actual murders, gruesome enough though they are, give no impression of being committed in a frenzy of blood-lust. Carol is not, to her, killing human beings at all, but rather destroying some threatening obscenity as one might stamp repeatedly on a loathsome insect. In the second, that of the landlord, she uses no violence until the last possible moment, even after he has made one attempt to assault her. Only when he comes at her again (after the sound of the convent bell) does she destroy him.

Very important are the various wanderings round the South Kensington and neighbouring streets on which we accompany her. Starting with the reasonably normal walk to lunch already noticed, each subsequent journey reflects her growing withdrawal until on her final one, before shutting herself up for ever, not even that most attention-drawing of all events, a car accident, has the power to rouse her. It is difficult to account for the powerful influence these wanderings, often photographed in large close-up, have in drawing us closer to her, in helping us, so to speak, to "know" her.

Sound is brilliantly used. It is hard to imagine a more apt musical accompaniment, from the sad, touching little tune which might be called Carol's "theme" (resolving most beautifully into its closing chord at the end), to the sinister *arpeggios* as she moves down the darkened passage, and the drumbeats or clashing cymbals of her hallucinations. Natural noises heighten the atmosphere—dripping taps, distant piano scales, clanking lift doors, a group of musicians playing "Waltzing Matilda" on a guitar accompanied by spoon-castanets (a weird trio, with its crab-like spoon-player), the convent bell. Note how subtly the last stroke is emphasised and cut off just before the landlord's murder. Then there are the distortions—the loud clock-tick during the silent hallucinations, the *apparent* cries and grunts during the murders, the ever more piercing 'phone and door bells, the ghastly travesty of sexual ecstasy in the final nightmare of rape. Note, too, how Helen's hysterical sobs at the end are made a grotesque echo of her own earlier cries of pleasure.

Catherine Deneuve is superb as Carol—it is quite unnerving to see her in some other film shortly afterwards. Yvonne Furneaux could not be bettered as her sister—lacking understanding rather than sympathy, yet cleverly hinting at some secret knowledge of Carol, in a little scene in the lift with Michael. Ian Hendry as Michael, conventional enough in earlier scenes, has some impressive moments on the return from the holiday. His indecision, shock, bewilderment, realisation that the publicity resulting from all this must break up his affair, if not his home—none of this mentioned in words—his mingled horror and fascination, above all that final enigmatic look at Carol.

At the very end of the film, after her inert form has been carried out of the flat and the neighbours (a cleverly selected group) have taken away the collapsing Helen, the camera slowly travels right round the sitting-room, passing over the strangely pathetic debris of that dreadful fortnight—a broken biscuit, the crumpled Pisa postcard, some half-finished sewing. Then it moves up to the family photograph. This time it does not stop at the frame. It moves, inexorably, right into the group, past the smiling elder daughter, the cheerful mother, the complacent father and others, to the small girl in the background. Standing behind her mother's chair, out of the enclosed little circle, her eyes are fixed on the man—her father. The expression on the child's face is terrifying, and the more so for being inscrutable. Loathing, fear, resentment, a longing for affection turned sour—it could be any of these, and it is unforgettable. The camera advances further—to the girl's eye, to the pupil—until nothing is left but the darkness of the mind from which, at the opening of the film, it slowly withdrew.

Inevitably, so controversial a film aroused criticism as well as high praise. Polanski was accused of generating no sympathy for his heroine. This is incomprehensible. Anyone who could hear unmoved (to take only two facile examples) Carol's last, hopeless plea to her sister, "Oh please—don't go!", or her broken voice as she sits in the flat after the first murder crooning a monotonous little chant such as children sing to comfort themselves in the dark, must indeed be devoid of understanding.

The two public house scenes, in which Carol is not involved, have been condemned as irrelevant. On the contrary, they are vital. One of the few moments where credulity might be slightly strained is when so harmless and gentle a young man as Colin takes a running jump at Carol's door and smashes it down. As it is, we can understand how his frustration and worry are fanned to the necessary heat by the chaffing and petty obscenities of his pub companions in the second scene— and the first is a necessary preparation for this.

One or two shots through a lensed Judas window in the front door have been described as affectation. In actual fact, Carol's last view of Colin is through this distorting medium (she does not look at him once he is in the hall), and this adds to her panic, leading to the murder.

Like any worthwhile film, *Repulsion* demands more than a single viewing. There is hardly a frame which has not a dual purpose—simultaneously developing and commenting on the story. A shot of the sprouting potatoes, for instance serves (a) to mark the passage of time, (b) to reflect the growing distortion of Carol's mind, and (c) to make a parallel cut to Madame Denise's wrinkled face. To take one simple instance of the film's complexity—the crack in the kitchen wall. Some time in her wanderings Carol becomes fascinated by a crack in some paving on a traffic island—actually sitting down to gaze at it and forgetting a date with Colin. The next time we see the kitchen crack, it has taken on the exact shape of the flaw in the paving. There is no close-up, the crack is seen from a different angle; it is probable that not one viewer in a hundred would notice this subtlety on a first visit, and it is only one of many.

Opinions will differ as to the most "shocking" moment in this film so crowded with shocks—the man in the mirror, perhaps, the opening of the unused door, or the last sudden thrust of a pair of hands through a patch in the wall. It may well be, however, that the most unnerving moment of all is a quieter one. Carol is sitting alone in the little basement of the beauty salon after listening to Bridget's tearful complaints of her boy-friend's "beastliness". She is staring idly in front of her, abstracted and withdrawn. Suddenly a shaft of sunlight comes through the dusty little window and falls on a chair beside her. For a moment she gazes at it blankly, then slowly leans forward and tries to brush the ray off the seat. On the quiet sound of her hand against the wood the scene fades. This brief intimation of the failing of reason, the remorseless approach of madness, is more fearful than any screaming shock cut would be. The dark door is opening, for Carol—and for us.*

*For a fuller analysis of this masterly film, including a detailed sequence of Carol's hallucinations, see my book *The Cinema of Roman Polanski* (London/New York, 1970).

13. British and American Horror, 1966-1976

Both British and American horror films of the period inevitably suffered to some degree from the grubby blight of "permissiveness," many of their makers appearing to feel obliged to introduce moments—however irrelevant—of needless nudity or silly sensationalism, suggesting an insultingly low opinion of the intelligence of the audiences for whom they were made; though neither Britain nor America descended quite to the abysmal depths of the Canadian *Shivers,* as nasty and puerile a film as has yet been seen in the aboveground cinema.

*Films featuring Dracula and Frankenstein are discussed in Chapter 4, and one or two British films of 1966 in Chapter 7.

Witch and victim. Two scenes from *The Witches*—Kay Walsh presiding.

Britain

Michael Reeves, to die tragically young, brought out his second film (after *Revenge of the Blood Beast,* 1965) entitled *The Sorcerers,* from a new stable, Tigon. Karloff is in good form as a hypnotising professor who is beaten at his own game by his wife, played with great relish by Catherine Lacey. Tigon also produced David Greene's *The Shuttered Room* in the same year, 1966. A really credible (and thus all the more terrifying) "thing in the attic," indicated by splendidly eerie sound effects, raises this conventionally shaped thriller into the realm of superior horror. The introductory sequence, photographed subjectively through a distorting lens, is a masterly hint of terror to come. Carol Lynley is vulnerable enough to arouse the most dormant protective instincts, and Flora Robson is grandly eccentric. *The Shuttered Room* has a reasonably believable story, characters to hold the interest, fine photography and tense, often subtle direction, and is one of numerous examples of a minor, low-budgetted film that proves far better of its kind than many a costly, over-publicised, wider-known "masterpiece."

In 1967 Amicus (Max J. Rosenberg and Milton Subotsky) followed up their earlier short-story anthology, *Dr. Terror's House of Horrors* with *Torture Garden,* from tales by Robert Bloch (of *Psycho*). The success of this splendidly macabre collection, together with the even better *House That Dripped Blood* (1971), the less effective *Tales from the Crypt* (1972), and *Vault of Horror* (1973) and *From Beyond the Grave* (1973), raises the question whether the linked-short-story method is not the best of all for the macabre movie. Some of the best television horrors have

Carol Lynley menaced in *The Shuttered Room*.

Judith Arthy also menaced in *The Shuttered Room*.

The climactic scene from *The Shuttered Room:* Carol Lynley.

been one hour or less in length. In the famous Grand Guignol Theatre four or five short plays, generally alternating horror with farce, made up a highly satisfying evening's fare.

After a remake of *The Old Dark House,* which is best forgotten as quickly as possible, Hammer brought out *The Witches,* a modest, unpretentious, but credible and altogether above average essay in black magic set in the present-day English countryside, with a script by Nigel Kneale from a novel by Peter Curtis. After a shaky start with an unnecessary Prologue, characters, situations and settings settle down into a nice example of sinister activities beneath the surface of everyday rural life, with Kay Walsh imposingly presiding over the village coven.

Roy Dotrice and Barbara Murray, with an inhabited coffin, in *Tales from the Crypt.*

An unrecognisable Peter Cushing rises from the grave in
Tales from the Crypt.

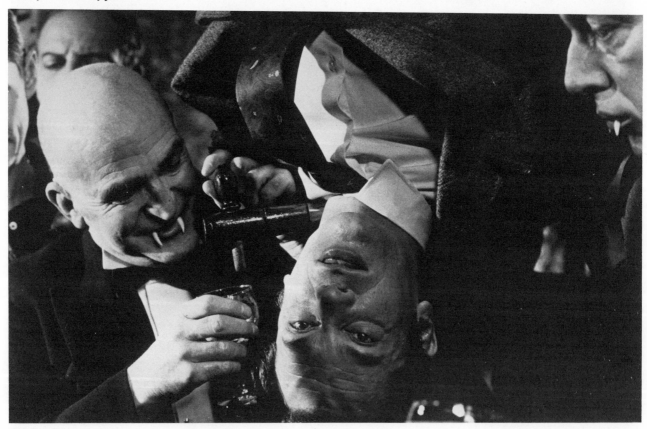

Daniel Massey "on tap" in a very peculiar restaurant: a
scene from *Vault of Horror.*

Peter Cushing and Jack Palance in *Torture Garden*.

Of the films mentioned above, *Torture Garden,* with its memorable final episode introducing Poe himself, and its tantalisingly ambiguous ending, is probably the most noteworthy taken as a whole, but nothing in any of them can approach the *Sweets to the Sweet* episode in *The House That Dripped Blood.* This brief tale of the pretty, innocent-seeming little girl who proves to have the powers of a witch is told with an economy and power (Peter Duffell directing) that truly chills the blood. The three participants—suffering father, horrified governess, angelic-satanic child—are superbly played by Christopher Lee, Nyree Dawn Porter and Chloe Franks. The last, incidentally, has more horror awaiting her the following year, in *Whoever Slew Auntie Roo?,* when she is imprisoned by a demented woman (Shelley Winters) who keeps the skeleton of her own child in a coffin. Helped by her slightly older brother, the little girl manages to escape, leaving the woman to burn to death in her own house, and the children the richer by a box of jewels. A resourceful small girl, Miss Franks, and not to be trifled with.

The last episode of *The House That Dripped Blood* is a gorgeous spoof about a veteran horror film star who inadvertently buys Dracula's cloak from a shabbily sinister old costumier, with bloodcurdling—if not entirely unexpected—results, affording Jon Pertwee and Ingrid Pitt some splendid moments in the grand Transylvanian tradition.

A somewhat different portfolio film—from the same firm, Amicus, and written by Robert Bloch—is *Asylum,* in which a young doctor (Robert Powell), accompanied, with notable irrelevance, by thunderous bars from Moussorgsky's "Night on the Bare Mountain," arrives at a lonely Home for the Insane to be interviewed for a post on the staff.

Seeing who is responsible for the script, the young doctor should have known better: it is quickly obvious to everyone except himself that he is bound to come to a sticky (in this case a stethoscopic) end. The decidedly improbable condition for his engagement is that he should recognise among the patients the erstwhile Head of the institution, now a madman himself. The incorporated stories are related, with some courage, by four of the inmates. Unfortunately, towards the end the film—which has some good moments—betrays the logic even of its own conventions, and becomes chaotic.

It is very noticeable that during the period under survey the interest swings away from vampires and monsters towards various aspects of witchcraft—perhaps in reflection of the growth of "real-life" activities in England.

Among such films we may note *The Devil Rides Out* (1967) and *To the Devil a Daughter* (1976) from novels by Dennis Wheatley—the latter a British/West German production; *Witchfinder General* (1968), the third and last film from Michael Reeves; *The Curse of the Crimson Altar* (1969), one of Boris Karloff's final appearances; *Cry of the Banshee* (1970); *Virgin Witch* (1970), combining hexing with sexing; and *Twins of Evil* (1971).

Of these, *Witchfinder General,* from Tigon, is the most interesting. It concerns the career of the notorious East Anglian witch-hunter Matthew Hopkins. The atmosphere of menace, cruelty and general misery during the English Civil War is well suggested, but the film collapses into an absurd, gratuitously disgusting axe-hacking blood-spattering welter. It thus entirely misses the true horror of Matthew Hopkins—which is that he died warmly in his bed. Had he met the end given him here one could comfortably feel that at least he had only received his due.

The entrance to the *Torture Garden*.

Innocence or original sin? Chloe Franks as the little witch in
The House That Dripped Blood.

Chloe Franks and Mark Lester as the not-so-gullible children in *Whoever Slew Auntie Roo?*

Ingrid Pitt and Jon Pertwee in the "old vampire cloak" episode: a lively burlesque from *The House That Dripped Blood.*

An atmospheric scene from Michael Reeves' *Witchfinder General*.

The Devil Rides Out (directed by Terence Fisher) has interesting details of black magic rites, but the resultant evil is rather tamely vanquished. *Twins of Evil* has the advantage of the redoubtable Peter Cushing fighting both vampires and witches. Unfortunately he overreaches himself: after beheading a vampire girl he suspects of being a witch he is himself axed by a male vampire who is in turn killed by a local choirmaster. The rather exceptional run of events is directed very stylishly by John Hough out of Hammer, courtesy of characters from Sheridan Le Fanu.

Non-Draculan vampires made several other appearances, among them being *The Vampire Lovers* (1970), *Lust for a Vampire* (1971) and *Vampire Circus* (1972)—all from Hammer, the first in association with American International. *The Vampire Lovers* and *Lust for a Vampire* made further use of Le Fanu's conveniently to hand characters. *Vampire Circus,* more enterprisingly, took full advantage of an original idea—a circus staffed by vampires able to transform themselves into animals. Provided the necessary liquid sustenance could be regularly supplied, one would imagine such casting could considerably reduce the cost of running this expensive form of entertainment. All three are among the better Hammer offerings, and all three are trendily titivating.

Much less enjoyable is the would-be parody, *Vampira* (1974). Cod horror is notoriously tricky to bring off successfully, though it has been tried *ad nauseam* by would-be jokers who think they are on to an easy thing. Roman Polanski achieved it brilliantly in the much underrated *Dance of the Vampires (The Fearless Vampire-Killers)* and Vincent Price is, of course, a master in the art of the gentle send-up, but these are exceptions. In *Vampira* David Niven, of all people, plays a modern-day Dracula who is looking for blood to inject into his long-dead spouse, Vampira. When a very trendy (and thus already old-fashioned) party of girls visits his castle on a publicity stunt for a famous

99

Ingrid Pitt in action again: in *The Vampire Lovers.*

splendid style. The film could perfectly well have stood on its own feet without the introduction (entirely out of place) of such famous Victorian murders as Burke and Hare and Jack (or Jill) the Ripper—but no matter, this is a horror film with implications beyond its obvious thrills and enjoyable on several levels. A possible flaw is that Martine Beswick as Hyde looks so alluring that any potential victim worthy of his sex might well consider her company worth the inevitable consequences.

An entertaining new addition to the horror portrait gallery appeared in 1971, in the person of *The Abominable Dr. Phibes,* portrayed by Vincent Price at his sardonic and tongue-half-in-cheek best; though completely hidden at times under a skull-like mask. Even his voice comes to us only by courtesy of a speaker wired to his throat, for the unfortunate Doctor, who now spends most of his time playing his magnificently garish cinema organ when not planning ingenious murders, was very cut up in a car crash, and even more so by the death of his wife during an operation. Now demented, he determines to wreak vengeance on the medical men he holds responsible for her death and, to add savour to a somewhat monotonous task (for there are a surprising number of them) he determines to

magazine they meet more than they had bargained for. Dracula obtains samples from the young ladies' veins, but unfortunately the test-tubes get mixed up, with the result that Vampira receives the blood of a Negress and wakes up black. In his efforts to rectify the error Dracula follows the party back to London, but after a series of increasingly tedious events he finishes up black himself. Even the directorial skill of Clive Donner and the suave charm of Niven cannot altogether avoid the unpleasant taste inherent in such a mishmash. Despite a few amusing lines early on, one or two attractive settings (such as the dark, crumbling castle with its modern gadget-crammed laboratories) *Vampira* soon becomes bogged down in its foolish script.

Of other standard monsters, *Blood from the Mummy's Tomb* (1971), from a tale by Bram Stoker, rings the changes by presenting a *female* Mummy, and *Dr. Jekyll and Sister Hyde* (1971) by presenting a female Hyde. Both came from Hammer, and the former follows well-trodden paths despite the sex-change. *Dr. Jekyll and Sister Hyde,* however, is done with a flair and ingenuity that fully justifies the boldness of the basic idea. Directed by Roy Ward Baker, it is in fact among the most enjoyable horror films of the period. Ralph Bates and Martine Beswick pair off remarkably well, and merge in and out of each other in

Ralph Bates as Jekyll in *Dr. Jekyll and Sister Hyde.*

100

Vincent Price offering Virginia North a somewhat uncomfortable salutation in *The Abominable Dr. Phibes.*

kill them off by modern parallels to the Plagues of Egypt. The connection is strained, but such ingenuity (aided by a marvellous cameo by Hugh Griffith as a rabbi-historian) all adds to the general enjoyment. Finally he shuts himself up in a gorgeously decorated self-designed tomb with the preserved corpse of his wife—the last Plague being that of Darkness. A stylish telephone in the tomb suggests this may not be the absolute end. The film (directed by Robert Fuest) is a garish joy to look at, with Phibes's organ room resembling an old super-super-cinema, complete with full-size model orchestra; and the ingenuity of the Pharaoh parallels are as intriguing as they are outrageous. The Thirties period is quite satisfactorily suggested, and the deliberately flat dialogue (script by James Whiton and William Goldstein) is a pretty parody in itself.

As one might have expected, Phibes reappeared in 1972—hurrying off to Egypt in search of an

Seated one day at the organ...Vincent Price in *The Abominable Dr. Phibes.*

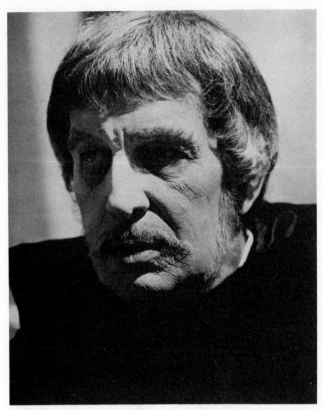

Vincent Price in his more familiar "mask" in *The Abominable Dr. Phibes.*

descends (or erupts) into insanity. These lurid goings-on are given surprising credibility, at least while the lights are still down, by the director, Alan Gibson, and a *frisson* or two can be guaranteed. James Olson, doubling the brothers, switches from addiction to lunacy with enviable ease.

The second film, *Fright* (1971), is directed by Peter Collinson, who had earlier made a remarkable, grim, little known and underrated war film with only four characters titled *The Long Day's Dying.* When a pretty young girl comes to baby-sit in a desolate and eerie house whose owners seem excessively anxious to lock every door and window before spending an evening in a restaurant, we can be reasonably certain, that she has no quiet evening watching the television before her—especially when it is revealed that the gentleman diner is not the lady diner's husband and that the husband himself is an escaped homicidal maniac. Collinson uses every type of cinematic device—shock cuts, low-angle shots, dripping taps, faces reflected in a swinging pendulum, horror-film conveniently showing on television—to ensure edge-of-seat attention, but surprisingly allows this to slacken periodically by visits to the dining couple. There are moments when we are apt to feel we are being too artificially manipulated by tricks, but the horrific

elixir for his still extinct wife. For a sequel the film *(Dr. Phibes Rises Again)* holds up fairly well, but it has not the originality, nor the advantage of surprise, to be found in its predecessor. The conclusion of the film leaves the way open for another successor. As I write, this has not materialised, which may be as well. One views the prospect of Phibes "carrying-on" indefinitely with a certain apprehension.

Finally we may glance at two British horror films which have no truck with the supernatural or inexplicable—except for a nightmare or two. The first, and better, is *Crescendo* (1969), notable for a strong performance by Margaretta Scott as the widow of a famous composer and mother of twin sons, one a madman and the other a crippled drug addict. One might imagine that, having been so unfortunate in her offspring, she might not be anxious to prolong the family line, but in fact she is quite the opposite. When a young girl (Stefanie Powers) arrives at her villa in the South of France, the scheming matriarch tries to pair her off with the addict. A series of increasingly sinister and mysterious events, including the stabbing to death of a very French French maid, culminates in the mad son threatening to kill both girl and addict, only to be shot by his mother, who finally herself

Crescendo: **Stefanie Powers shrinks from an approaching hand.**

Stefanie Powers confronts the lady waxworks: two scenes from *Crescendo*.

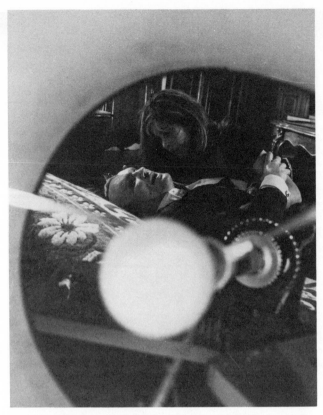

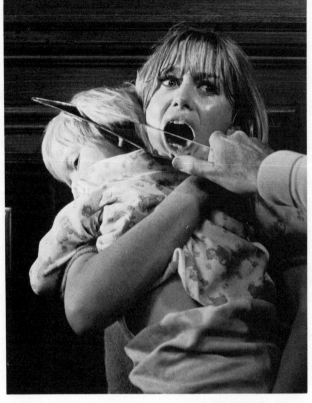

Through the table lamp: an effective still from *Crescendo*.

Fright: "first-rate screaming from Susan George."

climax is vice-like in its grip, aided by some first-rate screaming from Susan George and a performance from Ian Bannen that conjures pity as well as terror. The morality of basing the thrills of a purely commercial shocker on insanity has been questioned, and this may have some justification, but comes a little hypocritically from anyone prepared to accept as a similar basis war, murder, alcoholism, sexual deviation, deprivation of one sort or another, even physical deformity. Indeed, if every form of human aberration, mental, physical, moral, were to be excluded from all commercial films except those of serious, clinical import, the cinemas might as well close down and the television screens remain wholly occupied by advertisements.

America

Apart from such horror-busters as *The Exorcist* and *The Omen* (see Chapter Fourteen) and, in a different category, the Revised Version of *King Kong,* the American output of significant films in the *genre* was relatively quiet during the period under review. There were, however, two vampire films of unusual intelligence, featuring a Count Yorga, a cheaply budgeted but outstanding Zombie film, *The Night of the Living Dead,* a genuinely

unnerving witch film, *The Dunwich Horror* (which sounds as if it should come from England, but doesn't), and a strange obsession with nasty-little-beings films; rats, frogs and worms taking up where mutated ants, spiders and others left off.

Count Yorga, Vampire (1970), directed by Bob Kelljan with Robert Quarry in the title role, accomplishes the rarely successful feat of placing vampirism in a present-day period and place (Los Angeles), playing cleverly, and with a satirical touch which nevertheless does not weaken the horror, on the disbelief with which such a being would be regarded in the contemporary world of self-satisfied scepticism. This makes the gradual realisation of what is actually occurring (an actual vampire in the midst) all the more unnerving. The director's handling is in keeping with the cool approach, avoiding the Gothic trappings and effects of the conventional horror film. For all that, the thrills are there, and expertly engineered to turn the screw. The sequel, *The Return of Count Yorga* (1971) is equally effective, perhaps more so. Kelljan even injects a certain amount of fashionable, if mild, social criticism. There is a marvellously macabre opening and an ending which, if not wholly unexpected, is nicely ironic. A good twin, then, the Yorga films, and apparently (to date at any rate) with sense enough not to attempt a triplet.

Night of the Living Dead (1969) is one of those encouraging surprises which occur occasionally in the field of horror—a cheaply made, unpretentious production which turns out to have been handled with a sense of the macabre and a skill in continually springing the unexpected twist of plot on the flinching spectator, that puts many a larger scale effort to shame. In this instance it is pleasant to be able to record that virtue has not gone unrewarded, for *Night of the Living Dead* has become a highly prized film among the horror *élite*. It tells, briefly, of an upsurge of zombies who menace visitors to the graveyard of a country church, and later in the lonely hours in which they have taken refuge. As the tension mounts relentlessly from the first sight of a single creature to their terrifying attack in massed swarms, one waits—unnerved but expecting relief in the end—for the climax. But it turns out to be a ghastly one. For once, *everything* goes wrong, *every* plan fails, and the final moment—even with the defeat of the zombies in sight—is a straight blow to the chin.

The Dunwich Horror (1969), directed by Daniel Haller who was earlier responsible for some fine art direction on the Corman/Poe series, also has considerable merit. Its subject is village witchcraft (strange how often this seems to bring out the best in a film-maker), and the attempt of a young man of demonic ancestry to bring back the magic powers once possessed by his family. Fertility rites, ancient manuscripts and an attic-incarcerated monster all add to the general enjoyment (from a master horror-writer H.P. Lovecraft), but Haller gets his effects with notable restraint, something in the manner of Lewton—and thereby frightens us all the more thoroughly. Dunwich, incidentally, is an American village, not the ghostly drowned seaport of old Suffolk—but the name undoubtedly has apposite reverberations for an Englishman.

And so to *Willard, Ben, Frogs* and *Squirm*.

Willard (1970) starts off with a built-in advantage because it is about rats. For those many people in whom the very word induces a shiver of loathing, the mere idea of a screenful of rampant rodents will be enough to bring on a state of near panic. The story, from a novel by Stephen Gilbert, concerns a strange, lonely youth who finds he has an odd *rapport* with rats, and starts training some of the large numbers that live in the old garden of the house where he lives. His purpose is far from altruistic, far from a selfless desire to improve the rats' welfare. It is to revenge himself on his dead

Count Yorga, Vampire: **the progress of Erica (Judith Lang).**

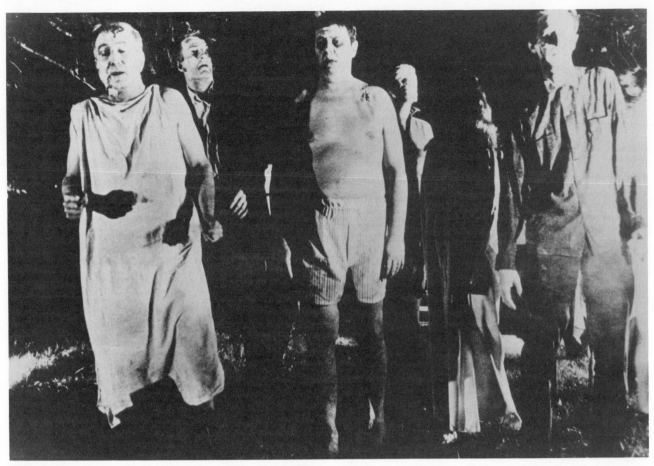

Night of the Living Dead: assorted zombies in a minor masterpiece.

father's business partner, a coarse bully whom he suspects of nefarious practices. Inevitably, like all monsters of filmdom whether of flesh, clay, stone or atomic waste, they get out of control, biting off more than they were intended to chew. The concerted attack on Ernest Borgnine is nasty, but otherwise, surprisingly, the sight of all the scampering little beings is unexpectedly unhorrific—far less terrifying than the unseen beastliness of Nigel Kneale's television play referred to earlier. The leading rat, indeed, so won the hearts of all concerned that he was awarded a name (Ben) and a sequel all to himself. And to a rat-lover, of course (as to a cat-lover in the case of *The Eye of the Cat*—see page 144) they will all appear merely as interesting, if voracious, fellow inhabitants of our common earth. Not everybody shudders even at spiders, as tarantula-film makers must have discovered.

Ben, the sequel, is even milder. Admittedly, the rats, having disposed of the young man who trained them, are totally in command, and widen their spheres considerably, creating quite a number of unpleasant situations: but the affectionate relationship between a lonely little boy and the equally lonely little Ben is enough to take the edge off things in general—with shades of Disney closing round the growing rat. Ben, by the way, is surely the first live rat in cinema history to have his own theme song?

Sandra Dee and unwelcome visitors in *The Dunwich Horror*.

Ernest Borgnine in *Willard*.

Willard: **the rats attack.**

With *Frogs* · (1971) we are on much more realistic ground. The idea is similar to that of Hitchcock's *The Birds*—the sudden, stealthy and apparently motiveless attack on human beings by animals: in this case not only frogs but snakes, lizards and other denizens of the waters and swamplands surrounding a small island. The owner of the island (played with gusto by Ray Milland) has, in this casem provided the attackers with a conceivable motive of revenge by his use of anti-pest chemicals, but this is not strongly emphasised. The allegorical warning is, of course, too obvious to need underlining: there may be a limit to what "nature" will put up with from man. The trick (or, more accurately, induced) photography whereby animals are made to appear to be working to an end with unusual intelligence is excellent—but apart from this there is no hint of anthropomorphism.

Keep worms away from your electric wiring, would seem to be the moral of *Squirm* (1976), or they may turn into man-eaters. This somewhat unlikely premise accepted, there is plenty to bring squirms to the squeamish as massed battallions invade houses and public buildings. Jeff Lieberman, the director, has the good sense (and taste) to exercise restraint on the appearances of his horrors—who are rarely seen and thus have the added threat of the *un*seen. An unusual amount of comedy—if grim—and good playing from a largely unfamiliar cast also help this minor but enjoyable horror offering. The Squirm Company produced.

*

Further titles of both British and American films during this period appear in the Chronology.

108

14. An Unholy Trinity ?

The Big Three of the period 1967-1977 were undoubtedly *Rosemary's Baby* at the beginning (1968), *The Exorcist* in the middle (1973) and *The Omen* at the end (1976). All three dealt with aspects of the same subject, Satanic possession, all three hailed from America, all three were big box-office successes, and all three (particularly the first) deserved that success.

Rosemary's Baby, the film that finally brought Roman Polanski world recognition, was the first of which he was not the absolute originator—in all his earlier productions he was at least partially responsible for the script. In this case it was based on (and followed extremely closely) a novel by Ira Levin. Its basic theme (should there be anyone still unaware of it) is the birth of anti-Christ—the dawn of the Satanic Year One. A young couple, Rosemary Woodhouse and her husband Guy, a struggling, unrecognised actor, take an apartment in a dingy old New York block, the Bramford. From the very beginning they notice one or two odd things about the place—a huge cupboard recently

John Cassavetes and Mia Farrow in *Rosemary's Baby*.

moved to block an adjoining door, a half-finished letter of slightly sinister import left by the former, now deceased, owner, strange herbs growing, "not-quite-right" voices heard from the occupants of the adjacent flat. Then they are advised by Rosemary's uncle, Hutch, that the block has long had an unsavoury reputation—witchcraft is hinted at. Shortly after they move in a girl living with the neighbours is found dead on the pavement outside, having apparently flung herself from the window. Through this ghastly event they meet, and become increasingly involved with, the neighbours themselves—a somewhat eccentric but apparently harmless elderly couple, Roman Castevet and his wife Minnie. Guy in particular seems to come under their influence, but at first Rosemary, though a little puzzled, is only mildly—indeed amusedly—concerned. (The entire film is told from her point of view and she is present throughout the action.) An evening arrives when Guy and Rosemary decide to "make a baby": while they are having a preliminary meal a special delicacy, "chocolate mousse," prepared that day (apparently by chance) is brought to their door by Minnie. Despite Rosemary's protestations that it has "a chalky undertaste" Guy is strangely insistent that she should eat it so as not to offend the old lady. Rosemary gives in, but when Guy is absent from the table for a moment she manages to wrap most of the stuff in a napkin, and later disposes of it. She has therefore had only half a "dose." Later that night, after feeling ill, she has a vivid and terrible nightmare—one that seems, in fact, *too* vivid to be just a nightmare. "This is not a dream," she cries out at one point, "this is really happening!" She imagines she is being raped by a demoniac figure with horns and strange, inhuman eyes. On awakening she is told by Guy that, despite her condition, he has made love to her during the night. When later she finds she is pregnant, the Castevets (and Guy) persuade her to leave her own doctor and put herself into the care

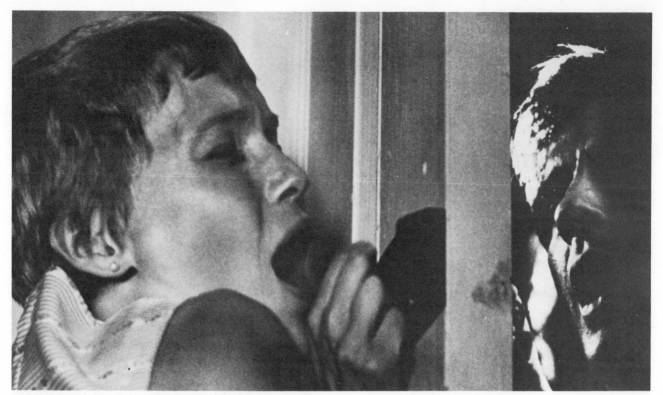

Mia Farrow takes refuge: climax to one of the most terrifying sequences in *Rosemary's Baby*.

Mia Farrow, John Cassavetes, Ralph Bellamy and members
of the coven in *Rosemary's Baby*.

Rosemary's Baby: **Mia Farrow determines to rescue her child.**

of a well-known gynaecologist, Dr. Sapirstein. Meanwhile Guy's career takes an unexpected turn for the better, but at a terrible cost to the man whose part in a play Guy is now asked to take over—the man has suddenly, for no apparent cause, gone blind. Rosemary becomes more and more distressed—and not only because of the strangeness of the Castevets and their friends, who at a New Year party drink a toast proposed by Roman "to the Year One!" Her pregnancy causes her savage and continuous pain, not noticeably eased by a mixture of herbs which Minnie assiduously urges upon her. One day, after suddenly finding herself eating uncooked offal, she catches sight of her gaunt, shadowed, totally altered face in a polished electric toaster. Rebelling in disgust, she makes a frantic attempt to escape from the misery surrounding her. She gives a party for her own, *young* friends (Minnie and Roman are not invited, she tells the protesting Guy) who are horrified at her appearance. Afterwards, alone with Guy, she insists on returning to her own Dr. Hill—but suddenly her pain ceases, and at the same moment the baby moves. The suggested change of doctor is dropped.

Next comes the sudden and mysterious death of her uncle, Hutch, after he had visited her, told her (in front of Castevet) in no uncertain terms what he thought of her condition under Sapirstein's treatment, and arranged to meet her for an im-

portant talk. At his funeral she is given a book Hutch had left for her—a book on witchcraft, from which she gathers that Roman is the son of a Satanist. She becomes convinced, in the face of various pieces of evidence, that she, and her unborn baby, are part of some terrible occult plot. Guy ridicules the idea, but later throws away the book. Rosemary, horrified, grows more and more certain that her husband is deeply involved. She goes to Sapirstein for help, only to find that he himself is a member of the group. Frantically she telephones Dr. Hill and persuades him to see her. As she pours out her story he seems to believe her, but later betrays her to Sapirstein and Guy, who arrive to fetch her home. In the hallway of the Bramford she makes a last desperate effort to escape—culminating in some of the most hair-raising moments in the history of the cinema. The attempt fails, she finds herself in labour, and Sapirstein delivers the child. Later she is told the baby died, but refuses to believe this, especially after suspecting that she hears a child crying in a room or apartment nearby. Eventually she makes her way secretly into the Castevets' flat. All the disciples, and Guy, are gathered there to celebrate the birth of a son—to Satan. In a corner of the room is a black-draped cradle with an inverted crucifix. She approaches and stares, horrified, into the face of her baby—a baby with Satan's eyes. At first she rejects it, rejects them all; but when a member of the group rocks the cradle clumsily and the baby cries, Rosemary moves instinctively towards it. Roman dismisses the other woman and tells Rosemary to rock the cradle. "You're trying to get me to be his mother," she says. "Aren't you his mother?" Roman asks gently. Slowly, Rosemary starts to rock the cradle.

*

In *Rosemary's Baby,* Polanski sets out to induce our belief in what we feel to be impossible—because no other belief is possible. Once we enter the building from the travelling rooftops shot of the opening, he achieves just that. Indeed, we start to believe—or at least to wonder—even before Rosemary does, perhaps on account of the uncle's warning, or perhaps because of a foreknowledge (from the book or reviews of the film) of the events that lie ahead. It is, in fact, impossible for the audience to identify with Rosemary (as they must, for the whole film is, as stated earlier, made from her viewpoint) until she *does* begin to believe in the witchcraft. I do not think it is true to say, as some have, that during her final interview with Dr. Hill the

Roman Polanski directing a scene from *Rosemary's Baby*.

audience begins to doubt her sanity. By this time suspension of disbelief is so complete that we must consider Hill to be stupidly slow in understanding, rather than that Rosemary is insane. Later, of course, we realise that Hill, in betraying her, may be either deferring to a much respected colleague (Sapirstein), or be an actual member of the witch coven himself. As everywhere in this brilliantly created film, the very ground itself shifts uncertainly beneath our feet.

The stages in the breakdown of Rosemary's preliminary disbelief follow a steadily and ever more convincing pressure of facts on her consciousness. It is only in the closing moments of the film that the "supernatural" is actually encountered. Until then, everything *could* have a "natural explanation." But by the closing moments, so cunningly has the web been woven that we are ensnared in the conviction that only the impossible is possible. The whole film moves towards compelling our belief in the actuality of those final moments. Rosemary

herself needs no compulsion: she has the evidence before her eyes—in the cradle. But as we with the camera move to join her and look at the child ourselves everything fades and we are outside the building, above the New York rooftops as we were at the beginning, hearing only her lullaby. All that we ourselves have seen is a subliminal flash of what appeared to be the Satanic eyes of her nightmare ravisher. Polanski's achievement (and, indeed, Levin's in the book) is to make our acceptance as certain after Rosemary's look into the cradle as it was before. Quite simply, we have no alternative—there is no way out for us.

In the space available here it is impossible to do justice to the consummate skill and subtlety with which Polanski has interpreted—and enriched—Levin's novel in translating it into visual and audible terms. (The soundtrack is masterly throughout—a worthy successor to that of *Repulsion*.) The density of the imagery, the unnerving ambiguity of scene after scene, make it a film that

112

demands to be seen many more times than once if it is to be fully appreciated.

Out of dozens, two brief scenes may be instanced here as admirable examples of claustrophobic horror. The first is the sequence in the telephone booth as Rosemary calls for help from the unenthusiastic Dr. Hill, and suffers agonisingly from the not uncommon delays of inefficient service. It is made in one long take, with William Castle (producer of the film) playing a potentially sinister—and perhaps symbolic—figure waiting impatiently for the occupier of the booth to finish.

The second is the attempted escape referred to earlier. Rosemary's flight up in the apartment block's elevator is immeasurably aided by a sound-track of mounting, beating screams, done partly by means of a siren, that seems to be trying to burst out of itself. The sequence ends, after she has managed to shut her pursuers out of the apartment and is frantically phoning a friend for help, in a splendid moment of *frisson* as two out-of-focus figures tiptoe across a room they should have had no means of entering.

Suggestions have been put forward that what happens to Rosemary is not real—"it's all in her mind." But neither in the book nor in the film are there any grounds for this comforting conclusion. Except for two dream sequences, no part of the film is presented as more or less "real" than any other. Where, then, does the onset of hallucination begin? When she and Guy take the flat? When they find the dead girl on the pavement? When they return from a dinner with the Castevets? When Rosemary eats the mousse? When Hutch dies? When she reads his book on witchcraft? Before the baby is born? After the baby is born? Any moment can be selected—and each is as arbitrary as any other. It might be pointed out that each separate suspicion of Rosemary's might have a perfectly normal explanation—but for all of them to do so entails a string of coincidences as unlikely and as abnormal as anything Rosemary believes. "I show people something so obviously impossible as witchcraft," says Polanski, "and I say to them—are you *certain* it is not true?"*

*

The Exorcist, directed by William Friedkin, with a script by William Peter Blatty from his own novel, is a good example—in Britain at least—of a film being to some extent oversold in advance. So much had been proclaimed about its sensational-

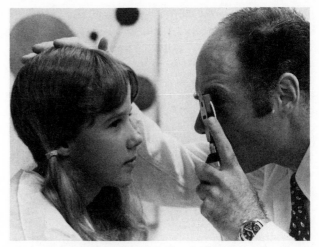
Linda Blair under medical scrutiny in *The Exorcist.*

ism, its record-breaking receipts, its fainting and exit-rushing audiences, its incredible but true sources—that when at last it arrived it had to face an implanted prejudice, resulting in some remarkably unimaginative and unjustified criticism. Nevertheless, it has achieved an enviable commercial success, and has also been recognised in many and varied quarters for the superb essay in the occult that it undoubtedly is.

The well-known story need only be outlined here. We first visit an archaeological site in Iraq where an elderly Jesuit priest, Father Merrin, discovers a strangely carved stone amulet and a medal, and later has an awe-inspiring visionary encounter with Pazuzu, one of the Satanic demons—a scene splendidly photographed by Billy Williams. We are then shifted abruptly to Georgetown, Washington, D.C., in what appears to be a completely new start to the film. In the first—later rejected—script Batty wrote, this Prologue was omitted altogether, but it forms a highly atmospheric opening and is full of subtly unsettling moments. In Georgetown a house has been temporarily taken over by Chris MacNeil (a superb performance by Ellen Burstyn), a film actress working on location at a Jesuit college. With her is her daughter Regan, a hitherto normal healthy girl of twelve, whose recent rather odd behaviour has been causing some concern—including references to a weird imaginary companion she calls Captain Howdy. Menacing noises at night, a most embarrassing moment when Regan appears unexpectedly in the living-room during a small party, and later the apparently uncontrollable shaking and rocking of the girl's bed drive Chris to consult the doctors, who are puzzled and helpless to explain what is going on. Further disquieting events, including the desecration of the College chapel, culminate horrifyingly in the violent death

* A fuller analysis of Rosemary's Baby, from which I have made one or two brief quotations here, is to be found in my book *The Cinema of Roman Polanski,* referred to earlier.

of the director of Chris's film. He is discovered dead at the bottom of a long flight of exterior steps (a wonderfully sinister flight, and a credit to the location-hunter who found them), outside the girl's window. His head had been twisted completely round, facing backward. He had been in the bedroom along with Regan, and Chris, realising that if, as the police think, he was murdered, then her daughter was responsible, asks a Catholic priest, Father Karras, to "get an exorcism." The Father, who is the psychiatric counsellor of the College, has his own spiritual and emotional problems—a loss of religious faith and a tormented feeling that he had neglected his recently dead mother. He is at first reluctant to involve himself with Chris's problems but later, after seeing the dreadful "thing" that Regan has become, he allows himself to be persuaded, and seeks the assistance of Father Merrin after permission to perform the rite has

been sought and granted. Regan had earlier undergone some appalling examinations in hospital, which proved totally unrevealing and totally useless, and was now transformed into a lewd, obscene horror, wholly unrecognisable as a child at all. The work of expelling the evil power that has possessed her begins. During a terrible contest of wills Father Merrin dies of a heart attack. Trying frantically to pump life back into the old man, Father Karras hears Regan giggling foully at him from the filthy bed on which she has been lying. In a frenzy he grabs her, shaking and beating her, and screaming to the demon to "Take *me*! Come into *me*!" A change occurs in both of them. Father Karras has seemed about to strangle the girl to death but suddenly—with a literally superhuman effort—he regains control of his body, and plunges out of the window through which the film director had earlier met his death. Regan is found on the floor, herself

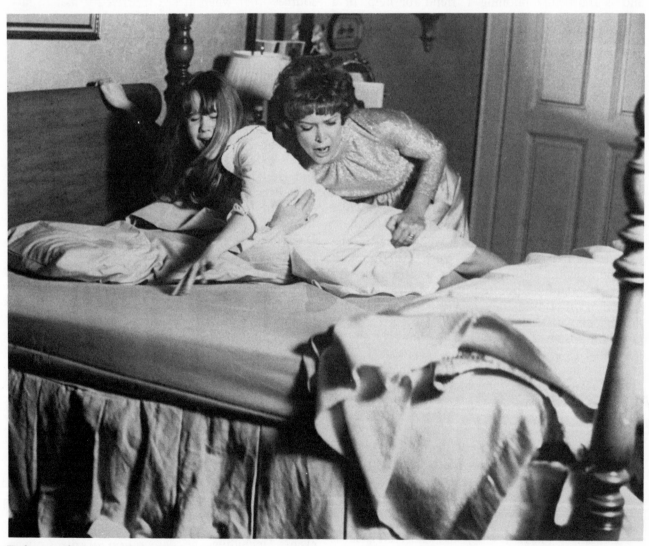

Early manifestations of the Devil in *The Exorcist*: Linda Blair and Ellen Burstyn.

114

Max von Sydow as *The Exorcist*.

again, unconscious and serene. Later she leaves with her mother for home, totally ignorant of what has occurred—though, understandably, looking a little off colour.

A crude outline, necessarily emphasising the surface sensationalism of the film, cannot do it justice—to its power, its compassion, its integrity within its own conventions, to the interest it arouses in its characters—even, on a more superficial level, to its impact merely as a macabre story of the utmost intensity. It is not unflawed. The tightness of construction which makes *Rosemary's Baby* a film from which not a frame should be cut is not always evident here. Rather too much is made of the drunken film director before he meets his death—the character never really comes alive. There is an unnecessarily protracted scene in which the detective improbably watches Father Karras running round a race-track and they start comparing each other to film stars (though the detective's reference to John Garfield in *Body and Soul* obviously has point), which seems brought in just to provide a change of setting. The chapel desecration is inconclusive: if she did it, then when, and how? The mystery of the ex-Nazi servant Karl's behaviour is undeveloped—it was, says Blatty, a major casualty of the re-write he made. The scene where Chris, after hearing a strange creaking, grunting noise, climbs into the dark attic and is scared out of her wits is (though an effective horror moment) on a more conventional level than the rest of the film, and indeed invites the "relieved laugh" which the remainder sedulously avoids.

These minor reservations apart, however, there is much to acclaim. The dread with which we accompany one of the characters into that fearful bedroom (what awaits us *this* time?) is an indication of the extent to which we have been involved. Never, incidentally, has sheer *coldness* been so brilliantly conjured up in the cinema as in the later scenes in that room. Seen on the hottest summer's day, they can leave one shivering. The mechanical tricks—flying objects, shaking beds, violently moving cupboards, even the final horrifying levitation, are totally convincing, and timed to a split second so as to attain their maximum effect and then cut. The soundtrack has rightly been praised—whether consisting of quiet, sinister taps and whispers or howling, shattering tumult it freezes the nerves. These, however, are the mechanics. More important is our concern for the characters and our belief in what is happening to them. Here the film is almost wholly successful. The steps taken to underline the authenticity of the various pro-

cedures are hardly necessary, so complete is the suspension of disbelief by the time they are seen: though Fathers Thomas Bermingham and William O'Malley manage to be wholly convincing even if not attaining the topmost heights of genius as film actors.

The mental and spiritual torment of Father Karras (most sensitively portrayed by Jason Miller) adds a further dimension to the purely macabre element, as well as providing an entirely credible motivation for his final act of redemption. It also, incidentally, causes a notable moment of true—inexplicable—terror, when he enters Regan's room and finds her place on the bed taken, momentarily, by the tiny, reproachful figure of his dead mother.

Horribly effective is the way in which the scenes of Regan's examination in the hospital are made to appear almost as brutal and terrifying as anything which occurs in her ghastly bedroom. Here the soundtrack excels itself, as the clicking, clanking, clashing machinery of modern healing lowers over and probes into the frail human flesh strapped beneath it.

William Blatty apparently had considerable difficulty in condensing his fairly lengthy and detailed novel into a two-hour screenplay: indeed, his first version would have run for something like four hours. He himself liked his first draft (which is available in book form together with the actual transcript and two essays of great interest) but a number of objections, together with its length, caused him to make the revised one which was eventually filmed.

*

Our last member of the unholy three, *The Omen,* directed by Richard Donner, is somewhat lesser in scope—and also, perhaps, in achievement—but still stands out above the general run. Though American-made, a large part of the action is set in England, with Gregory Peck and Lee Remick in good form as a suave diplomat and his wife, and Billie Whitelaw in superb form as a sort of witch-nanny. The diplomat, Robert Thorn, arrives at a hospital in Rome to hear that his wife's baby has been still-born. Realising the shock this would be to her, he agrees to a priest's suggestion that another baby—a boy whose "mother," (they tell him) has "died"—should be substituted. A slight knowledge of horror films would, of course, have warned him of the dire risk he was taking by falling in with this sort of arrangement. Nor would he have burdened the child with the emotive name of Damien.

116

Lee Remick in *The Omen*.

We now move on five years, at which time, though apparently there has been no sign of anything untoward hitherto, it becomes evident that the child is not all that (or rather, is a great deal more than) he appears to be. What in fact he is—and what we realise him to be a good deal earlier than most of those close to him—is a little anti-Christ. The first sign that something is wrong is fairly startling—the simultaneous appearance of a sinister black dog and the suicide of his nanny; both events occurring on the little devil's fifth birthday, and providing an excellently contrived shock moment. Thorn is now U.S. Ambassador to Britain—a post which seems to burden him with surprisingly little work, leaving him plenty of time to agonise over developments in his family. A strange, uncouth-looking priest warns him of sinister things in store, and begs him to consult an exorcist in Megiddo: but his manner is so wild that Thorn ignores him. The priest is killed during a violent storm by what could be regarded as a macabre accident (if we didn't know better); and later the child, aided and abetted by his unpleasant new nanny (Billie Whitelaw) causes his mother,

who is pregnant, to fall over a balcony—apparently through an accident—a horridly vertiginous sequence. Meanwhile a photographer named Jennings, who has been around a good deal, discovers strange markings on pictures of the priest and the first nanny which seem to have some bearing on their deaths. (Shadows of *Blow-up!*) Subsequently he finds a similar sign on a photograph of himself. Eventually Thorn and Jennings go to Rome to try to discover just what is going on, but are very unpleasantly thwarted. They then proceed at last to Megiddo for a bizarre (and, to be honest, somewhat unbelievable) session with the most peculiarly situated exorcist. Thenceforward the Satanic pace rapidly increases, with the death of Thorn's wife (engineered by the wicked nanny), the decapitation of the photographer through a lightning combination of unforeseen circumstances, the killing of the nanny by Thorn himself (and no-one could say she didn't deserve it), and his own death as he is about to perform the gruesome final exorcism on Damien. The final shot, ironic and very effective, is of little Damien turning to look at us with anticipatory gloating, having been taken

117

The devil child: Harvey Stephens in *The Omen*.

when they see one, make a wild attack on the car, leaping on the bonnet, beating on the windscreen, gibbering and grabbing with terrifying ferocity in a technically brilliant few moments of filmmaking.

Perhaps the reason that *The Omen* does not make quite so much impression as the two former films is that, in contrast with them, we never find ourselves very closely involved with the characters. The child is little more than a cipher—carefully photographed so that now and again we might catch an expression which *could,* to carefully predisposed eyes, be seen as sinister. The Ambassador and his wife are pleasant enough people (Gregory Peck at his most sympathetic, Lee Remick at her most attractively vulnerable) who get caught up in some extremely unpleasant circumstances. It has been suggested that Thorn has to expiate a sin he committed in his baby-substituting: but it all seems a somewhat disproportionate punishment for a deception practised from the very best of motives—and what about the unfortunate first nanny, and the intrusive but well-intentioned warning priest, and even the persistent photographer?

However, taken as a whole, *The Omen* is a highly effective shocker—and perhaps a salutary warning to us all to watch out for any untoward expressions in the faces of our five-year-olds.

into the care of a close friend of the late Ambassador—no less than the President of the United States. The political implications are ambiguous but tantalising.

Where *Rosemary's Baby* and *The Exorcist* each have one pill of improbability, which, if swallowed, permits the viewer to swallow all that follows with ease, *The Omen* has, frankly, a whole bottle of pills, each of which has to be taken separately. It says a lot for the skill of director, players and writer (David Seltzer) that the act of swallowing is made so smooth. The film, not entirely satisfactory as a whole, is full of incidental felicities. Perhaps the *tour-de-force* is the seemingly fortuitous decapitation of the photographer—starting with an unexpectedly moving vehicle and ending with the slicing off of the man's head by a sheet of plate-glass. Done in a flash of speed, what could so easily have been ludicrous is in fact a stunning shock of horror. Then there is the Ambassador's wife's fall over the balcony—a brilliant touch sends a glass bowl spinning crazily down to shatter into fragments as she clings desperately to the rail. Finally, among the most frightening sequences of the film, there is the episode in which the boy's mother takes him on a visit to a free-range zoo. A number of vicious-looking baboons, knowing a bad thing

Gregory Peck as the distraught father faces a grim necessity in *The Omen*.

118

Annotated Chronology of Horror in the Cinema

The following is not intended to present a complete list, as it is felt that mere pages full of titles of ephemeral and often worthless films would be of little interest. I have, however, tried to make it as representative as possible, and the inclusion of a title is not necessarily meant as an indication of merit.

Credits are given for all films discussed in detail in the text or given special notice in the chronology: others are listed with the director's name only.

1908 **DR. JEKYLL AND MR. HYDE**
A Selig Polyscope Production.
1910 **FRANKENSTEIN** (Edison 1-reel).
1912 **DR. JEKYLL AND MR. HYDE.** *Dir:* Lucius Henderson.
players: James Cruze, Marguerite Snow.
1912 **THE SYSTEM OF DR. GOUDRON AND PROFESSOR PLUME (LE SYSTÈME DU DOCTEUR GOUDRON ET DU PROFESSEUR PLUME).**
1913 **THE STUDENT OF PRAGUE (DER STUDENT VON PRAG)** *Dir:* D. Stellan Rye.
1913 **BALAOO.** *Dir:* Victorin Jasset. *sc:* (from a story by Gaston Leroux).
1913 **THE VAMPIRE.** *Dir:* Robert Vignola.
1914 **THE GOLEM (DER GOLEM).** *Dir:* Paul Wegener, Henrik Galeen.
1915 **THE PORTRAIT OF DORIAN GRAY.** *Dir:* Vsevolod Meyerhold.
1915 **THE MADNESS OF DR. TUBE (LA FOLIE DU DOCTEUR TUBE).** *Dir:* Abel Gance.
1915 **LIFE WITHOUT SOUL.** *Dir:* J.W. Smiley. sc: from Mary Shelley's novel *Frankenstein.*
It was all a dream!
1916 **THE VICTIM (LA PROIE).** *Dir:* Monca.
1919 **THE CABINET OF DR. CALIGARI (DAS CABINET DES DR. CALIGARI).** *Prod:* Delca-Bioskop. *dir:* Robert Wiene. *sc:* Carl Mayer, Hans Janowitz. *ph:* Willy Hameister. *des:* Walther Reimann, Hermann Warm. *mus:* Walther Röhrig. *players:* Conrad Veidt, Werner Krauss, Lil Dagover, Hans von Tvardovski, Friedrich Feher.

1919 **BROKEN BLOSSOMS.** *Dir:* D. W. Griffith.
Lillian Gish's panic-stricken screams in the closet scene referred to in the text are said to have shocked cynical, hardbitten studio hands into white-faced silence. No greater compliment could have been paid to her performance in this horrifying sequence.
1920 **THE GOLEM (DER GOLEM).** *Prod:* Union-Ufa. *dir:* Paul Wegener, Carl Boese. *sc:* Paul Wegener, from a story by Gustav Meyrink, and a film scenario by Paul Wegener and Henrik Galeen (1915). *ph:* Karl Freund, Guido Seeber. *des:* Hans Polezig, Rochus Gleise. *players:* Paul Wegener, Albert Steinrück, Lydia Salmonova, Ernst Deutsch.
1920 **THE PHANTOM CARRIAGE (KORKARLEN).** *Dir:* Victor Sjöström.
1920 **DR. JEKYLL AND MR. HYDE.** *Dir:* John S. Robertson. John Barrymore as Jekyll.
1920 **LOVE'S MOCKERY (DER JANUSKOPF).** *Dir:* F. W. Murnau.
1920 **DESTINY (DER MUEDE TOD).** *Dir:* Fritz Lang.
1922 **NOSFERATU.** *Dir:* F. W. Murnau. *sc:* Henrik Galeen, from the novel *Dracula* by Bram Stoker. *ph:* Fritz Arno Wagner, Gunther Krampf. *des:* Albin Grau. *players:* Max Schreck, Alexander Granach, Gustav von Wangenheim, Greta Schröder, John Gottowt.
1922 **WITCHCRAFT THROUGH THE AGES (HAXAN).** *Dir:* Benjamin Christensen.
1922 **DR. MABUSE, THE GAMBLER (DR. MABUSE, DER SPIELER).** *Dir:* Fritz Lang.

1923 **THE HUNCHBACK OF NOTRE DAME.** *Dir:* Wallace Worsley.

One of Lon Chaney's most famous (and painful) makeups. It is interesting to compare his performance with that of Charles Laughton in the 1939 version (q.v.)

1924 **THE HANDS OF ORLAC (ORLACS HAENDE).** *Dir:* Robert Wiene.

1924 **WAXWORKS (DAS WACHSFIGURENKABINETT).** *Dir:* Paul Leni.

Notably the third of the three episodes, a nightmarish pursuit of two lovers by the figure of Jack-the-Ripper (Werner Krauss) through Caligari-like settings.

1925 **THE PHANTOM OF THE OPERA.** *Prod:* Universal. *dir:* Rupert Julian. *sc:* Elliott J. Clawson (from the novel by Gaston Leroux). *ph:* Charles Van Enger. *des:* Dan Hall. *players:* Lon Chaney, Mary Philbin, Norman Kerry, Arthur Edmund Carewe, Gibson Gowland.

In a letter to *Films in Review* (October 1962) Rudy Behlmer gives some interesting details of Chaney's make-up as the Phantom, which ". . . gave his face the appearance of a skull. His nostrils were distended by hairpin-like devices which also lifted the tip of his nose. To protruding, rotted and jagged false teeth he attached small prongs which drew back the corners of his lips. Cotton wadding and celluloid discs in his mouth distorted the cheekbones. His eyes were popped and dilated by chemicals." Chaney's face is not seen without the mask until the fifth reel, and no stills were permitted to be shown until after the film's release. In 1930 some dialogue sequences were added and the film re-issued in a dubbed version. It was not an improvement.

1925 **THE LOST WORLD.** *Dir:* Harry D. Hoyt.

1926 **METROPOLIS.** *Prod:* UFA. *dir:* Fritz Lang. *sc:* Thea von Harbou. *ph:* Karl Freund, Gunther Rittau. *des:* Otto Húnte, Erich Kettlehut, Karl Vollbrecht. *players:* Alfred Abel, Brigitte Helm, Gustav Frolich, Rudolf Klein-Rogge, Fritz Rasp.

1926 **SECRETS OF A SOUL (GEHEIMNISSE EINER SEELE).** *Prod:* UFA. *dir:* G. W. Pabst. *ph:* Guido Seeber, Curt Oertel. *players:* Werner Krauss, Ruth Weyher, Jack Trevor.

1926 **THE STUDENT OF PRAGUE (DER STUDENT VON PRAG).** *Dir:* Henrik Galeen.

1926 **THE CLOAK (SHINEL).** *Dir:* Grigori Kozintsev, Leonid Trauberg.

1927 **THE CAT AND THE CANARY.** *Prod:* Universal (Paul Leni). *dir:* Paul Leni. *sc:* Robert F. Hill, Alfreda Cohn (from the play by John Willard). *ph:* Paul Leni. *players:* Laura la Plante, Creighton Hale, Tully Marshall, Lucien Littlefield, Martha Mattox.

1927 **LONDON AFTER MIDNIGHT.** *Dir:* Tod Browing. *Leading player:* Lon Chaney.

1928 **ALRAUNE.** *Dir:* Henrik Galeen. *sc:* Henrik Galeen (from a novel by H. H. Ewers). *ph:* Franz Planer. *des:* Walter Reimann. *players:* Brigitte Helm, Paul Wegener, Ivan Petrovich.

The horror content of this "fantastic horror film" (Kracauer) is mild even by the standards of its period. The actual experiment by which the being is brought to life is so briefly treated as to be obscure, and the development of the theme suffers badly in that we see nothing whatsoever of the baby—or childhood of the creature, first meeting her as an adolescent girl in a convent. Most of her actions are merely those of a normal human being with a rather more than average share of callousness. Our first sight of her, pushing an escaping fly back into a cup of milk, is presumably intended to emphasise her abnormal cruelty—but how many schoolchildren of either sex have not done something similar? The sentimental ending, where she cries to her young lover to give her a real heart, is ludicrous. However, Brigitte Helm gives a bravura performance—her early close-up, tempting a young man to steal for her, and later ones showing her approaching her sleeping creator after reading his secret diary, convey a sort of pale menace which is quite formidable—and some of the sets are among the best of the German Gothic period.

1928 **THE FALL OF THE HOUSE OF USHER (LA CHUTE DE LA MAISON USHER).** *Dir:* Jean Epstein. *ph:* Lucas. *sc:* (from the story by Edgar Allan Poe). *players:* Margaret Gance, Jean Dubencourt, Charles Lamay.

1928 **THE SPY (SPIONE).** *Dir:* Fritz Lang.

1928 **AN ANDALUSIAN DOG (UN CHIEN ANDALOU).** *Dir:* Luis Buñuel.

1929 **THE LAST WARNING.** *Dir:* Paul Leni.

1930 **DRACULA.** *Prod:* Universal. *dir:* Tod Browning. *sc:* Garrett Fort (from the play by Hamilton Deane and John Balderston, based on the novel by Bram Stoker). *dial:* Dudley Murphy. *ph:* Karl Freund. *des:* Charles D. Hall. *mus:* Tchaikovsky. *ed:* Milton Carruth, Maurice Pivar. *players:* Bela Lugosi, Helen Chandler, Dwight Frye, David Manners, Edward van Sloan.

1930 **THE BLUE ANGEL (DER BLAUE ENGEL).** *Prod:* UFA (Erich Pommer). *dir:* Josef von Sternberg. *sc:* Karl Zuckmayer, Karl Vollmöller, Robert Liebmann (from a novel by Heinrich Mann). *ph:* Gunther Rittau, Hans Schneeberger. *des:* Otto Hunte, Emil Hasler. *mus:* Friedrich Holländer. *players:* Emil Jannings, Marlene Dietrich, Kurt Gerron, Rosa Valletti, Hans Albers.

Emil Jannings's towering performance as the German professor wrings every once of horror from the terrible climactic scene. Having given up position, livelihood and self-respect for the travelling concert artiste Lola-Lola, he is forced, when the troupe revisits the town where he once taught, to stand on the stage in the grubby little tavern where he first met her and, grotesquely apparelled, crow like a cock as eggs are broken over his head. His mind finally gives way and, crying out like a wounded animal, he stumbles from view, attempts to strangle Lola-Lola, gropes his way back to his old class-room, and there dies. The progressive path of self-degradation which led to this final catastrophe is traced by Sternberg with unrelenting cruelty, and the scene of the climax, in a din and confusion of smoke, netted draperies, half-lights, yelling voices and clattering tankards, is as shattering in its effect today as when it first stunned its audiences over thirty years ago. If tragedy is truly defined as the ruin of the hero through some flaw in himself, then this performance of Jannings raises the film very close to this high level.

1930 **THE CAT CREEPS.** *Dir:* Rupert Julian.

1930 **ALRAUNE.** *Dir:* Richard Oswald.

A sound version of the story made in 1928 by Henrik Galeen.

1931 **FRANKENSTEIN.** *Prod:* Universal (Carl Laemmle, Jr.). *dir:* James Whale. *sc:* Garrett Fort, F. E. Faragoh, Robert Florey (after the play by Peggy Webling based on the romance by Mary Shelley). *ph:* Arthur Edeson. *ed:* Clarence Kolster. *players:* Colin Clive, Boris Karloff, Mae Clarke, John Boles, Edward van Sloan.

1931 **VAMPYR.** *Prod:* Carl Dreyer. *dir:* Carl Dreyer. *sc:* Carl Dreyer, Christen Jul (freely adapted from a story by Sheridan le Fanu). *ph:* Rudolph Maté. *mus:* Wolfgang Zeller. *players:* Julian West (Baron Nicolas de Gunzburg), Henriette Gerard, Rena Mandel, Sybille Schmitz, Jan Hieronimko.

1931 **THE MURDERS IN THE RUE MORGUE.** *Dir:* Robert Florey.

1931 **M.** *Dir:* Fritz Lang. *leading player:* Peter Lorre.

1931 **MURDER BY THE CLOCK.** *Dir:* Edward Sloman.

1932 **THE LIVING DEAD (UNHEIMLICHE GESCHICHTEN).** *Dir:* Paul Wegener.

The great German horror pioneer's first sound film, based on stories by Edgar Allan Poe.

1932 **DR. JEKYLL AND MR. HYDE.** *Prod:* Paramount. *dir:* Rouben Mamoulian. *sc:* Samuel Hoffenstein, Percy Heath (from the story by Robert Louis Stevenson). *ph:* Karl Struss. *des:* Hans Dreier. *players:* Fredric March, Miriam Hopkins, Rose Hobart, Edgar Norton, Holmes Herbert.

1932 **THE OLD DARK HOUSE.** *Prod:* Universal. *dir:* James Whale. *sc:* Benn Levy (from the novel *Benighted* by J. B. Priestley). *dial:* R. C. Sherriff. *ph:* Arthur Edeson. *players:* Boris Karloff, Melvyn Douglas, Charles Laughton, Gloria Stuart, Ernest Thesiger, Raymond Massey.

1932 **FREAKS.** *Prod:* M-G-M (Tod Browning). *dir:* Tod Browning. *sc:* Willis Goldbeck, Leon Gordon (from the novel *Spurs* by Tod Robbins). *dial:* Al Boasberg. *ph:* Merritt B. Gerstad. *des:* Cedric Gibbons. *ed:* Basil Wrangell. *players:* Olga Baclanova, Henry Victor, Leila Hyams, Wallace Ford, Harry Earles, Daisy Earles.

1932 **THE MYSTERY OF THE WAX MUSEUM.** *Prod:* Warner Bros. *dir:* Michael Curtiz. *sc:* Charles Beldon. *dial:* Don Mullaly, Carl Erickson. *ph:* Ray Rennahan. *ed:* George Amy. *players:* Lionel Atwill, Fay Wray, Glenda Farrell, Frank McHugh, Allen Vincent.

1932 **THE MOST DANGEROUS GAME (THE HOUNDS OF ZAROFF).** *Prod:* Merian C. Cooper. *dir:* Ernest B. Schoedsack, Irving Pichel. *sc:* J. A. Creelman (from a novel by Richard Connell). *ph:* Henry Gerrard. *des:* Carroll Clark. *mus:* Max Steiner. *ed:* Archie Marshek. *players:* Leslie Banks, Fay Wray, Joel McCrea, Robert Armstrong.

Described in glowing terms by Ado Kyrou *(Le Surréalisme au cinéma)* as "the perfect example of the good sadistic film . . . a masterpiece of surrealist cinema." Despite the very obviously studio origin of much of the setting (particularly the exterior of the Count's castle), much of the photography is atmospheric and imaginative, notably the latter part of the chase where black hounds loom out of the mist, and one brief sequence of telescopic shots from hunter to hunted and back. Characterisation is almost nil, but Leslie Banks as the Count who, bored with hunting animals, turns to men for his victims, is an impressively sadistic and megalomaniacal figure—fingering the lion's scar on his forehead when the mood comes upon him, blowing his hunting horn and drawing his crossbow in the chase, falling finally to his doom among his own hounds.

1932 **THE ISLE OF LOST SOULS.** *Dir:* Erle C. Kenton.

1932 **THE MUMMY.** *Dir:* Karl Freund.

1932 **THE GHOUL.** *Dir:* T. Hayes Hunter.

1933 **KING KONG.** *Prod:* RKO (Ernest B. Schoedsack, Merian C. Cooper). *dir:* Ernest B. Schoedsack, Merian C. Cooper. *sc:* James Creelman, Ruth Rose (after a story by Merian C. Cooper and Edgar Wallace). *ph:* Edward Lindon, Verne Walker, J. O. Taylor. *sp. ef-*

Fay Wray, the perfect heroine, in the 1933 *King Kong*.

King Kong himself, in 1933.

fects: Willis O'Brien. *des:* Carroll Clark, Al Herman. *mus:* Max Steiner. *ed:* Ted Cheesman. *players:* Fay Wray, Robert Armstrong, Bruce Cabot, Frank Reicher.

The most famous of all the prehistoric animal films. Despite the obviously artificial setting, the first approach of the ship to the island is genuinely eerie, and the events leading up to the first appearance of Kong are full of excitement, only weakened by some unfortunately anti-climactic lines. Kong himself radiates charm, and easily wins our sympathy from his captors, who deserve worse than they get. Fay Wray, the perfect heroine in such circumstances, would have softened tougher hearts than the old ape's, and their scenes together, as she lies cradled in his gentle palm, make us wish that he could have had a better chance of winning her over to a greater appreciation of his warm regard for her.

1933 **THE INVISIBLE MAN.** *Prod:* Universal. *dir:* James Whale. *sc:* R. C. Sherriff (from the story by H. G. Wells). *ph:* Arthur Edeson, John Mescall. *players:* Claude Rains, Gloria Stuart, William Harrigan, Henry Travers, Una O'Connor.

The trick camerawork stands up well even by present standards. There is little of the really horrific in the film, but the moment when the Man (Claude Rains) first unwraps his bandaged face and reveals— nothing, is a genuine touch of the macabre.

1933 **THE LAST WILL OF DR. MABUSE (DAS TESTAMENT DES DR. MABUSE).** *Dir:* Fritz Lang.

From the nerve-wracking opening sequence—of a man walking uneasily through a huge empty warehouse which is continuously shaken by a great roaring rattle—the tension rarely slackens, and although it is fundamentally a mastercrook thriller, Lang's treatment of the fantastic story of madness, hypnotism and mass crime fills the screen with the horror of imminent chaos, of dark forces barely controlled. In this he is greatly aided by the photography of Fritz Arno Wagner. It is significant that the film, completed just before the seizure of power by the Nazis, was immediately banned.

1933 **SON OF KONG.** *Dir:* Ernest B. Schoedsack.

Alas, he does not come up to his father's standard.

1933 **WHITE ZOMBIE.** *Dir:* Victor Halperin.

1934 **THE BLACK CAT** (reissued in America under the title *The Vanishing Body,* and released in Europe as *The House of Doom*). *Prod:* E. M. Asher. *dir:* Edgar G. Ulmer. *sc:* Peter Ruric (from the story by Edgar Allan Poe). *ph:* John Mescall. *players:* Boris Karloff, Bela Lugosi, David Manners, Jacqueline Wells.

There is not much Poe in this, and in spite of a splendidly sinister performance by Karloff and a surprisingly moving one from Lugosi the final result is a rather scrappy and ineffectual film. Karloff's Latin incantations are impressively delivered, but otherwise the Satanic rites, admittedly interrupted before they can get under way, look like being even less diabolical than English Druid junketings, and the guests are clearly not going to allow any orgiastic carryings-on to disarrange their elegant evening dresses and coiffeurs. The black cat of the title (and Lugosi's abhorrence of it) is completely expendable. Even the final revenge fizzles out in shadows and switch-triggered castle-dynamiting.

1934 **THE HANDS OF ORLAC**. *Dir:* Karl Freund.

1935 **THE BRIDE OF FRANKENSTEIN**. *Prod:* Universal. *dir:* James Whale. *sc:* John L. Balderston, William Hurlbut. *ph:* John Mescall. *mus:* Franz Waxman. *ed:* Ted Kent. *players:* Colin Clive, Boris Karloff, Ernest Thesiger, Elsa Lanchester, Valerie Hobson.

1935 **THE MARK OF THE VAMPIRE**. *Dir:* Tod Browning.

Though Carol Borland makes an extremely fetching female vampire, the film does not match the earlier silent *London After Midnight*.

1935 **WEREWOLF OF LONDON**. *Dir:* Stuart Walker.

1935 **MAD LOVE**. *Dir:* Karl Freund. *players:* Peter Lorre, Colin Clive.

A long-lost remake of *The Hands of Orlac*, part-authored by John Balderston who had a share in the Lugosi *Dracula*.

1935 **CONDEMNED TO LIVE**. *Dir:* Frank Strayer.

A girl is bitten by a vampire bat in Africa, and dies giving birth to a mad child who later tries to have the best of both worlds by becoming both half-vampire and half-werewolf.

1936 **THE DEVIL DOLL**. *Dir:* Tod Browning.

Carol Borland in 1935's *Mark of the Vampire.*

1936 **THE GOLEM (LE GOLEM).** *Dir:* Julien Duvivier.

1936 **THE WALKING DEAD.** *Dir:* Michael Curtiz.

1936 **REVOLT OF THE ZOMBIES.** *Dir:* Victor Halperin.

1936 **DRACULA'S DAUGHTER.** *Dir:* Lambert Hillyer.

1939 **THE CAT AND THE CANARY.** *Prod:* Paramount (Arthur Hornblow). *dir:* Elliott Nugent. *sc:* Walter de Leon, Lynn Starling (from the play by John Willard). *ph:* Charles Lang. *des:* Hans Dreier, Robert Usher. *ed:* Archie Marshek. *players:* Bob Hope, Paulette Goddard, John Beal, Douglass Montgomery, Gale Sondergaard, George Zucco.

Though it has its effective moments (the Cat's appearance being a distinct improvement on the Leni version), much of the atmosphere is lost in far too cheerful a setting, by the completely inexplicable omission of the mysterious doctor, by the insertion of typical Hope gags regardless of context, by too much use of exteriors, and by an insufficiently formidable housekeeper.

1939 **THE HUNCHBACK OF NOTRE DAME.** *Dir:* William Dieterle.

All things considered, probably the most successful of the three best-known versions, though Chaney's contains unmatchable moments. Laughton's portrayal is somewhat less grotesque in appearance, though, more sinister in conception. Each, however, manages to project a pitiful human being through the mountains of make-up.

1939 **THE SON OF FRANKENSTEIN.** *Dir:* Rowland V. Lee.

1940 **DR. CYCLOPS.** *Prod:* Paramount (Dale van Every). *dir:* Ernest B. Schoedsack. *sc:* Tom Kilpatrick. *ph:* Henry Sharp. *players:* Albert Dekker, Thomas Coley, Janice Logan, Victor Kilian.

Quite an effective "mad scientist" example. This time the "doctor" reduces a group of people to six-inch miniatures by "atomic rays"—dressing them, with more modesty than probability, in pieces of handkerchief during their period of unconsciousness. The film loses some chances of imaginative treatment in that the obstacles and animals they have to contend with are very prosaically normal objects seen large, no attempt being made to communicate the unnatural horror of their appearance to the little people—an aspect well brought out in *The Incredible Shrinking Man* of Jack Arnold (1957). Their predicament thus becomes surprisingly ordinary, if unusual. However, the film has good moments, such as the efforts of the group to train a colossal rifle on the sleeping Cyclops—a splendidly sinister performance by Albert Dekker.

1940 **THE INVISIBLE MAN RETURNS.** *Dir:* Joe May.

He would have done better to have stayed away.

1940 **THE PHANTOM OF THE OPERA.** *Dir:* Arthur Lubin.

But a pale shadow of the Lon Chaney epic, with Claude Rains as the Phantom.

1940 **THE FACE BEHIND THE MASK.** *Dir:* Robert Florey.

1940 **THE DEVIL BAT.** *Dir:* Jean Yarborough.

A minor Lugosi offering.

1940 **THE MUMMY'S HAND.**

1940 **THE MUMMY'S HAND.** *Dir:* Christy Cabanne.

1941 **DR. JEKYLL AND MR. HYDE.** *Prod:* M-G-M. *dir:* Victor Fleming. *sc:* (from the story by Robert Louis Stevenson). *ph:* Joseph Ruttenberg. *des:* Cedric Gibbons, Daniel Cathcart. *mus:* Franz Waxman. *players:* Spencer Tracy, Ingrid Bergman, Lana Turner.

The approach is on a more psychological level than in the Mamoulian film, emphasising the mental rather than the physical. Despite a sensitive perfromance by Spencer Tracy the result lacks the impact—the gusto and panache—of the older version, and also the photographic virtuosity.

1941 **THE INVISIBLE WOMAN.** *Dir:* A. E. Sutherland.

1941 **THE WOLF-MAN.** *Prod:* George Waggner. *dir:* George Waggner. *sc:* Curt Siodmak. *ph:* Joseph Valentine. *des:* Jack Otterson. *mus:* Charles Previn. *ed:* Ted Kent. *players:* Lon Chaney, Claude Rains, Ralph Bellamy, Bela Lugosi, Maria Ouspenskaya.

In spite of one of the strangest depictions of English village life to come even from America, the misty atmospheric photography, believable script and unforced dialogue, and restrained sincere playing by Lon Chaney and others could have made this a really convincing study of the oldest and most universal of all superstitions—lycanthropy. Unfortunately Waggner has not realised, as Lewton was to realise a year or two later in *The Cat People*, the power of the unseen as against the seen. He allows his wolf man to be clearly, and often, visible. Chaney's make-up results in quite a good monster, and might pass among apes, but it bears not the slightest resemblance to any wolf that ever was, would have been disclaimed with horror by the most devoted wolf-mother, and would not have deceived the hunters for an instant. Had his appearances been as shadowy and mysterious as those of Lewton's panther, this could have been a classic of its kind.

1941 **THE INVISIBLE WOMAN.** *Dir:* A. E. Sutherland.

She was, of course, inevitable.

1942 **THE GHOST OF FRANKENSTEIN.** *Dir:* Erle C. Kenton.

Another step on the downward path.

1942 **SON OF DRACULA.** *Dir:* Robert Siodmak.

See above.

1943 **THE UNINVITED.** *Assoc. prod:* Charles Brackett. *dir:* Lewis Allen. *sc:* Dodie Smith, Frank Partos (from the novel by Dorothy Macardle). *ph:* Charles Lang. *des:* Hans Dreier, Ernst Fegté. *mus:* Victor Young. *ed:* Doane Harrison. *players:* Ray Milland, Ruth Hussey, Gail Russell, Donald Crisp, Cornelia Otis Skinner.

A really chilling little ghost story, splendidly atmospheric, with an evil spirit which is all the more frightening for being only vaguely seen.

1943 **THE CAT PEOPLE.** *Prod:* Val Lewton. *dir:* Jacques Tourneur. *sc:* DeWitt Bodeen. *ph:* Nick Musuraca. *des:* A. S. D'Agostino, Walter E. Keller. *mus:* Roy Webb. *ed:* Mark Robson. *players:* Simone Simon,

Kent Smith, Tom Conway, Jane Randolph, Jack Holt.

1943 **THE LEOPARD MAN.** *Prod:* Val Lawton. *dir:* Jacques Tourneur. *sc:* Ardel Wray (after a story by Cornell Woolrich). *ph:* Robert de Grasse. *mus:* Roy Webb. *ed:* Mark Robson. *players:* Dennis O'Keefe, Margo, Jean Brooks, Isabel Jewell, James Bell.

1943 **DAY OF WRATH (DIES IRAE).** *Dir:* Carl Dreyer.

The horror of the witch's burning is real enough, but the true strength of this most beautiful and haunting film is in the all-pervading sense of unseen evil, of primitive beliefs and dark rites—the "respectable" ones no less than the diabolical. Notable is the indefinable sense of overpowering menace as the parson walks home through the windy, moonlit countryside.

1943 **I WALKED WITH A ZOMBIE.** *Prod:* Val Lewton. *dir:* Jacques Tourneur. *sc:* Curt Siodmak, Ardel Wray (after a story by Inez Wallace). *ph:* J. Roy Hunt. *mus:* Roy Webb, C. Bakaleinikoff. *ed:* Mark Robson. *players:* James Ellison, Frances Dee, Tom Conway.

Tourneur is said to prefer this to almost all his other films on account of its poetry.

1943 **THE RETURN OF THE VAMPIRE.** *Dir:* Lew Landers.

1943 **FRANKENSTEIN MEETS THE WOLF MAN.** *Dir:* Roy W. Neill.

1943 **DEAD MEN WALK (CREATURE DU DIABLE).** *Dir:* Sam Newfield.

George Zucco as a little-known vampire, Dwight Frye in attendance.

1944 **THE CURSE OF THE CAT PEOPLE.** *Prod:* Val Lewton. *dir:* Robert Wise. *sc:* DeWitt Bodeen. *players:* Simone Simon, Kent Smith.

1944 **THE HOUSE OF FRANKENSTEIN.** *Dir:* Erle C. Kenton.

1944 **THE CRY OF THE WEREWOLF.** *Dir:* Henry Levin.

1944 **WEIRD WOMAN.** *Dir:* Reginald LeBorg.

1944 **DEAD MAN'S EYES.** *Dir:* Reginald LeBorg.

THE MUMMY'S CURSE. *Dir:* Reginald LeBorg.

THE MUMMY'S GHOST. *Dir:* Leslie Goodwins.

Four Lon Chaney Jr. offerings in a busy year. *Weird Woman* reappeared in 1962 as *Night of the Eagle*, considerably altered.

1945 **THE SPIRAL STAIRCASE.** *Dir:* Robert Siodmak.

A notable example of claustrophobic terror—a girl (Dorothy McGuire) shut in, not only by the grim old house, but also by her own lack of the power of communication, for she is dumb. One by one the "normal" people around her—the props on whom she has been relying for protection against an unknown threat—fail her: layers of safety relentlessly peeled away. Splendidly atmospheric direction by Siodmak.

1945 **DEAD OF NIGHT.** *Prod:* Michael Balcon. *dir:* Cavalcanti *(Ventriloquist's Dummy, Christmas Party)*, Basil Dearden *(Hearse-Driver, Linking story)*. Robert Hamer *(Haunted Mirror)*, Charles Crichton *(Golfing story)*, John V. Baines, Angus MacPhail, from the stories by John V. Baines *(Ventriloquist's Dummy, Haunted Mirror)*, Angus MacPhail *(Christmas Party)*,

E. F. Benson *(Hearse-Driver, Linking story)*, H. G. Wells *(Golfing story)*. *dial:* T. E. B. Clarke. *ph:* Jack Parker, H. Julius. *des:* Michael Relph. *mus:* Georges Auric. *ed:* Charles Hassey. *players:* Mervyn Johns, Roland Culver, Googie Withers, Frederick Valk, Antony Baird, Sally Ann Howes, Robert Wyndham, Judy Kelly, Miles Malleson, Ralph Michael, Basil Radford, Naunton Wayne, Michael Redgrave, Mary Merrall, Michael Allan.

1945 **THE LOST WEEKEND.** *Dir:* Billy Wilder.

Ray Milland's alcoholic hallucination—the invasion of his room by a bat, the mouse crawling from a hole which suddenly appears in the wall, the killing and the slow dropping line of blood—is horrific enough to serve as a warning to any pub crawler. The cracking wall is an interesting prefiguration of one of the most terrifying hallucinations in Polanski's *Repulsion*.

1945 **ISLE OF THE DEAD.** *Prod:* Val Lewton. *dir:* Mark Robson.

1945 **THE BODY SNATCHER.** *Prod:* Val Lewton. *dir:* Robert Wise. *sc:* Philip MacDonald, Carlos Keith (from a story by Robert Louis Stevenson). *ph:* Robert de Grasse. *mus:* Roy Webb. *ed:* J. R. Whittredge. *players:* Boris Karloff, Henry Daniell, Bela Lugosi, Russell Wade, Edith Attwater.

1945 **THE HOUSE OF DRACULA.** *Dir:* Erle C. Kenton.

1945 **THE PICTURE OF DORIAN GRAY.** *Dir:* Albert Lewin.

1946 **BEDLAM.** *Prod:* Val Lewton. *dir:* Mark Robson. *sc:* Carlos Keith, Mark Robson. *ph:* Nicolas Musuraca. *mus:* Roy Webb. *ed:* Lyle Boyer. *players:* Boris Karloff, Anna Lee, Billy House, Richard Fraser.

1946 **FACE OF MARBLE.** *Dir:* William Beaudine.

John Carradine achieves a variation by resuscitating a *dog* vampire.

1946 **THE VALLEY OF THE ZOMBIES.** *Dir:* Philip Ford.

1947 **THE BEAST WITH FIVE FINGERS.** *Dir:* Robert Florey.

1947 **THE PHANTOM CREEPS.** *Dir:* Ford Beebe.

1949 **VOODOO MAN.** *Dir:* William Beaudine.

1949 **MIGHTY JOE YOUNG.** *Dir:* Ernest B. Schoedsack.

1950 **THE YOUNG AND THE DAMNED (LOS OLVIDADOS).** *Dir:* Luis Buñuel.

Apart from its appalling picture of delinquency, violence, perversion and criminal neglect—specifically in Mexico, but by implication in the darker environs of any large city—the film contains a masterly nightmare sequence filmed in slow motion and occurring in the dreamer's own communal bedroom. His mother floats slowly across the room towards his bed like a sort of monstrous bird. The change from the brightly lit terror of the dream to quiet, dark normality as the dreamer soundlessly screams himself awake brilliantly reproduces the familiar horror of the nightmare's climax.

1950 **THE THING FROM ANOTHER WORLD.** *Dir:* Christian Nyby.

1950 **THE FALL OF THE HOUSE OF USHER.** *Dir:* Ivan Barnett.

1951 **THE MEDIUM.** *Dir:* Gian-Carlo Menotti.

A highly successful translation of opera into film, Menotti's dramatic story and musical style probably presenting fewer difficulties than more conventional works. Most—not, I think, all—of the eerie quality of the original has been preserved. Marie Powers as the fake medium who feels a hand on her throat while in a supposed trance, gives a commanding performance, particularly in the later sequences where she tries frantically to force a confession from the dumb boy who assists her, that he was the culprit. The gradual crumbling of her bluff cynicism until having unintentionally shot the boy dead, she crouches by his body in drunken, abject terror asking uselessly "Was it you?", is in the true tradition of horror.

1951 **THE SON OF DR. JEKYLL.** *Dir:* Seymour Friedman.
He would better have remained childless.

1952 **THE BLACK CASTLE.** *Dir:* Nathan Juran.

1952 **ALRAUNE.** *Dir:* A. M. Rabernatt.
Another victim of the descending series.

1952 **THE EMPEROR'S BAKER.** *Dir:* Martin Fric.

1953 **THE WAR OF THE WORLDS.** *Dir:* Byron Haskin.

The spate of other-world beings and things really starts from this film, one of the earliest and still one of the best. There is real menace in the slow unscrewing of the huge cap of the flying saucer and the electronic clickings of the slowly emerging periscope. The invading beings are seen only in glimpses and thus preserve their mystery, especially in the sequence where they feel their way around and into the smashed and barricaded house. The nasty sucker-ended tentacle which gropes affectionately for the heroine looks uncomfortably alive. Excellent too are the scenes of panic and flight.

1953 **HOUSE OF WAX.** *Dir:* André de Toth.

The addition of 3-D cannot compensate in any way for the lack of imaginative treatment which was present in the 1932 version. The film was later reissued "flat", with no discernable difference.

1953 **THEM.** *Dir:* Gordon Douglas.

The preliminary suspense is so well built up that Their appearance is an almost inevitable let-down. Even so, the giant ants manage to stir up an occasional gentle *frisson.*

1953 **THE BEAST FROM 20,000 FATHOMS.** *Dir:* Eugène Lourie.

1953 **THE MAGNETIC MONSTER.** *Dir:* Curt Siodmak.

1953 **CAT-WOMEN OF THE MOON.** *Dir:* Arthur Hilton.
Making the best of both worlds.

1953 **ZOMBIES OF THE STRATOSPHERE.** *Dir:* Fred C. Brannon.

1953 **IT CAME FROM OUTER SPACE.** *Dir:* Jack Arnold.

1954 **THE PHANTOM OF THE RUE MORGUE.** *Dir:* Roy del Ruth.
In 3-D.

1954 **REAR WINDOW.** *Dir:* Alfred Hitchcock.

1954 **ROBOT MONSTER.** *Dir:* Phil Tucker.

1955 **THE FIENDS (LES DIABOLIQUES).** *Dir:* Henri-Georges Clouzot. *sc:* Henri-Georges Clouzot, Jérome Geronimi (from the novel *Celle qui n'était plus* by Boileau and Narcejac). *ph:* Armand Thirard. *des:* Léon Barsacq. *mus:* Georges van Parys. *ed:* Madeleine Gug. *players:* Simone Signoret, Véra Clouzot, Paul Meurisse, Charles Vanel, Pierre Larquey.

1955 **IT CAME FROM BENEATH THE SEA.** *Dir:* Robert Gordon.

1955 **THE QUATERMASS XPERIMENT.** *Dir:* Val Guest.

1955 **TARANTULA.** *Dir:* Jack Arnold.

1955 **THE DAY THE WORLD ENDED.** *Dir:* Roger Corman.

1955 **GODZILLA.** *Dir:* Terry Morse, Inoshiro Honda.
A Japanese water-monster.

1955 **NIGHT OF THE HUNTER.** *Dir:* Charles Laughton.

A strange, haunting film, supremely beautifully photographed by Stanley Cortez, about the pursuit of a small boy and girl by a psychopathic preacher. An allegorical story of the powers of darkness and light, the film powerfully conveys an immediate sense of the presence of evil and horror, notably in the death of the widow and the subsequent pursuit of the children through the moonlit countryside. The result makes one regret that Laughton did not direct more movies.

1956 **THE INVASION OF THE BODY SNATCHERS.** *Dir:* Don Siegel.

An unusually intelligent and well-made science horror. The "invasion" of real people by their mysterious doubles, and their consequent change of personality, are treated with considerable subtlety and, though there is visual eeriness in plenty, the emphasis is more intellectual than is the case in most "thing" films.

1956 **THE UNDEAD.** *Dir:* Roger Corman.

1956 **IT CONQUERED THE WORLD.** *Dir:* Roger Corman.

1956 **THE CYCLOPS.** *Dir:* Bert I. Gordon.

1957 **WILD STRAWBERRIES (SMULTRONSTÄLLET).** *Dir:* Ingmar Bergman.

The opening dream marvellously conveys the horror of nightmare. The dreamer, an elderly man, imagines he is taking his usual early morning stroll through the streets. But everything is strangely empty—and silent. The sun shines with an unnaturally brilliant glare, rendering the shadows intensely black. But it gives off no heat. He passes a watchmaker's who always had a large clock outside his shop, and an optician's sign of large eye-glasses and eyes, beneath it. To his astonishment the hands of the clock have disappeared, and the eyes behind the glasses are smashed and look like infected sores. He pulls out his own watch—to find that this also has no hands. The sound of his own heart-beats fills the silence and overpowers him. Suddenly he sees a man dressed in black standing in the street, with his back to him. In relief he goes up and touches the motionless figure. The man turns, and reveals that under his black hat he has but a clay face—the next instant the figure collapses into a bundle of clothes on the pavement. The silence is broken by the harsh clatter of hooves and grating wheels. A hearse is driven round the corner—and crashes into a lamp-post. The coffin is

Battle with a cat: one of the many gripping sequences in Jack Arnold's remarkable *Incredible Shrinking Man.*

ejected and smashed. A hand protrudes. The dreamer approaches—the hand grasps his own and pulls him down to the coffin.

Slowly the corpse rises—it is a man dressed in a frock-coat—and faces the dreamer. The corpse is himself. Each of these incidents has symbolic significance in the story which follows, but even taken out of context it is difficult to recall a more convincing representation of the terror of the bad dream. It is, in fact, one of the most frightening sequences in cinema.

1957 **THE INCREDIBLE SHRINKING MAN.** *Prod:* Universal-International (Albert Zugsmith). *dir:* Jack Arnold. *sc:* Richard Matheson (from his own novel). *ph:* Ellis W. Carter. *des:* Alexander Golitzen, Robert Clatworthy. *mus:* Joseph Gershenson. *ed:* Al Joseph. *players:* Grant Williams, Randy Stuart, April Kent, Paul Langton, Raymond Bailey.

One of the very best "effects of radiation" films. The fantastic story of an infected man who slowly dwindles in size to an invisible atom is worked out with complete logic from its original premise. Disbelief remains completely suspended, and the terror of the victims' changing situations is maintained throughout. Potentially ludicrous moments are ren-

dered acceptable by restrained and sincere treatment—even the first sight of the man shrunk to a third of normal size, seated in an enormous armchair. Only his grappling with the giant telephone receiver is unfortunately misjudged, inviting the unwanted laugh. His panic-stricken flight in a doll's house from a clawing cat, his efforts to obtain the cheese from a mousetrap for food without being crushed by the spring, his frightful battle with a spider his own size—all these and other details, aided by excellent trick photography, carry complete conviction, assuming, indeed, an epic quality of man's struggle for survival. The ending is uncompromising. A horror film with the courage of its conclusions.

1957 **THE CURSE OF FRANKENSTEIN.** *Prod:* Hammer Films (Anthony Hinds). *dir:* Terence Fisher. *sc:* Jimmy Sangster (from the romance by Mary Shelley). *ph:* Jack Asher. *des:* Ted Marshall. *mus:* James Barnard. *ed:* James Needs. *players:* Peter Cushing, Christopher Lee, Hazel Court, Robert Urquhart, Valérie Gaunt.

1957 **THE BLOOD OF DRACULA.** *Dir:* Herbert L. Strock.

1957 **DAUGHTER OF DR. JEKYLL.** *Dir:* Edgar Ulmer.

More unfortunate progeny of the indestructible Doctor.

Sandra Harrison in *Blood of Dracula.*

1957 **THE BLACK SCORPION.** *Dir:* Edward Ludwig.
1957 **THE HUNCHBACK OF NOTRE DAME.** *Dir:* Jean Delannoy.

    With Anthony Quinn as the Hunchback. Third in the race.

1957 **THE MONOLITH MONSTERS.** *Dir:* John Sherwood, from a story by Jack Arnold (director of *Tarantula*).
1957 **QUATERMASS II.** *Dir:* Val Guest.
1958 **NIGHT OF THE DEMON.** *Prod:* Sabre Films (Frank Bevis). *dir:* Jacques Tourneur. *sc:* Charles Bennett, Hal E. Chester (from the story *Casting the Runes* by M. R. James). *ph:* Ted Scaife. *des:* Ken Adam. *mus:* Clifton Parker. *ed:* Michael Gordon. *players:* Dana Andrews, Peggy Cummings, Niall McGinnis, Athene Seyler, Maurice Denham.

    A story of the occult which is distinctly better than average. Several scenes, such as the calling up of the storm, are highly effective—the devil, however, when he becomes visible, is less so. Unseen demons are best.

1958 **THE FLY.** *Prod:* Twentieth-Century Fox. *dir:* Kurt Neumann. *ph:* Karl Struss. *players:* Patricia Owens, Al Hedison, Vincent Price (in a minor part).

Included here on account of its notoriety, this is probably the most ludicrous, and certainly one of the nastiest science-horror films. Attempting a sort of X-ray transference of solids from one place to another by the dispersal and reassembly of their molecular constitution, a scientist, André, tries the experiment on himself, but gets his own atoms mixed up with those of a fly, ending up with its head and one leg in place of his own head and one arm. After quite a tense opening, with not much sillier-than-usual pseudo-scientific discussion and a nice moment when a deatomised cat yowls from all over the room at once, the film degenerates from the moment we see the insected man, plumbing lower and lower depths of inanity, and ending by revelling in mere sadistic beastliness when his wife squashes his fly-head in a large press—an episode dwelt on with disgusting relish. The final sequence is perhaps the most unintentionally risible of any film. A fly appears with André's tiny head and little white arm, squealing "Help me!" in a Disney cartoon voice, prior to being devoured by a spider. If the film had been intended as a parody of some of the sillier science-fiction efforts it might pass, but this is apparently not the case. Nothing, anyway, could excuse the head-crushing business. Even the much-publicised trick camerawork, including a not very ingenious fly's-eye view of his wife, is unremarkable.

1958 **THE HORROR OF DRACULA (DRACULA).** *Prod:* Anthony Hinds. *dir:* Terence Fisher. *sc:* Jimmy Sangster (from the novel by Bram Stoker). *ph:* Jack Asher. *des:* Bernard Robinson. *mus:* Malcolm Williamson. *ed:* Bill Lenny. *players:* Christopher Lee, Peter Cushing, Michael Gough, Melissa Stribling, Valérie Gaunt.

1958 **THE RETURN OF DRACULA.** *Dir:* Paul Landres.

1958 **BLOOD OF THE VAMPIRE.** *Dir:* Henry Cass.

1958 **MACABRE.** *Dir:* William Castle.

1958 **THE HOUSE ON HAUNTED HILL.** *Dir:* William Castle.

1958 **THE FACE or THE MAGICIAN (ANSIKTET).** *Dir:* Ingmar Bergman.

Towards the end of the film, the "magician" Vogler (Max von Sydow) plays a series of illusionist tricks on the Counsellor on Medicine, Vergérus (Gunnar Björnstrand) who, earlier on, with the rest of the local authorities, has accused him of charlatanism. Vergérus is perfoming a post-mortem on a body which he mistakenly supposes to be that of Vogler. Supposing himself alone in the attic where he has been doing the job, he sits down to write his report—then pauses, pen in hand. A human eye stares up at him from the inkwell. A moment later the autopsy report falls to the floor. An old clock behind him starts striking quickly—then as suddenly stops. A hand lays itself over his own on the table—he starts up—it is severed at the wrist—a model. He hurries to the door, to find it locked. In a mirror a face floats behind his own—that of the "dead" man. His spectacles are ripped off. Terrors multiply until he is reduced to hysterical collapse—all dignity gone. We share his terror, and also—strangely enough—his disappointment when he realises it was caused merely by a conjuror's tricks. As Peter Cowie points out in his book *(Swedish Cinema)* "It is society that longs to be duped."

1958 **THE REVENGE OF FRANKENSTEIN.** *Prod:* Hammer. *dir:* Terence Fisher. *sc:* Jimmy Sangster. *ph:* Jack Asher. *mus:* Leonard Salzedo. *players:* Peter Cushing, Eunice Grayson, Francis Matthews, Michael Gwynn.

1959 **PEEPING TOM.** *Prod:* Michael Powell. *dir:* Michael Powell. *sc:* Leo Marks. *ph:* Otto Heller. *des:* Arthur Lawson. *mus:* Brian Easdale. *ed:* Noreen Ackland. *players:* Carl Boehm, Anna Massey, Moira Shearer, Maxine Audley, Esmond Knight.

1959 **WASP WOMAN.** *Prod:* Roger Corman. *dir:* Roger Corman. *sc:* Leo Gordon. *ph:* Harry C. Newman. *des:* Daniel Haller. *mus:* Fred Katz. *ed:* Carlo Lodato. *players:* Susan Cabot, Fred Eisley, Barboura Morris, Michael Marks, William Roerick.

1959 **EYES WITHOUT A FACE (LES YEUX SANS VISAGE).** *Prod:* Jules Borkon. *dir:* Georges Franju. *sc:* Jean Redon (from his own novel). *adapt:* Georges Franju, Jean Redon, Claude Sautet, Pierre Boileau, Thomas Narcejac. *ph:* Eugène Schuftan. *des:* Auguste Capelier. *mus:* Maurice Jarre. *ed:* Gilbert Natot. *players:* Pierre Brasseur, Alida Valli, Edith Scob, François Guerin, Beatrice Altariba.

Despite the fact that it contains three of the most horrid scenes yet filmed—the deaths of Louise and the Professor, and above all the surgical removal of the skin from the girl's face—the main impression left by the film is strangely one of austere beauty, due mainly to Schuftan's lovely and sombre photography and to Edith Scob's miraculous achievement in endowing her white masked face (only the tragic eyes visible) with life and character. It is the scenes of her wandering about the house and cellars, ringing up her fiancé to hear his voice though she may not reply, and, most of all, gazing down on the pretty face which is to be so horrifyingly used to restore her own happiness, that remain most strongly in the memory. Franju's purpose is not altogether clear—the film could be regarded as an attack on the *hubris* of medical scientists, or even as a melodramatic tract against vivisection. What it certainly is not, is just another "mad doctor movie." Following on such films as his *Le sang des bêtes,* Franju's sincerity of approach is

Edith Scob, who, though hidden behind a blank mask, gives an unforgettable performance in Georges Franju's superior shocker *Eyes Without a Face (Les Yeux sans Visage).*

unquestionable. On the framework of a gruesome Boileau-Narcejac mystery thriller (they had a hand in the adaptation), Franju has constructed a work which transcends its horrific content and leaves the spectator haunted, thoughtful and disturbed, even if not quite knowing why he should be.

1959 **THE STRANGLERS OF BOMBAY.** *Dir:* Terence Fisher.

Although reputedly founded on fact, and more original in setting (much of which is convincing) this film about religious thuggee is essentially in the Hammer horror/sadism tradition. It is said to have horrified "even its director." The general approach is perhaps indicated by the announcement that the film is made in Strangloscope.

1959 **THE RETURN OF THE FLY.** *Dir:* Edward L. Bernds.

Back again, but no better.

1959 **EXPERIMENT IN EVIL (LE TESTAMENT DU DOCTEUR CORDELIER).** *Dir:* Jean Renoir.

1959 **FRANKENSTEIN'S DAUGHTER.** *Dir:* Richard E. Cunha.

1959 **THE MUMMY.** *Dir:* Terence Fisher.

1959 **THE TINGLER.** *Dir:* William Castle.

Spoof, but really rather fun, if only to watch Vincent Price enjoying himself so hugely.

1959 **BUCKET OF BLOOD.** *Dir:* Roger Corman.

1960 **PSYCHO.** *Prod:* Paramount (Alfred Hitchcock). *Dir:* Alfred Hitchcock. *sc:* Joseph Stefano (from the novel by Robert Bloch). *ph:* John L. Russell. *des:* Joseph Hurley, Robert Clatworthy. *mus:* Bernard Herrmann. *ed:* George Tomasini. *players:* Anthony Perkins, Janet Leigh, Vera Miles, Martin Balsam, John Gavin.

1960 **GORGO.** *Dir:* Eugène Lourié.

One of the better prehistoric monster films, demonstrating the strength of maternal devotion. As the enormous primeval monster proceeds slowly down the river to the sea, bearing in its loving embrace the child which human beings had been exhibiting for sordid gain, the devastated city all around bears solemn witness to the righteous fury of its affection for its offspring, leaving us with a satisfying feeling of justice done—and seen to be done.

1960 **BLOOD AND ROSES (ET MOURIR DE PLAISIR).** *Dir:* Roger Vadim.

A somewhat pretentious version of Sheridan le Fanu's story *Carmilla* (the basis also of Dreyer's *Vampyr*) which, despite some effective and beautiful moments, does not really succeed. Dubbed dialogue does not help matters.

1960 **THE FALL OF THE HOUSE OF USHER.** *Dir:* Roger Corman. *sc:* Richard Matheson (from the story by Edgar Allan Poe). *ph:* Floyd Crosby. *des:* Daniel Haller. *mus:* Les Baxter. *ed:* Anthony Carras. *players:* Vincent Price, Mark Damon, Myrna Fahey, Harry Ellerbe.

1960 **THIRTEEN GHOSTS.** *Dir:* William Castle.

1960 **THE TWO FACES OF DR. JEKYLL.** *Dir:* Terence Fisher.

1960 **THE BRIDES OF DRACULA.** *Dir:* Terence Fisher.

1960 **THE VILLAGE OF THE DAMNED.** *Dir:* Wolf Rilla.

1960 **THE HANDS OF ORLAC.** *Dir:* Godfrey Grayson.

1960 **BLACK SUNDAY.** *Dir:* Mario Bava.

Barbara Steele as a reincarnated witch in an Italian/American film which appears to combine horror, beauty and the ludicrous in about equal proportions.

1960 **THE LITTLE SHOP OF HORRORS.** *Dir:* Roger Corman.

It took over a dozen years for this engaging little oddity to reach Britain, preceded by its reputation of having been made in two days flat. There was no need to apologise for this and other stringent economies, because this is a very entertaining horror-comic about a man-eating plant which insistently demands (in an *Alphaville* voice) blood and human flesh, and reflects the tormented faces of its mealtime victims when its buds open. Among a largely unknown cast of fine comic grotesques it is interesting to catch a glimpse of a young Jack Nicholson.

1960/2 **THE PIT.** *Prod:, dir:, sc:* Edward Abraham (from Edgar Allan Poe's story *The Pit and the Pendulum*). *player:* Brian Peck.

A fine macabre short film. Using only one word of dialogue (as Abraham points out, Poe's story has none), it relies on sound effects and silence to underline the terror—and succeeds. Outside one's nightmares, has one even seen anything as nasty as the bottom of this pit? As Dilys Powell described it: "a genuine essay in horror."

1961 **THE INNOCENTS.** *Prod:* Twentieth-Century Fox/Achilles (Jack Clayton). *dir:* Jack Clayton. *sc:* William Archibald, Truman Capote (from *The Turn of the Screw,* by Henry James). *add. scenes:* John Mortimer. *ph:* Freddie Francis. *des:* Wilfrid Shingleton. *mus:* Georges Auric. *ed:* James Clark. *players:* Deborah Kerr, Martin Stephens, Pamela Franklin, Megs Jenkins, Michael Redgrave.

1961 **THE DAMNED.** *Prod:* Hammer/Swallow (Anthony Hinds). *dir:* Joseph Losey. *sc:* Evan Jones (from the novel *The Children of Light,* by H. L. Lawrence). *ph:* Arthur Grant. *des:* Don Mingaye. *mus:* James Bernard. *ed:* Reginald Mills. *players:* Macdonald Carey, Shirley Ann Field, Viveca Lindfors, Alexander Knox, Oliver Reed.

1961 **THE PIT AND THE PENDULUM.** *Prod:* Roger Corman. *dir:* Roger Corman. *sc:* Richard Matheson (from the story by Edgar Allan Poe). *ph:* Floyd Crosby. *des:* Daniel Haller. *mus:* Les Baxter. *ed:* Anthony Carras. *players:* Vincent Price, John Kerr, Barbara Steele, Luana Anders, Anthony Carbone.

1961 **THE PREMATURE BURIAL.** *Prod:* Roger Corman. *dir:* Roger Corman. *sc:* Charles Beaumont, Ray Russell (from the story by Edgar Allan Poe). *ph:* Floyd Crosby. *des:* Daniel Haller. *mus:* Ronald Stein. *ed:* Ronald Sinclair. *players:* Ray Milland, Hazel Court, Richard Ney, John Dierkes.

1961 **INCIDENT AT OWL CREEK (LA RIVIÈRE DU HIBOU).** *Dir:* Robert Enrico. *sc:* Robert Enrico (from the story *An Occurrence at Owl Creek Bridge* by Ambrose Bierce). *ph:* Jean Boffety.

Barbara Steele, horror stalwart, in 1960's *Black Sunday* (alternatively titled *Revenge of the Vampire*).

This exquisitely photographed short film beautifully illustrates the gradual encroachment of fear—the sense of "something not quite right"—upon an apparent situation of joyous escape from danger. The opening is grim: a civilian who has been condemned for "resistance" work during the American Civil War is about to be hanged from a bridge over a river. As he falls, the noose slips and he plunges down into the water. Overwhelmed with happiness, he escapes from the firing soldiers and begins his long run home to his wife. Most of the film is taken up by this trek, through beautiful woodland, the sounds of pursuit and rifle fire dying away to a silence broken only by his panting breath and running footsteps. As he travels, almost imperceptibly the atmosphere changes, the surroundings very gradually acquire an oddly sinister aspect. A glimpse of an opening in the wood ahead seems unnaturally dark—a gateway looks strangely menacing. The graduations of this are most subtly done. He runs on, and at last sees his wife approaching—but in slow motion. His own progress is slowed up in the same nightmare fashion. Though well in sight of her, however far he runs he is never any nearer to her. At last he seems to break the spell—there is a shock cut—and he falls to his death

by the rope from which he has never escaped, save in his own mind during the last seconds of life. The high quality of the film is shown by the fact that on a second viewing, when the end is known, the feeling of suspense and unease is as great as ever.

Roger Jacquet in Robert Enrico's *Incident at Owl Creek*.

1961 TASTE OF FEAR. *Dir:* Seth Holt.

1961 HOUSE OF MYSTERY. *Dir:* Vernon Sewell.

1962 TALES OF TERROR. *Prod:* Roger Corman. *dir:* Roger Corman. *sc:* Richard Matheson (based on short stories by Edgar Allan Poe). *ph:* Floyd Crosby. *des:* Daniel Haller. *mus:* Les Baxter. *ed:* Anthony Carras. *players:* Vincent Price, Peter Lorre, Basil Rathbone, Debra Paget.

1962 THE TERROR OF DR. HICHCOCK (ORRIBILE SEGRETO DEL DOTTOR HICHCOCK, L'). *Prod:* Panda (Louis Mann, i.e. Luigi Carpentieri and Ermanno Donati). *dir:* Robert Hampton (Riccardo Freda). *sc:* Julyan Perry. *ph:* Donald Green (Raffaele Masciocchi). *des:* Frank Smokecocks (Franco Fumagalli). *mus:* Roman Vlad. *ed:* Donna Christie (Arnella Micheli). *players:* Robert Flemyng, Barbara Steele, Teresa Fitzgerald (Maria Teresa Vianello)

1962 WHATEVER HAPPENED TO BABY JANE? *Dir:* Robert Aldrich.

1962 THE DAY OF THE TRIFFIDS. *Dir:* Steve Sekely.

1962 THE DIARY OF A MADMAN. *Dir:* Al Westen.

1962 KISS OF THE VAMPIRE. *Dir:* Don Sharp.

1962 THE EXTERMINATING ANGEL (EL ANGEL EXTERMINADOR). *Dir:* Luis Buñuel.

Buñuel shows us the horror of disintegration—the disintegration of conventional civilisation from polite society manners to degradation and filth—stripped of veneers. The lack of any reason for the collapse—the inexplicable inability of the trapped people to walk from the room—adds a further dimension to the horror, and the sardonic comedy does nothing to relieve it. There is a moment of typical Buñuel nightmare, when a disembodied hand starts to crawl from the cupboard into which a corpse has been thrust: a familiar horror-film ingredient, but treated here with just the extra turn of the screw.

1962 HARAKIRI (SEPPUKU). *Dir:* Masaki Kobayashi.

The horrible savagery beneath the dignified ritual is ruthlessly exposed, and the fact that the scenes of brutality are contrasted with a stylised treatment of much of the film enhances their effect.

1963 THE BIRDS. *Prod:* Universal-International (Alfred Hitchcock). *dir:* Alfred Hitchcock. *sc:* Evan Hunter (from the story by Daphne du Maurier). *ph:* Robert Burks. *des:* George Milo. *ed:* George Tomasini. *players:* Tippi Hedren, Rod Taylor, Suzanne Pleshette, Jessica Tandy, Veronica Cartwright.

1963 NIGHT OF THE EAGLE. *Dir:* Sidney Hayers. *sc:* Charles Beaumont, Richard Matheson, George Baxt, from a story by Fritz Leiber. *ph:* Reginald Wyer. *ed:* Ralph Sheldon. *mus:* William Alwyn. *players:* Janet Blair, John Wyngarde, Margaret Johnston, Anthony Nicholls, Colin Gordon.

An excellently atmospheric Gothic horror, set in a medical school. The Eagle is a huge, threatening stone bird which dominates the school and, egged on by black magic, behaves in a way no respectable stone eagle should. Director and cast succeed in making the distinctly improbable almost credible.

1963 THE HAUNTED PALACE. *Prod:* Alta Vista (Roger Corman). *dir:* Roger Corman. *sc:* Charles Beaumont (based on stories by Edgar Allan Poe and H. P. Lovecraft). *ph:* Floyd Crosby. *des:* Daniel Haller. *mus:* Ronald Stein. *ed:* Ronald Sinclair. *players:* Vincent Price, Debra Paget, Lon Chaney, Jr., Frank Maxwell, Elisha Cook, John Dierkes.

1963 THE MAN WITH THE X-RAY EYES. *Prod:* Alta Vista (Roger Corman). *dir:* Roger Corman. *sc:* Robert Dillon, Ray Russell (from a story by Ray Russell). *ph:* Floyd Crosby. *des:* Daniel Haller. *mus:* Les Baxter. *ed:* Anthony Carras. *players:* Ray Milland, Diana Van Der Vlis, Harold J. Stone, John Hoyt, Don Rickles, John Dierkes.

1963 THE RAVEN. *Prod:* Alta Vista/American International (Roger Corman). *dir:* Roger Corman. *sc:* Richard Matheson. *ph:* Floyd Crosby. *des:* Daniel Haller. *mus:* Lex Baxter. *ed:* Ronald Sinclair. *players:* Vincent Price, Peter Lorre, Boris Karloff, Hazel Court.

Included here for sake of completeness, this is very much fringe-horror and fringe-Poe, being more or less a parody of both. It is amusingly done, however, which is refreshingly unusual in a *genre* only too easy to mimic feebly, and Vincent Price manages to laugh at himself without guying himself.

1963 THE HAUNTED AND THE HUNTED. *Prod:* Roger Corman. *dir:* Francis Coppola. *sc:* Francis Coppola. *ph:* Charles Hannawalt. *des:* Albert Locatelli. *mus:* Ronald Stein. *ed:* Stewart O'Brien. *players:* William Campbell, Luana Anders, Bart Patton, Patrick Magee.

Roger Corman only produced this film, but Francis Coppola's direction has many touches of the authentic Corman atmosphere. Conventional old castle and lakeside settings are imaginatively photographed, and at least two incidents—the axe attack on Louise Halloran (Luana Anders), and the appearance of the wax figure under the water—are moments of genuine shock.

1963 THE HAUNTING. *Dir:* Robert Wise.

1963 THE TERROR. *Dir:* Roger Corman.

1963 INSOMNIA (INSOMNIE). *Dir:* Pierre Etaix.

A brief, hilarious satire on the vampire cult.

1964 THE MASQUE OF THE RED DEATH. *Prod:* Alta Vista/Anglo Amalgamated (George Willoughby). *dir:* Roger Corman. *sc:* Charles Beaumont, R. Wright Campbell (from the story by Edgar Allan Poe). *ph:* Nicolas Roeg. *des:* Robert Jones. *set dec:* Colin Southcott. *mus:* David Lee. *ed:* Ann Chegwidden. *players:* Vincent Price, Hazel Court, Jane Asher, Skip Martin, Patrick Magee, John Westbrook, David Weston.

1964 THE TOMB OF LIGEIA. *Prod:* Alta Vista (Roger Corman, Pat Green). *dir:* Roger Corman. *sc:* Robert Towne (from the story by Edgar Allan Poe). *ph:* Arthur Grant. *des:* Colin Southcott. *mus:* Kenneth V. Jones. *ed:* Alfred Cox. *players:* Vincent Price, Elizabeth Shepherd, John Westbrook, Oliver Johnston, Derek Francis.

1964 DR. TERROR'S HOUSE OF HORRORS. *Prod:* Amicus (Milton Subotsky, Max J. Rosenberg). *dir:*

Hitchcock's *The Birds.*
The small birds attack: Tippie Hedren, Rod Taylor.

The big birds attack.

Freddie Francis. *sc:* Milton Subotsky. *ph:* Alan Hume. *des:* Bill Constable. *mus:* Elizabeth Lutyens. *ed:* Thelma Connell. *players:* Peter Cushing, Neil McCallum, Alan Freeman, Christopher Lee, Roy Castle, Max Adrian.

1964 **WITCHCRAFT**. *Prod:* Lippert Films (Robert Lippert, Jack Parsons). *dir:* Don Sharp. *sc:* Harry Spald-ing. *ph:* Arthur Lavis. *des:* George Provis. *mus:* Carlo Martelli. *ed:* Robert Winter. *players:* Jack Hedley, Jill Dixon, Marie Ney, Lon Chaney, Jr., Diane Claire, Yvette Rees, David Weston.

1964 **THE EARTH DIES SCREAMING**. *Prod:* Lippert Films (Robert Lippert). *dir:* Terence Fisher. *sc:* Henry Cass. *ph:* Arthur Lavis. *des:* George Provis. *mus:* Elizabeth Lutyens. *ed:* Robert Winter. *players:* Willard Parker, Virginia Field, Dennis Price, Thorley Walters, David Spenser, Anna Palk.

1964 **KWAIDAN**. *Dir:* Masaki Kobayashi.

A collection of three fantastic tales of old Japan. The first, *The Black Hair,* is most conventionally a horror story, but all three are fine studies in the macabre, and ravishingly photographed by Yoshio Miyajima. A fourth story, equally impressive, is issued separately as *The Woman of the Snow.*

1964 **THE LONG HAIR OF DEATH (I LUNGHI CAPELLI DELLA MORTE)**. *Dir:* Anthony Dawson (Antonio Margheriti).

Noteworthy, as always, for Barbara Steele.

1964 **SIX IN PARIS (PARIS VU PAR . . .), LA MUETTE** episode. *Dir:* Claude Chabrol.

This final episode in a 16 mm. six-director anthology starts off as a devastating exposition of the inane futilities and squabblings of a bourgeois family, and culminates in sudden death when the wife (Stéphane

Images from two Japanese films
Kwaidan (1964).

134

Onibaba (1965).

Audran), screaming after her departing husband (Claude Chabrol), falls headlong down a flight of stairs. As she lies dying in the poky little hallway, her ghastly semi-conscious moans go unheeded by her small son who has plugged his ears to protect himself from the incessant quarrelling. Sympathy is not aroused, the characters being too unpleasant, and the episode too brief, for real involvement, but the horror of violent, unexpected and stupidly unnecessary death is shown with brutal force.

1964 **BLOOD AND BLACK LACE (SEI DONNE PER L'ASSASSINO).** *Dir:* Mario Bava.

Despite wooden acting, several unfortunate anticlimaxes, and the usual appalling dubbing (when will it be realised that subtitles are infinitely less destructive to atmosphere than this abominable process of foisting on actors a voice and a language not their own?), the film is beautifully photographed, with imaginative touches.

1964 **THE EVIL OF FRANKENSTEIN.** *Dir:* Freddie Francis.

1964 **THE GORGON.** *Dir:* Terence Fisher.

1964 **THE CURSE OF THE MUMMY'S TOMB.** *Dir:* Michael Carreras.

1964 **HYSTERIA.** *Dir:* Freddie Francis.

1965 **REPULSION.** *Prod:* Gene Gutowski. *dir:* Roman Polanski. *sc:* Roman Polanski, Gerard Brach. *ph:* Gilbert Taylor. *des:* Seamus Flannery. *mus:* Chico Hamilton. *ed:* Alistair McIntyre. *players:* Catherine Deneuve, Yvonne Furneaux, Ian Hendry, John Fraser, Patrick Wymark, Valerie Taylor, Helen Fraser.

1965 **THE COLLECTOR.** *Prod:* Jud Kinberg, John Kohn. *dir:* William Wyler. *sc:* Stanley Mann, John Kohn (from a novel by John Fowles). *ph:* Robert L. Surtees. *des:* John Stoll. *mus:* Maurice Jarre. *ed:* Robert Swink, David Hawkins. *players:* Terence Stamp, Samantha Eggar.

1965 **FANATIC.** *Prod:* Hammer/Seven Arts (Anthony Hinds). *dir:* Silvio Narizzano. *sc:* Richard Matheson (from the novel *Nightmare* by Anne Blaisdell). *ph:* Arthur Ibbetson. *des:* Peter Proud. *mus:* Wilfred Josephs. *ed:* John Dunsford. *players:* Tallulah Bankhead, Stefanie Powers, Peter Vaughan, Yootha Joyce, Maurice Kaufman.

1965 **BUNNY LAKE IS MISSING.** *Prod:* Otto Preminger. *dir:* Otto Preminger. *sc:* John and Penelope Mortimer (from the novel by Evelyn Piper). *ph:* Denys Coop. *des:* Don Ashton. *mus:* Paul Glass. *ed:* Peter Thornton. *players:* Keir Dullea, Carol Lynley, Laurence Olivier, Martita Hunt, Noël Coward, Anna Massey.

1965 **THE NANNY.** *Prod:* Hammer (Jimmy Sangster). *dir:* Seth Holt. *sc:* Jimmy Sangster (from the novel by Evelyn Piper). *ph:* Harry Waxman. *mus:* Richard Rodney Bennett. *ed:* Tom Simpson. *players:* Bette Davis, Jill Bennett, Wendy Craig, James Villiers, William Dix, Pamela Franklin.

1965 **DRACULA, PRINCE OF DARKNESS.** *Prod:* Hammer (A. Nelson Keys). *dir:* Terence Fisher. *sc:* John Sansom (from an idea by John Elder, based on the characters of Bram Stoker). *ph:* Michael Reed. *des:* John Mingaye. *mus:* James Bernard. *ed:* Chris Barnes. *players:* Christopher Lee, Barbara Shelley, Andrew Keir, Francis Matthews, Suzan Farmer, Charles Tingwell.

1965 **RASPUTIN, THE MAD MONK.** *Prod:* Hammer. *dir:* Don Sharp. *sc:* John Elder. *ph:* Michael Reed. *des:* Don Mingaye. *mus:* Don Banks. *ed:* Roy Hyde. *players:* Christopher Lee, Barbara Shelley, Richard Pasco, Francis Matthews, Suzan Farmer.

1965 **THE HOLE (ONIBABA).** *Dir:* Kaneto Shindo.

Set entirely among vast fields of man-high grass (offering opportunities, always taken, of very beautiful photography), the film starts off as a grim story of a mother and daughter-in-law who earn a precarious living by trapping and killing soldiers escaping from war (Samurai, not modern), stripping off their armour to sell, and hiding their bodies in the hole. This is gruesome enough, but from the moment when the sword of one such fugitive crashes through teh wall of their reed hut it becomes pure Grand Guignol, and first-class Grand Guignol at that. This particular soldier is wearing a mask, and forces the terrified older woman to show him an escape route. She traps him into the hole, however, climbs down after him and strips the mask from his dead body, revealing a hideously disfigured face beneath. Later she uses the mask to deter her daughter-in-law from an affair she is having with the only other inhabitant of the field—an ex-farmer who has returned from the wars in somewhat dubious circumstances, and who the mother fears will entice the girl away and ruin their trade in the stolen armour. Wearing the mask one night for this purpose in the rain, she finds it will not come off. The girl, who has been genuinely terrified, realises how she was fooled. In response to the woman's entreaties she exultantly and viciously smashes the mask—revealing the woman's face beneath disfigured as dreadfully as that of the soldier. The bare outline conveys little of the horror of the scene as the girl hacks and bashes at the screaming woman's tortured head. Yet with all this the film has an austere dignity which lifts it above the conventional. Much of the effectiveness of the latter part is due to the mask itself—a magnificently alive and

menacing creation, which seems to change expression in differing circumstances and from differing angles. It is, in fact, as fine an actor as the rest of the cast. The sight of the apparition starting up from the ground should be enough to cool any amorous ardour, but ironically it is instrumental finally in triggering off the most vigorous outburst of all. (The slow drooping of the masked woman's arms as she watches the failure of her plan is surprisingly moving). There is one unforgettably beautiful and sinister scene of the woman leading the masked soldier, in bright moonlight, through the waving grass—to his death.

1965 **THE REVENGE OF THE BLOOD BEAST (LA SORELLA DI SATAN).** *Dir:* Michael Reeves, Charles Griffiths.

An Italian-made vampire film which achieves the rarely successful task of laughing at itself without altogether losing the sense of horror. Barbara Steele is, as usual, splendiferous, though in a comparatively small role. Released in an English version—i.e. dubbed by the players themselves.

1965 **THE CURSE OF THE FLY.** *Dir:* Don Sharp.

Even so accomplished a director can do little with yet another fly film—though in fact the wretched insect does not appear, and the title is a blatant box-office catch-penny.

1965 **TERROR CREATURES FROM THE GRAVE (CINQUE TOMBE PER UN MEDIUM).** *Dir:* Ralph Zucker (Massimo Pupillo).

1965 **BILLY THE KID V. DRACULA.** *Dir:* William Beaudine.

John Carradine as the Count.

1965 **JULIET OF THE SPIRITS (GIULIETTA DEGLI SPIRITI).** *Dir:* Federico Fellini. *sc:* Federico Fellini, Tullio Pinelli, Brunello Romdi, Ennio Flaiano. *ph:* Gianni Di Venazo. *des:* Piero Gherardi. *mus:* Nino Rota. *players:* Giulietta Masina, Mario Pisu, Sandra Milo, Valentina Cortese, Sylva Koscina, Catherina Boratto.

It may seem strange to find this unforgettably beautiful film in a book on horror—but the constant visions which haunt the lonely woman in her suburban villa are true ingredients of *frisson*. The nightmare effect that certain aspects of religious teaching can have on children is an important theme in the film. Memories of gruesome and, one would have thought, totally unsuitable convent school plays in which an eight-year-old girl takes part, return to her long after she is a grown woman, in distorted and terrifying forms. Representing a martyr who is grilled alive, the little girl had been raised on a pulley high up to the ceiling of the stage while the other children chant a doleful dirge. In memory, God becomes a dark, sinister, elongated figure in the domed roof; the convent nuns become a row of black, faceless cowled figures moving in a menacing, relentless procession; her own child-self turns into a grotesque, obscene parody of innocence. Towards the end of the film the nuns and other figures silently invade the entire

Juliet of the Spirits: **nightmare childhood memories**.

house in a scene which rises to a climax of fear—finally dispelled, after a confrontation, in the exquisite closing moments. Enormously aided by Nino Rota's music, this is an unforgettably moving experience. The whole film is a subtle and compassionate (and marvellously imaginative) study, which for some reason has often been grossly underrated in comparison with others of Fellini's productions.

1965 **THE FACE OF FU MANCHU.** *Dir:* Don Sharp.

1965 **DEVILS OF DARKNESS.** *Dir:* Lance Comfort.

1965 **MONSTER OF TERROR** (Alternative U.S. title **DIE, MONSTER, DIE**). *Dir:* Daniel Haller.

1965 **PLANET OF THE VAMPIRES (TERRORE NELLO SPAZIO).** *Dir:* Mario Bava.

1965 **THE BLACK CAT.** *Dir:* Harold Hoffman.

Not to be confused with the 1934 version of Poe's story, and with not much more resemblance to the original.

1966 **THE REPTILE.** *Prod:* Hammer (Anthony Nelson Keys). *dir:* John Gilling. *sc:* John Elder. *ph:* Arthur Grant. *des:* Don Mingaye. *mus:* Don Banks. *ed:* Roy Hyde. *players:* Noel Willman, Jennifer Daniel, Ray Barrett, Jacqueline Pearce, John Laurie.

Juliet of the Spirits: **the phantoms invade the house.**

1966 **THE PLAGUE OF THE ZOMBIES**. *Prod:* Hammer (Anthony Nelson Keys). *dir:* John Gilling. *sc:* Peter Bryan. *ph:* Arthur Grant. *des:* Don Mingaye. *mus:* James Bernard. *ed:* Chris Barnes. *players:* Andre Morell, Diane Clare, Brook Williams, Jacqueline Pearce, John Carson.

1966 **THE SKULL**. *Prod:* Amicus (Milton Subotsky). *dir:* Freddie Francis. *sc:* Milton Subotsky (from the story *The Skull of the Marquis de Sade* by Robert Bloch). *ph:* John Wilcox. *des:* Scott Slimon. *mus:* Elizabeth Lutyens. *ed:* Oswald Hafenrichter. *players:* Peter Cushing, Christopher Lee, Patrick Wymark, Jill Bennett, Nigel Green.

1966 **THE PSYCHOPATH**. *Prod:* Amicus (Max J. Rosenberg, Milton Subotsky). *dir:* Freddie Francis. *sc:* Robert Bloch. *ph:* John Wilcox. *des:* Bill Constable. *mus:* Elizabeth Lutyens. *ed:* Oswald Hafenrichter. *players:* Patrick Wymark, Margaret Johnston, John Standing, Alexander Knox, Judy Huxtable.

1966 **CUL-DE-SAC**. *Dir:* Roman Polanski.

How "black" must comedy be to qualify for the description "horrific"? This prize-winning film received widely divergent criticisms, and probably more than most depends on individual reactions as to what is laughable, and what is not. Certainly the comedy is sufficiently off-key and underlaid with cruelty—from the sinister opening with the water lapping round the wheels of the broken-down car on the lonely causeway, and the croaking man crouched over the wheel, to the closing shot of the weeping, demented husband perched on his lonely rock—to ensure that the laughter is not that of simplehearted innocence. The film may be admired or detested—it cannot be forgotten.

1966 **THE PROJECTED MAN**. *Dir:* Ian Curteis.

Interesting surroundings, but a monster unworthy of them.

1966 **ISLAND OF TERROR**. *Dir:* Terence Fisher.

Donald Pleasence, Lionel Stander and, receiving her come-uppance, Francoise Dorléac, in Polanski's nightmarish black comedy *Cul-de-Sac*.

138

Cul-de-Sac: **death of the gangster.**

The striking closing moments of *Cul-de-Sac:* Donald Pleasence.

1966 **SECONDS.** *Dir:* John Frankenheimer.

A chill monitory tale concerning the provision of a new personality—almost literally to a new life—to the bored and jaded rich. The distorted scenes of the operation, the revelation that everyone around the hero has also been "re-made," and the ending when he realises he is to be the means of providing a new "life" for the next customer, are horrific highlights.

1966 **THE WITCHES.** *Prod:* Hammer. *dir:* Cyril Frankel. *sc:* Nigel Kneale, from *The Devil's Own,* by Peter Curtis. *ph:* Arthur Grant. *des:* Bernard Robinson. *mus:* Richard Rodney Bennett. *ed:* James Needs, Chris Barnes. *players:* Joan Fontaine, Kay Walsh, Alec McCowen, Ingrid Brett, Martin Stephens, Gwen Ffrangcon-Davies.

1966 **SLAVE GIRLS.** *Dir:* Michael Carreras.

Wildly incredible yet somehow ingratiatingly entertaining horror-comic about a hunter in the jungle who finds himself (courtesy of a flash of lightning in a kingdom of Amazonian women—all brunettes—who use captured blondes as slaves. Some quite nasty moments (particularly those involving a rhinoceros horn) are encountered. When the hunter is returned to more prosaic surroundings (courtesy of another flash of lightning) he finds that time has been oddly compressed: he then meets a young woman who mysteriously resembles his favourite blonde of the between-flashes era. Shades of *She* haunt this very minor but oddly enjoyable example of cod-horror.

1966 **BLOODSUCKERS.** *Dir:* Mel Welles.

1966 **BLOW-UP.** *Dir:* Michelangelo Antonioni.

Whatever significances are read into the events which occur in it, the strange, tree-rustling, grey-green, eerie, hushed, out-of-this-world little park is a noteworthy example of the edgy unease which can be conjured up simply by skilful treatment of an outwardly very ordinary setting.

1966 **FRANKENSTEIN CREATED WOMAN.** *Prod:* Hammer. *dir:* Terence Fisher.

1966 **THE MUMMY'S SHROUD.** *Prod:* Hammer. *dir:* John Gilling.

1966 **THE SORCERERS.** *Prod:* Tigon. *dir:* Michael Reeves. *sc:* Michael Reeves, Tom Baker, from an idea by John Burke. *ph:* Stanley Long. *des:* Tony Curtis. *mus:* Paul Ferris. *ed:* David Woodward. *players:* Boris Karloff, Catherine Lacey, Ian Ogilvy, Elizabeth Ercy, Susan George.

Mean, moody and menacing: Martine Beswick in *Slave Girls.*

The blonde slaves and their rulers: a scene from *Slave Girls*.

Martine Beswick is impaled on the stone rhinoceros in *Slave Girls*.

1966 **THE SHUTTERED ROOM**. *Prod:* Phillip Hazelton. *dir:* David Greene. *sc:* D. B. Ledrov, Nathaniel Tanchuk, from the novel by H. P. Lovecraft and August Derleth. *ph:* Ken Hodges. *des:* Brian Eatwell. *mus:* Basil Kirchin. *ed:* Brian Smedley-Aston. *players:* Carol Lynley, Flora Robson, Gig Young, Oliver Reed, William Devlin, Robert Cawdron.

1966 **THE DEADLY BEES**. *Dir:* Freddie Francis.

1966 **THE DIABOLICAL DOCTOR Z (MISS MUERTE)**. *Dir:* Jésus Franco.

1966 **THE WITCH IN LOVE (LA STREGA IN AMORE)**. *Dir:* Damiano Damiani.

1966 **STING OF DEATH**. *Dir:* William Grefé.

1966 **EYE OF THE DEVIL**. *Dir:* J. Lee Thompson.

An oddity, dealing with a cult wherein the head of a French family has to offer himself up as a sacrifice whenever the vineyards fail to produce. Complete with hooded initiates, high turret walls, bows and arrows, and Donald Pleasence as a highly unconventional priest.

1967 **THE BLOOD BEAST TERROR**. *Prod:* Tigon. *dir:* Vernon Sewell.

1967 **QUATERMASS AND THE PIT**. *Prod:* Hammer. *dir:* Roy Ward Baker.

"Things" in the London tube. Good build-up but the usual monstrous let-down when the evil power is personified.

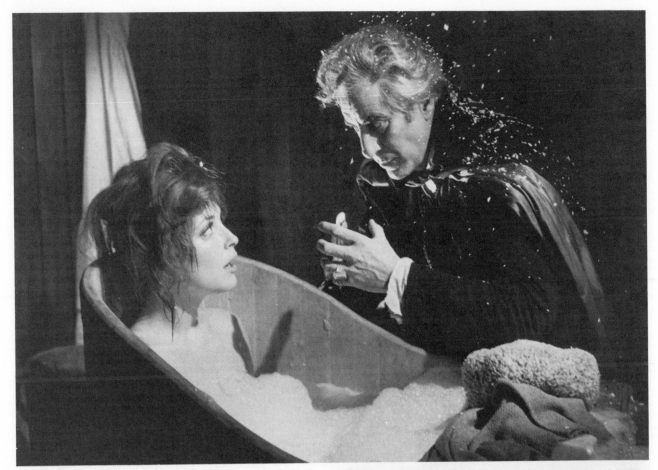

Sharon Tate and Ferdy Mayne in *Dance of the Vampires*
(The Fearless Vampire Killers).

1967 **BERSERK!** *Dir:* Jim O'Connolly.
    Joan Crawford presiding.
1967 **TORTURE GARDEN.** *Prod:* Amicus. *dir:* Freddie
    Francis. *sc:* Robert Bloch. *ph:* Norman Warwick. *des:*
    Don Mingaye. *ed:* Peter Elliot. *players:* Burgess Mere-
    dith, Jack Palance, Michael Bryant, Peter Cushing,
    Beverly Adams, Michael Ripper.
1967 **CORRUPTION.** *Dir:* Robert Hartford-Davis.
1967 **DANCE OF THE VAMPIRES.** *Prod:* Gene Gutowski.
    dir: Roman Polanski. *sc:* Gerard Brach, Roman
    Polanski. *ph:* Douglas Slocombe. *des:* Wilfrid Shingle-
    ton. *mus:* Krzysztof Komeda. *players:* Jack Mac-
    Gowran, Roman Polanski, Alfie Bass, Sharon Tate,
    Ferdy Mayne.

    Insensitively dismissed in some quarters as a mere
attempt to parody the vampire *genre,* this affectionate, visually beautiful, subtle and unfailingly entertaining film has not, in England at any rate, had the
success it deserves. Ferdy Mayne is the best vampire
count yet, and, even at the level of a shocker, there
have been few more chilling moments than his
descent through the skylight to gorge on the bathing
Miss Tate. The actual dance is a brilliant *tour-de-
force.*

    Viewers are warned that the version generally

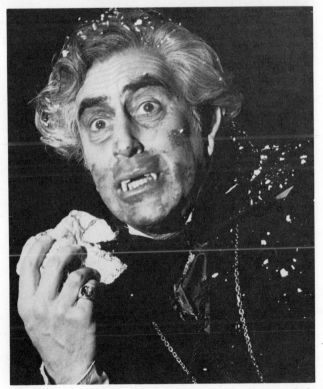

Ferdy Mayne, top-class vampire Count, in *Dance of the
Vampires*.

The vampire foretells the great triumphs in store for his kind. Roman Polanski, Jack MacGowran and Ferdy Mayne in *Dance of the Vampires.*

shown on television is a shameful travesty, cut, "embellished" and disgracefully dubbed.

1967 **KING KONG ESCAPES (KING KONG NO GYAKU-SHU).** *Dir:* Inoshiro Honda.

A Japanese Kong was, of course, inevitable, and here he is even paid the compliment of having a robot replica of himself made; but Robert Armstrong's captive of 1933 is still Number One Ape.

1967 **GAMES.** *Dir:* Curtis Harrington.

Simone Signoret must have had old feelings of "I have been here before" while making this weird story of a young married couple whose outlandish games suddenly turn into something more serious, for memories of *Les diaboliques* are revived more than somewhat. Still, there is plenty of originality to shiver at here, and a *triple* twist (or two twists and a hint) to finish up with.

1967 **THE DEVIL RIDES OUT.** *Prod:* Hammer. *dir:* Terence Fisher. *ph:* Arthur Grant. *sc:* Richard Matheson, from the novel by Dennis Wheatley. *players:* Christopher Lee, Charles Gray, Nike Arrighi, Gwen

The splendidly macabre and brilliantly timed *Dance of the Vampires.*

Ffrangcon-Davies, Rosalyn Landor.

Interesting details of black magic rites, but evil is rather too tamely overcome.

1967 **TARGETS.** *Dir:* Peter Bogdanovich.

Boris Karloff's last American film, and a singularly apt and touching farewell from the great master of horror. An aging and disillusioned star of horror films, realising that his style of thing is now outdated and dead, attends a showing of one of his old pictures in a drive-in theatre, and there encounters real horror in the shape of a psychopathic sniper . . . an intensely exciting shocker brilliantly and tautly directed by Peter Bogdanovich as his first feature.

1968 **WITCHFINDER GENERAL.** *Prod:* Tigon. *dir:* Michael Reeves. *sc:* Michael Reeves, Tom Baker, from a novel by Ronald Bassett. *ph:* Johnny Coquillon. *des:* Jim Morahan. *mus:* Paul Ferris. *ed:* Howard Lannine. *players:* Vincent Price, Ian Ogilvy, Hilary Dwyer, Rupert Davies, Patrick Wymark, Wilfrid Brambell.

1968 **DRACULA HAS RISEN FROM THE GRAVE.** *Prod:* Hammer. *dir:* Freddie Francis. *sc:* John Elder. *ph:* Arthur Grant. *des:* Bernard Robinson. *mus:* James Bernard. *players:* Christopher Lee, Rupert Davies, Veronica Carlsson, Barbara Ewing, Barry Andrews.

1968 **THE CURSE OF THE CRIMSON ALTAR.** *Prod:* Tigon. *dir:* Vernon Sewell.

The promise of a combination of Lee, Karloff and Barbara Steele is not fulfilled in this surprisingly tame witch story, filmed in the late W. S. Gilbert's famous mansion.

1968 **TWISTED NERVE.** *Dir:* Roy Boulting.

Though no *Psycho* (an inevitable comparison, even

Pamela Franklin menaced by Richard Boone in *The Night of the Following Day.*

Hayley Mills and Hywel Bennett in the controversial *Twisted Nerve.*

to having the same composer, Bernard Herrmann), several scenes in this "psychological horror" work up to a certain tension, but the climax is overlong, and sensationalism generally is too much to the fore. The film caused a great outcry at the time of its release because of its alleged (but denied) deliberate linking of mongolism and psychopathy.

1968 **THE STALKING MOON.** *Dir:* Robert Mulligan.

An authentic Horror Western, with all the necessary ingredients of hidden menace ever growing closer (and seen only as a disappearing shape), creaking doors, padding footsteps, progressive stripping away of protective layers from heroine, final confrontation with monster—in this case an understandably cross Red Indian. In addition, much of the Western warmth and charm of the recognisable virtues.

1968 **THE NIGHT OF THE FOLLOWING DAY.** *Dir:* Hubert Cornfield.

An odd piece about a kidnapping that goes wrong, and provides several moments of *frisson* on the way. The film ends with the same sort of twist as *Dead of Night,* but without the blinding brief shot in that masterpiece which reveals that the circle of recurring time has been snapped. One is left wondering—if the whole thing really takes place in the young to-be-kidnapped girl's mind—just what sort of mind it is, concealed behind those bland, innocent features. This, perhaps, is the truly horrific touch. (There is

143

The Night of the Following Day: **Pamela Franklin hides from Marlon Brando.**

also a hint that it might all come from a play on her transistor radio.) Whatever the truth, however, the film consistently grips, and the deliberate touches of unreality throughout produce frequent shivers of unease. The version shown on television has been so appallingly mangled as to distort the entire story. The climax is omitted altogether, words are dubbed into a character's mouth that entirely alter his role and his personality, and a certain subtle ambiguity is thus totally destroyed. That even a minor and far from unflawed film should be so ravaged, without any reference to what has been done to it, is more shocking than any horror film.

1968 **KURONEKO (YABU NO KAKA NO KURONEKO).** *Dir:* Kaneto Shindo.

A more than worthy successor to the same director's celebrated *Onibaba.* An opening sequence of the rape and murder of two women in a lonely hut by marauding samurai moves swiftly from a long, quiet opening to sudden violence. Thereafter the ghosts of the women, appearing both as themselves and as a black cat, revenge themselves fearfully on their killers. By chance, the young warrior selected to destroy the fiends is the husband of one and the son of the other: the final outcome is as grim as might be expected. Some of the effects, wonderful at first meeting, are weakened by repetition—such as the somersaulting lady ghosts as they suddenly float

144

through the air to avoid the swords of the samurai: there are rather too many (admittedly beautiful) samurai-luring walks through the bamboo forest, and the final confrontation totters occasionally on the dangerous edge of ludicrous exaggeration. On the whole, however, this is a splendid essay in Japanese macabre.

1968 **ROSEMARY'S BABY.** *Prod:* William Castle. *dir:* Roman Polanski. *sc:* Roman Polanski, from the novel by Ira Levin. *ph:* William Fraker. *des:* Joel Schiller. *mus:* Krzysztof Komeda. *players:* Mia Farrow, John Cassavetes, Ruth Gordon, Sidney Blackmer, Maurice Evans, Ralph Bellamy.

1969 **FRANKENSTEIN MUST BE DESTROYED.** *Prod:* Hammer. *dir:* Terence Fisher. *sc:* Anthony Nelson Keys, Bert Batt. *des:* Bernard Robinson. *mus:* James Bernard. *players:* Peter Cushing, Veronica Carlson, Simon Ward, Freddie Jones, Maxine Audley.

1969 **EYE OF THE CAT.** *Dir:* David Lowell Rich.

A rather enjoyable essay in terror-by-beast, with cats instead of Hitchcockian birds, and a Boileau/Narcejac twist ending. The cats are trained by Ray Berwick, responsible for the birds in Hitchcock's film of that name, and Joseph Stefano, who wrote the scripts, also adapted *Psycho.* Several sequences, notably that of a bunch of cats fighting for their food in a car, aided by a splendidly spitting, snarling soundtrack, are effectively fierce, and there is a hair-raising, excitingly photographed murder attempt involving a runaway invalid chair, which includes a neat nod of recognition to *Night Must Fall* when the young man wheeling the chair sings "Danny Boy." The star cat gives a well rounded performance, but the trouble is that "aelurophobes" may well refuse to go near the film; and to their admirers, the cats, however much they are induced to spit and wave their tails and act nasty, still look like pretty pussies.

1969 **THE BODY STEALERS.** *Prod:* Tigon. *dir:* Gerry Levy.

1969 **NIGHT OF THE LIVING DEAD.** *Prod:* Image Ten. *dir:* George A. Romero. *sc:* John A. Russo. *ph:* George A. Romero. *players:* Judith O'Dea, Duane Jones, Karl Hardman.

The Eye of the Cat.
Gayle Hunnicutt and Michael Sarrazin attacked by felines.

Gayle Hunnicutt and unnamed character actor.

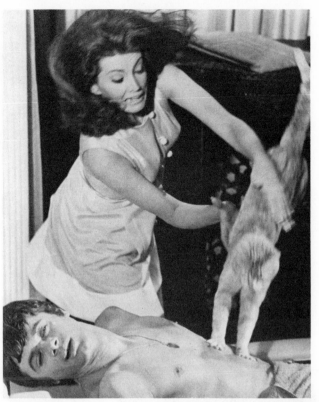

Gayle Hunnicutt uses a cat for her own purposes, with Michael Sarrazin.

1969 **BLOOD OF DRACULA'S CASTLE.** *Dir:* Al Adamson.

1969 **CRESCENDO.** *Prod:* Hammer. *sc:* Jimmy Sangster, Alfred Shaughnessy. *ph:* Paul Beeson. *des:* Scott MacGregor. *mus:* Malcolm Williamson. *ed:* Chris Barnes. *players:* Stephanie Powers, James Olson, Margaretta Scott, Jane Lapotaire.

1969 **TASTE THE BLOOD OF DRACULA.** *Prod:* Hammer. *sc:* John Elder. *ph:* Arthur Grant. *des:* Scott MacGregor. *mus:* James Bernard. *ed:* Chris Barnes. *players:* Christopher Lee, Geoffrey Keen, Gwen Watford, Peter Sallis, Linda Hayden, Ralph Bates.

1969 **THE DUNWICH HORROR.** *Prod:* American International. *dir:* Daniel Haller. *sc:* Curtis Lee Hanson, Henry Rosenbaum, Ronald Silkosky, from a story by H. P. Lovecraft. *ph:* Richard C. Glouner. *des:* Paul Sylos. *mus:* Les Baxter. *ed:* Fred Feitshans. *players:* Sandra Dee, Dean Stockwell, Ed Begley, Sam Jaffe.

1969 **FRANKENSTEIN ON CAMPUS.** *Dir:* Gilbert W. Taylor.

1970 **GUESS WHAT HAPPENED TO COUNT DRACULA.** *Dir:* Laurence Merrick.
Des Roberts as Dracula.

1970 **THE VAMPIRE LOVERS.** *Prod:* Hammer/American International. *Dir:* Roy Ward Baker, *sc:* Tudor Gates, from *Carmilla,* by Sheridan Le Fanu. *ph:* Moray Grant. *des:* Scott MacGregor. *mus:* Harry Robinson. *ed:* James Needs. *players:* Ingrid Pitt, Peter Cushing, Pippa Steele, George Cole, Madeline Smith, Ferdy Mayne.

1970 **THE HORROR OF FRANKENSTEIN.** *Prod:* Hammer. *dir:* Jimmy Sangster. *sc:* Jimmy Sangster, Jeremy Burnham. *ph:* Moray Grant. *des:* Scott MacGregor. *mus:* James Bernard. *ed:* Chris Barnes. *players:* Ralph Bates, Kate O'Mara, Graham James, Veronica Carlson, David Prowse, Dennis Price.

1970 **THE SCARS OF DRACULA.** *Prod:* Hammer. *dir:* Roy Ward Baker. *sc:* John Elder. *ph:* Moray Grant. *des:* Scott MacGregor. *mus:* James Bernard. *ed:* James Needs. *players:* Christopher Lee, Dennis Waterman, Jenny Hanley, Michael Gwynn, Christopher Matthews, Patrick Troughton.

1970 **COUNT YORGA, VAMPIRE.** *Prod:* Erica/A.I.P. *dir:* Bob Kelljan. *sc:* Bob Kelljan. *ph:* Arch Archambault. *des:* Bob Wilder. *mus:* William Marx. *ed:* Tony De Zarraga. *players:* Robert Quarry, Roger Perry, Michael Murphy, Michael Macready, Donna Andrews, Judith Lang.

1970 **CRY OF THE BANSHEE.** *Dir:* Gordon Hessler.

1970 **HOUSE OF DARK SHADOWS.** *Dir:* Dan Curtis.

1970 **LUST FOR A VAMPIRE.** *Prod:* Hammer. *dir:* Jimmy Sangster. *sc:* Tudor Gates, from characters created by Sheridan Le Fanu. *ph:* David Muir. *des:* Don Mingaye. *mus:* Harry Robinson. *ed:* Spencer Reeve. *players:* Ralph Bates, Suzanne Leigh, Barbara Jefford, Michael Johnson, Helen Christie, Pippa Steele.

1970 **COUNTESS DRACULA.** *Prod:* Hammer. *dir:* Peter Sasdy. *sc:* Jeremy Paul. *ph:* Ken Talbot. *des:* Philip Harrison. *mus:* Harry Robinson. *ed:* Henry Richard-

Victim awaits sacrifice: a scene from *Cry of the Banshee.*

son. *players:* Ingrid Pitt, Nigel Green, Sandor Eles, Maurice Denham, Patience Collier, Peter Jeffrey, Lesley-Anne Down.

1970 **THE HOUSE THAT DRIPPED BLOOD.** *Prod:* Amicus. *dir:* Peter Duffell. *sc:* Robert Bloch. *ph:* Ray Parslow. *des:* Tony Curtis. *mus:* Michael Dress. *ed:* Peter Tanner. *players:* Christopher Lee, Nyree Dawn Porter, Chloe Franks, Ingrid Pitt, John Pertwee, Denham Elliott, Peter Cushing, Joanna Dunham.

1970 **SATAN'S SKIN.** *Dir:* Piers Haggard.

1970 **THE BEAST IN THE CELLAR.** *Dir:* James Kelly.

1970 **DAUGHTERS OF DARKNESS (LE ROUGE AUX LEVRES).** *Dir:* Harry Kümel.

Delphine Seyrig would seem to be one of the less likely candidates for female vampirism, but she carries off this extraordinary mixture of thriller and sex-deviation shocker with remarkable aplomb. Some excellent photography by Eddy van der Enden helps the multi-national (Belgium/France/West Germany/Italy) on its way, and, though we may be wondering what on earth (or in hell) the director is at, we at least find it impossible to stop watching him at it.

1970 **THE INCREDIBLE TWO-HEADED TRANSPLANT.** *Dir:* Anthony M. Lanza.

The most incredible thing about it is that it should ever have reached the public screen. The two-headed monster itself is so blatantly botched a piece of creature-making that one can only admire the effrontery of those concerned.

1970 **WILLARD.** *Prod:* Bing Crosby Productions (Mort Briskin). *dir:* Daniel Mann. *sc:* Gilbert A. Ralston, from a novel by Stephen Gilbert. *ph:* Robert B. Hauser. *des:* Howard Hollander. *mus:* Alex North. *ed:* Warren Low. *players:* Bruce Davison, Sondra Locke, Elsa Lanchester, Ernest Borgnine, Michael Dante.

1970 **I, MONSTER.** *Dir:* Stephen Weeks.

Yet another Jekyll and Hyde version, with the name of the chief character changed for no apparent reason, for the story follows the original with considerable accuracy. Old stalwarts Lee and Cushing are in attendance, in good form. There is no apparent justification for the change of date to 1906, and none at all for the catch-penny title.

1970 **THE BROTHERHOOD OF SATAN.** *Dir:* Bernard

McEveety.

Witchcraft in the toy cupboard: an unusual and very effective minor offering.

1970 **VIRGIN WITCH.** *Dir:* Ray Austin.

Fashionably Lesbianic horrors.

1970 **COUNT DRACULA (EL CONDE DRACULA).** *Prod:* Harry Alan Towers. *dir:* Jésus Franco. *sc:* Peter Welbeck (Harry Alan Towers), based on Bram Stoker's *Dracula. ph:* Manuel Marino. *mus:* Bruno Nicolai. *players:* Christopher Lee, Herbert Lom, Klaus Kinski, Frederick Williams, Maria Rohm, Soledad Mitanda.

1970 **BLOOD OF FRANKENSTEIN.** *Dir:* Al Adamson.

1970 **AND SOON THE DARKNESS.** *Prod:* Albert Fennell, Brian Clemens. *dir:* Robert Fuest. *sc:* Brian Clemens, Terry Nation. *ph:* Ian Wilson. *des:* Philip Harrison. *mus:* Laurie Johnson. *ed:* Ann Chegwidden. *players:* Pamela Franklin, Michele Dotrice, Sandor Eles, John Nettleton, Clare Kelly.

Full of Hitchcockian suspense in bright sunshine and wide-open countryside, this too little-known minor masterpiece tells the story of two English girls on a bicycle tour in France who suspect they are being tracked by a killer, and mounts steadily and relentlessly to a magnificent height of tension. The terror of isolation among glum foreigners of whose speech one cannot understand a word, of trying to piece together what fearful hints they are dropping, is forcefully brought home to the viewer. As two of the most alluring cyclists one is likely to meet in a day on the open road, Pamela Franklin and Michele Dotrice make the most of every menacing moment. Robert Fuest's grip on us never falters, except perhaps very slightly in the rather overlong closing sequences.

1971 **THE ABOMINABLE DR. PHIBES.** *Prod:* American International. *dir:* Robert Fuest. *sc:* James Whiton, William Goldstein. *ph:* Norman Warwick. *des:* Brian Eatwell. *mus:* Basil Kirchen, Jack Nathan. *ed:* Tristam Cones. *players:* Vincent Price, Joseph Cotten, Hugh Griffith, Terry-Thomas, Virginia North, Peter Jeffrey, Aubrey Woods.

The two girls reflected in the glasses of their—attacker? Michele Dotrice, Pamela Franklin and Sandor Eles in the suspenseful *And Soon the Darkness.*

Two studies of Pamela Franklin under stress: giving a first-class performance in *And Soon the Darkness*.

1971 **DRACULA VS. FRANKENSTEIN (EL HOMBRE QUE VINO DE UMMO).** *Dir:* Tulio Demichelli.

1971 **BLOOD FROM THE MUMMY'S TOMB.** *Prod:* Hammer. *dir:* Seth Holt.

Seth Holt died before completing this film, and Michael Carreras took over. The story is taken from one of Bram Stoker's better-known non-Dracula novels, *The Jewel of the Seven Stars.*

1971 **DR. JEKYLL AND SISTER HYDE.** *Prod:* Hammer. *dir:* Roy Ward Baker. *sc:* Brian Clemens. *ph:* Norman Warwick. *des:* Robert Jones. *mus:* David Whitaker. *ed:* James Needs. *players:* Ralph Bates, Martine Beswick, Gerald Sim, Lewis Fiander, Susan Brodrick.

1971 **THE OMEGA MAN.** *Dir:* Boris Sagal.

Through being fortunate enough to have injected himself with a newly discovered antidote, Charlton Heston finds he is the only man in the world—or should we say Los Angeles—who is immune from a plague caused by a germ war between China and Russia which has reduced the world population by nine-tenths, not merely "decimated" it, as at least two critics erroneously stated. Most of those left have become mutated creatures cavorting rather ridiculously in black cowled garments, with pin-irised contact lenses. The "normal" remnants would probably themselves be infuriating enough to make Heston regret his survival, from what we see of them. This is the second film version of Richard Matheson's *I Am Legend,* originally done in 1964 as *The Last Man on Earth.* Technically quite efficient, and entertaining if totally unbelievable, but unable to stand any comparison at all with more serious treatments of the theme such as George R. Stewart's fine novel "Earth Abides," or the masterly British television series, *Survivors.*

1971 **FRIGHT.** *Prod:* Fantale Films. *dir:* Peter Collinson. *sc:* Tudor Gates. *ph:* Ian Wilson. *des:* Disley Jones. *mus:* Harry Robinson. *ed:* Raymond Poulton. *players:* Susan George, Ian Bannen, Honor Blackman, John Gregson, Dennis Waterman, George Cole.

1971 **TWINS OF EVIL.** *Prod:* Hammer. *dir:* John Hough. *sc:* Tudor Gates, from characters created by Sheridan Le Fanu. *ph:* Dick Bush. *des:* Roy Stannard. *mus:* Harry Robinson. *ed:* Spencer Reeve. *players:* Peter Cushing, Madeleine Collinson, Mary Collinson, Dennis Price, Kathleen Byron.

1971 **LET'S SCARE JESSICA TO DEATH.** *Dir:* John Hancock.

1971 **LADY FRANKENSTEIN (LA FIGLIA DI FRANKENSTEIN).** *Dir:* Mel Welles (Ernst von Theumer).

1971 **WHOEVER SLEW AUNTIE ROO;** *Prod:* American International/Hemdale.

1971 **WHOEVER SLEW AUNTIE ROO?** *Prod:* American International/Hemdale. *dir:* Curtis Harrington. *sc:* Robert Blees, James Sangster. *ph:* Desmond Dickinson. *des:* George Provis. *mus:* Kenneth Jones. *ed:* Tristam Cones. *players:* Shelley Winters, Mark Lester, Chloe Franks, Ralph Richardson, Lionel Jeffries, Hugh Griffith.

1971 **THE NIGHT COMERS.** *Dir:* Michael Winner.

Possibly the most arrogant piece of film-making to be found in these (or any other) pages. Director and scriptwriter take it on themselves to set down what happened at Bly *before* the Governess arrived, in Henry James's *The Turn of the Screw.* Even had it been done well, such unwarranted interference with a classic tale would have been a questionable proceeding. Henry James might have been given credit for knowing what he was doing when he started his story at a particular point. It has, however, been done very far from well—a botched-up piece of effrontery, totally incredible, with silly "permissive" scenes injected presumably in an attempt to liven things up. Not only rubbish, in fact, but ill-mannered rubbish.

1971 **VAMPIRE CIRCUS.** *Prod:* Hammer. *dir:* Robert Young.

1971 **DEMONS OF THE MIND.** *Dir:* Peter Sykes.

1971 **DR. JEKYLL AND THE WEREWOLF (DOCTOR JEKYLL Y EL HOMBRE LOBO).** *Dir:* Leon Klimovsky.

1971 **NIGHT HAIR CHILD** *Dir:* James Kelly.

A boy of twelve (Mark Lester) is expelled from school for drawing pornographic pictures in his exercise book and torturing a cat to death. "We can deal with homosexuality," says the bearded headmaster, but this. . . !" But this, indeed! Later, the boy forces his stepmother (Britt Ekland) to strip, confesses to having killed his mother, and generally plays havoc. A film about corruption that is as corrupt as its theme.

1971 **THE POSSESSION OF JOEL DELANEY.** *Dir:* Waris Hussein.

A horror film about demonic possession may seem an unlikely vehicle for Shirley MacLaine, which is perhaps why, when she is not in hysterics, she looks so puzzled: though not half as puzzled as Michael Hordern who, after half-a-dozen lines as an unidentifiable character, is last seen sitting on the edge of a bed in a long-held, incomprehensible shot. There is some excuse for Miss MacLaine's bewilderment when she suddenly finds her young brother possessed by the spirit of an embittered Puerto Rican murderer. The film is relentlessly ugly to look at, whether in the poorer districts of New York, or Shirley's hideous apartment. There are some quite chilling moments, but the trouble is that—as Lewis Carroll's carpenter might have said—"the horror's spread too thick."

1972 **FROGS.** *Prod:* American International. *dir:* George McCowan. *sc:* Robert Hutchison, Robert Blees. *ph:* Mario Tosi. *mus:* Les Baxter. *ed:* Fred Feitshans, Jr. *players:* Ray Milland, Sam Elliott, Joan Van Ark, Adam Roarke.

1972 **TALES FROM THE CRYPT.** *Prod:* Max J. Rosenberg/Milton Subotsky. *dir:* Freddie Francis. *sc:* Milton Subotsky, based on horror-comic magazine stories. *ph:* Norman Warwick. *des:* Tony Curtis. *mus:* Douglas Gamley. *ed:* Teddy Darvas.

1972 **ASYLUM.** *Prod:* Amicus. *dir:* Roy Ward Baker. *sc:* Robert Bloch. *ph:* Denys Coop. *des:* Tony Curtis. *mus:* Douglas Gamley. *ed:* Peter Tanner. *players:* Robert Powell, Patrick Magee, Sylvia Syms, Peter

Cushing, Britt Ekland, Herbert Lom, Barry Morse, Barbara Parkins, Charlotte Rampling.

1972 **DISCIPLE OF DEATH**. *Dir:* Tom Parkinson.

The apparent lesson to be learnt from this effort is "Don't cut your thumb on a suicide's tomb." If you do, you may release an agent of the devil who, to the music of mangled Bach, will indulge in a variety of unpleasant and disgusting activities.

1972 **DEATHLINE**. *Dir:* Gary Sherman.

After starting off rather interestingly as a straight-forward murder mystery in London's Russell Square tube station, with lively dialogue and amusing characterisation, this sadly degenerates into a welter of rat-bitten human flesh (lovingly displayed), rotting bodies, and a plague-ridden maniac with dirty water, saliva, blood and pus dripping plentifully from all points.

1972 **THE BLACK BELLY OF THE TARANTULA (LA TARANTULA DEL VENTRO NERO)**. *Dir:* Paolo Cavara.

The dubbing of this piece of glossy horror is so wholly dreadful that it would be unfair to comment on performers labouring under such disadvantages. Best acting comes from the spider itself, and a very pleasant gray cat. The film contains one nice line to be entered into any anthology of movie dialogue—a young girl's first words, over the telephone: "Why do you keep calling me a nymphomaniac? That's the way it goes."

1972 **DUEL**. *Dir:* Steven Spielberg.

Not a "horror" film in the accepted sense—though from the pen of the redoubtable Richard Matheson—this story of a salesman driving his family saloon across America and menaced on a country road by a huge tanker which becomes the very symbol of anonymous evil, keeps the skin crawling and the heart beating furiously throughout its superlatively directed length.

1972 **DR. PHIBES RISES AGAIN**. *Prod:* American International. *dir:* Robert Fuest. *sc:* Robert Fuest, Robert Blees, from characters created by James Whiton and William Goldstein. *ph:* Alex Thomson. *des:* Brian Eatwell. *mus:* John Gale. *ed:* Tristam Cones. *players:* Vincent Price, Robert Quarry, Peter Cushing, Valli Kemp, Fiona Lewis, Peter Jeffrey.

The true star of *The Black Belly of the Tarantula*.

Peter Cushing and Christopher Lee, two friends together again in *Horror Express*.

1972 **DRACULA - A.D. 1972.** *Prod:* Hammer/Warner. *dir:* Alan Gibson. *sc:* Don Houghton. *ph:* Richard Bush. *des:* Don Mingaye. *mus:* Michael Vickers. *ed:* James Needs. *players:* Christopher Lee, Peter Cushing, Stephanie Beacham, Michael Coles, Marsha Hunt, Christopher Neame.

1972 **THE CREEPING FLESH.** *Dir:* Freddie Francis.

1972 **NIGHT OF THE LEPUS.** *Dir:* William F. Claxton.
Lepus = rabbits, and very nasty giant ones, at that. No furry bunnies here.

1972 **BEN.** *Prod:* Bing Crosby Productions (Mort Briskin). *dir:* Philip Karlson. *sc:* Gilbert Ralston. *ph:* Russell Metty. *des:* Rolland M. Brooks. *mus:* Walter Black. *ed:* Harry Gerstad. *players:* Lee Harcourt Montgomery, Joseph Campanella, Arthur O'Connell, Rosemary Murphy, Ben the Rat.

1972 **BLACULA.** *Dir:* William Crain.

1972 **THE SPECTRE OF EDGAR ALLAN POE.** *Dir:* Mohy Quandour.

1972 **GRAVE OF THE VAMPIRE.** *Dir:* John Hayes.
A baby vampire makes his *début*, naturally preferring blood to mother's milk.

1972 **VAMPIRE WOMAN.** *Dir:* Ray Danton.
New footnote to history: the "bride" of King Louis VII of France (Crusader, thrice married, and father of Philip Augustus) was a vampire.

1972 **TOMB OF THE UNDEAD.** *Dir:* John Hayes.

1972 **CAPTAIN KRONOS—VAMPIRE HUNTER.** *Dir:* Brian Clemens.
A little-known film, written and directed by Brian Clemens, leading exponent of TV horror, and part-author of *And Soon the Darkness*.

1972 **HORROR EXPRESS (PANICO EN EL TRANS-IBERIANO).** *Dir:* Eugenio Martin.
Even in 1906, it seems, galactic monsters were busy at their nefarious activities on earth. This is, though frankly absurd, a rather intriguing and original oddity, with the ever-attractive train setting and a cast which includes stalwarts Christopher Lee and Peter Cushing, and a pre-*Kojak* Telly Savalas. The period, as may be seen, is not adhered to with any excessively pedantic accuracy.

1973 **HORROR HOSPITAL.** *Dir:* Antony Balch.
It is run (to nobody's surprise) by a mad doctor

Two monsters, and Helga Line, in 1972's *Horror Express.*

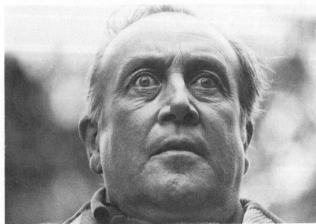

Dennis Price faces decapitation with understandable apprehension in *Horror Hospital.*

who was thwarted in his youth and now performs experimental operations on teenagers, transforming them into zombie acrobats. Michael Gough, as the horror-masked medico, relishes the parody intended in this offering, otherwise it is often difficult to tell the zombies from the humans. Some good macabre jokes, however, such as the decapitation of Dennis Price by a new kind of super-lethal limousine.

1973 **THE LEGEND OF HELL HOUSE.** *Dir:* John Hough.

Richard Matheson may not be at his best in this script (adapted from a novel of his own) but even so it has its quota of chills. A notably prestigious cast (Pamela Franklin, Roddy McDowall, Clive Revill, Peter Bowles, Roland Culver, Gayle Hunnicutt) stand up well against a fine performance from the haunted house itself. Michael Gough has an easier time in this one—as a corpse.

1973 **VAULT OF HORROR.** *Prod:* Amicus. *dir:* Roy Ward Baker. *sc:* Milton Subotsky, from horror-comic magazine stories. *ph:* Denys Coop. *des:* Tony Curtis. *mus:* Douglas Gamley. *ed:* Oswald Hafenrichter. *players:* Daniel Massey, Terry-Thomas, Glynis Johns, Curt Jurgens, Michael Craig, Denham Elliott.

1973 **FROM BEYOND THE GRAVE.** *Prod:* Amicus. *dir:* Kevin Connor. *sc:* Robin Clarke, Raymond Christodolou, from stories by R. Chetwynd-Hayes. *ph:* Alan Hume. *des:* Maurice Carter. *mus:* Douglas Gamley. *ed:* John Ireland. *players:* Peter Cushing, David Warner, Donald Pleasence, Ian Bannen, Diana Dors, Margaret Leighton, Ian Ogilvy.

1973 **DRACULA.** *Prod:* Dan Curtis. *dir:* Dan Curtis. *sc:* Richard Matheson, from Bram Stoker's novel. *ph:* Oswald Morris. *des:* Trevor Williams. *mus:* Robert Cobert. *ed:* Richard A. Harris. *players:* Jack Palance, Simon Ward, Nigel Davenport, Pamela Brown, Fiona Lewis, Penelope Horner.

1973 **THE EXORCIST.** *Prod:* William Peter Blatty. *dir:* William Friedkin. *sc:* William Peter Blatty, from his own novel. *ph:* Owen Roizman, Billy Williams. *des:* Bill Malley. *sup. ed:* Jordan Leondopoulos. *sound:* Chris Newman, Jean-Louis Ducarme. *players:* Ellen Burstyn, Max von Sydow, Linda Blair, Lee J. Cobb, Jason Miller, Jack MacGowran.

1973 **FRANKENSTEIN AND THE MONSTER FROM HELL.** *Prod:* Hammer. *dir:* Terence Fisher. *sc:* John Elder. *ph:* Brian Probyn. *des:* Scott MacGregor. *mus:* James Bernard. *ed:* James Needs. *players:* Peter Cushing, Shane Briant, Madeline Smith, John Stratton, Bernard Lee, Patrick Troughton.

1973 **FRANKENSTEIN—THE TRUE STORY.** *Prod:* Hunt Stromberg, Jr. *dir:* Jack Smight. *sc:* Christopher Isherwood, Don Bachardy, from Mary Shelley's novel. *ph:* Arthur Ibbetson. *des:* Wilfrid Shingleton. *mus:* Gil Mellé. *ed:* Richard Marden. *players:* Leonard Whiting, Michael Sarrazin, James Mason, Ralph Richardson, John Gielgud, David McCallum, Jane Seymour, Michael Wilding.

1973 **FLESH FOR FRANKENSTEIN (CARNE PER FRANKENSTEIN).** *Dir:* Paul Morrissey.

1973 **BLOOD FOR DRACULA (DRACULA VUOLE VIVERE: CERCA SANGUE DI VERGINE).** *Dir:* Paul Morrissey.

1973 **DRACULA'S VIRGIN LOVERS (EL GRAN AMOR DEL CONDE DRACULA).** *Dir:* Javier Aguirre.

1973 **SCREAM, BLACULA, SCREAM.** *Dir:* Bob Kelljan.

1973 **CHILDREN SHOULDN'T PLAY WITH DEAD THINGS.** *Dir:* Benjamin Clark.

1973 **IT'S ALIVE.** *Dir:* Larry Cohen.

A somewhat unsavoury tale of a woman who gives birth to a baby monster (or monster baby) after a painful delivery recorded in great detail. The newcomer at once kills all the medical attendants on its arrival and escapes through a skylight to start a reign of terror in Los Angeles. Some horror sequences involving toys which suddenly take on sinister aspects are quite well built up, and the Little Horror himself is rather appealing in the few glimpses we are afforded. What really makes the film worthy of mention, however, lifting it, indeed, to near-tragic heights, is the remarkably sincere and moving performance by John Ryan as the distracted father. Bernard (*Psycho*) Herrmann composed the music.

1973 **DARK PLACES.** *Dir:* Don Sharp.

Don Sharp has conjured up some very creditable horrors in the past (*Witchcraft*) but is only partially successful in manipulating the dark places in this haunted house, despite the always impressive Christopher Lee. However, it has its moment or two.

1973 **O LUCKY MAN!** *Dir:* Lindsay Anderson.

This brilliant caustic commentary on the modern human condition (disgracefully shorn of two key sequences on general release) does not, of course, fit into the accepted category of films represented here, but it contains—in one brief scene where the modern Everyman (Malcolm MacDowell) unexpectedly comes across the result of a voluntary "medical research" experiment—a moment as terrifying as anything in the whole range of horror in the cinema.

1973 **DON'T LOOK NOW.** *Dir:* Nicolas Roeg.

A strange, haunting film (from a story by Daphne du Maurier) which it is impossible to summarise in a short paragraph. A drowned child, bereaved parents, "second sight," eerie encounters in Venice, two weird sisters, a mysterious killer, a tiny furtive red-cloaked figure glimpsed in the streets, a shatteringly-timed near-fatal accident, a violent death, a surprising revelation, all superbly photographed by Anthony Richmond (and directed by a memorable photographer himself)—combine in a notable example of the ambiguous and macabre.

1973 **THE DEATHMASTER.** *Dir:* Ray Danton.

Robert Quarry (of Count Yorga fame) appears here as vampire Khorda, but there is little resemblance in this poor-relation production to his former glories.

1973 **THE WEREWOLF OF WASHINGTON.** *Dir:* Milton Moses Ginsberg.

Would-be political "satire" and horror-comic combination that does not come off, perhaps because the targets are too obvious and the shooting too cumber-

Sheila Keith, a magnificently evil stepmother in *Frightmare*.

some. All that remains are some rather pointless sniping and an occasional hit or two.

1974 **VAMPIRA**. *Prod:* Jack H. Wiener. *dir:* Clive Donner. *sc:* Jeremy Lloyd. *ph:* Tony Richmond. *des:* Philip Harrison. *mus:* David Whitaker. *ed:* Bill Butler. *players:* David Niven, Teresa Graves, Peter Bayliss, Veronica Carlson, Freddie Jones, Frank Thornton.

1974 **FRIGHTMARE**. *Dir:* Peter Walker.

Though crudely lurid, and suffering from a script that appears to revel in the nasty for its own sake, this is to some extent made watchable by a splendidly horrific performance by Sheila Keith as the villainous stepmother to end all villainous stepmothers.

1974 **YOUNG FRANKENSTEIN**. *Prod:* Michael Gruskoff. *dir:* Mel Brooks. *sc:* Gene Wilder, Mel Brooks. *ph:* Gerald Hirschfeld. *des:* Dale Hennesy. *mus:* John Morris. *ed:* John Howard. *players:* Gene Wilder, Peter Boyle, Marty Feldman, Cloris Leachman, Gene Hackman, Madeline Kahn.

1974 **THE LIVING DEAD OF THE MANCHESTER MORGUE**. *Dir:* Jorge Grau.

1974 **THE PHANTOM OF THE PARADISE**. *Dir:* Brian De Palma.

Set in a "Rock Palace," this whirligig turns out to be a rather gorgeous mess of photographic pyrotechnics, in which every conceivable kind of jazzed-up colour, sound and setting is mixed into a sort of parody horror extravaganza. It might excusably have been titled *The Phantom of the Popera*.

1974 **VOODOO GIRL**. *Dir:* Paul Maslansky.

1974 **THE DEVIL WITHIN HER (CHE SEI?)**. *Dir:* Oliver Hellman.

1974 **GHOST STORY**. *Dir:* Stephen Weeks.

Modest but very efficient little venture into the occult, exactly described by its unassuming title. A sinister toy is, once again, in evidence: it seems that the nursery cupboard is fast becoming the most sinister corner of the house.

1974 **SHIVERS (THE PARASITE MURDERS)**. *Dir:* David Cronenberg.

Some films are born nasty, some achieve nastiness and some have nastiness thrust upon them. When to the puerile desire to disgust are added tedium, silliness and a clear contempt for the audience's level of intelligence, the results are "horror" films such as this.

1974 **ABBY**. *Dir:* William Girder.

1974 **BLACK CHRISTMAS**. *Dir:* Robert Clark.

1974 **LEGEND OF THE WEREWOLF**. *Dir:* Freddie Francis.

1974 **SYMPTOMS**. *Dir:* Joseph Larraz.

Superficial resemblances to *Repulsion* in this study of an abnormal girl are too obvious to need emphasising, but Larraz is no Polanski. This remains stubbornly on the level of a reasonably effective shocker, neatly made, with Lesbianism as its fashionable basis.

1974 **VAMPYRES**. *Dir:* Joseph Larraz.

Another Lesbian sally by the same director, this time down the old vampire avenue. An altogether coarser film than *Symptoms,* it was awarded the British AA certificate against the other's X—perhaps because it was felt that, the worse the film, the younger the audience to whom it should be made available.

1974 **THE DAY OF THE LOCUST**. *Dir:* John Schlesinger.

The orgiastic fury of the climax—from the moment when the tormented Homer Simpson (marvellously portrayed by Donald Sutherland) turns against the loathsome child actor and the whole scene erupts into an unparalleled outburst of violence—demands that Schlesinger's film be included in any study of cinematic horror. It is a fine example (among many) of the fact that the most effective scenes of horror are not always to be found in the *genre* itself.

1975 **I DON'T WANT TO BE BORN**. *Dir:* Peter Sasdy.

A disappointing *Exorcist* cash-in from a director who, in the words of the school report, "could do better."

1975 **BUG**. *Dir:* Jeannot Szwarc.

More big insects, and quite effective too, demonstrating that you never know what an earthquake might throw up, and had better not meddle with

The Phantom at the consol in *The Phantom of the Paradise*.

Three grotesques from *The Phantom of the Paradise.*

what you do find—even if you are a biology professor.

1975 **THE GHOUL**. *Dir:* Freddie Francis.

A "different" type of ghoul appears in this story, in which the indefatigable Mr. Francis travels back to the nineteen-twenties—and on the whole captures the atmosphere of the period quite well, an atmosphere which seems strangely elusive for many film-makers. The characters menaced are more interesting than the menace, and include Peter Cushing, John Hurt, and Gwen Watford—as an *ayah*.

1975 **RACE WITH THE DEVIL**. *Prod:* Paul Maslansky. *Dir:* Jack Starrett. *sc:* Lee Forest. *ph:* Robert Jessup. *mus:* Leonard Rosenman. *players:* Peter Fonda, Warren Oates, Loretta Swit, Lara Parker, R. G. Armstrong.

An unexpectedly gripping story of devilry in the American West, starting quietly as two young business partners set off with their wives for a peaceful caravan holiday and mounting with ever-increasing tension from the moment they unwittingly intrude on a secret ceremony apparently involving a human

sacrifice. From then on they are menaced in a variety of increasingly unpleasant ways until the grim final twist—an excellent example of the dramatic effectiveness of false security suddenly shattered.

Peter Fonda is attacked by rattlesnakes left by devilworshippers in *Race with the Devil.*

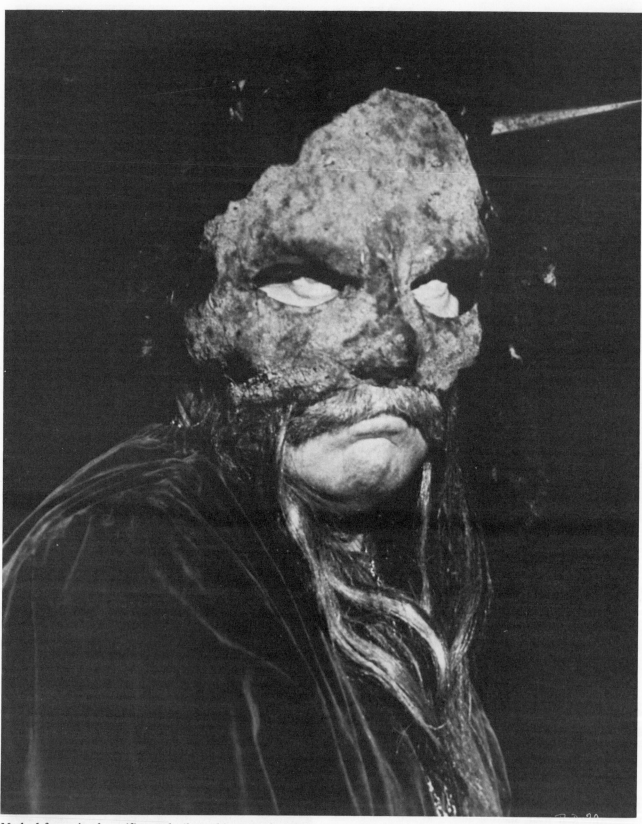

Masked for a ritual sacrifice: a devil-worshipper in the grim
and gripping *Race with the Devil*.

The 1976 victim: Jessica Lange in *King Kong*.

driven beyond all human bounds, she takes a horrify-ing vengeance on innocent and guilty alike. On the level of shocker alone this is a superb piece of film-making: the long build-up in the dance hall to the apocalyptic climax, for instance, is magnificently done—a considerable use of slow motion being for once entirely justified. As it reaches its culmination this sequence is guaranteed to send every heart in the cinema thumping against its ribs. From then on all is terror unconfined.

But the film is far more than mere shocker. It is, on one hand, an acute and moving study of adoles-cent shyness and loneliness and, on another, a grim realisation of the dreams of revenge of all such young people driven to a fury of despair by the torments of their tougher and brasher contemporaries. Much of the film's impact is due to a stunning portrayal by young Sissy Spacek—a star performance if ever there was one. Piper Laurie has perhaps the most difficult job as the religious fanatic: settings and actions are bizarre in the extreme—but no one with close know-ledge of the sort of behaviour in which such a mania can result would suggest that they are beyond belief.

Sissy Spacek, magnificent as the terrified and enraged Carrie White in the horrific and bizarre *Carrie*.

159

Owing to the publication of this book having been delayed by unavoidable circumstances, I have taken the opportunity to update the Chronology briefly in the following pages. As will be seen, nothing very notable has appeared in the world of Horror since the last entry above.

1974 **THE STEPFORD WIVES.** *Dir:* Bryan Forbes.

Ira Levin's monitory Women's Liberation parable is milder and less horrific than his *Rosemary's Baby* and *A Kiss Before Dying,* but Bryan Forbes manages to extract a few effectively uneasy moments from this tale of robot small-town wives created by their husbands as exact doubles to replace the less accommodating originals. The film's release was held up for some time.

1975 **THE GIANT SPIDER INVASION.** *Dir:* Bill Rebane.

Spiders join the ranks of Brobdingnagian insects, reptiles, etc. with depressingly foreseeable consequences, but providing, perhaps, a *frisson* or two for arachnephobes.

1976 **SHUDDER.** *Dir:* Chris Munger.

More spiders—merely life-size, but full of venom—owned by an unpleasant little girl (Suzanne Ling) who uses them to further her own ends.

1976 **BURNT OFFERINGS.** *Dir:* Dan Curtis.

A quite effective "villainous house", thanks to the hand of an experienced horror maker.

1976 **CATHY'S CURSE (CAUCHEMARS).** *Dir:* Eddy Matalon.

1976 **THE SAVAGE BEES.** *Dir:* Bruce Geller.

Still more wicked insects.

1976 **RABID.** *Dir:* David Cronenberg.

From the same stable whence issued the supremely repulsive SHIVERS (THE PARASITE MURDERS), this one is slightly less so.

1977 **KINGDOM OF THE SPIDERS.** *Dir:* John Cardos.

They finally take over (in Arizona).

1977 **EXORCIST II – THE HERETIC.** *Prod:* Richard Lederer. *dir:* John Boorman. *sc:* William Goodhart. *ph:* William A. Fraker. *des:* Richard MacDonald. *mus:* Ennio Morricone. *ed:* Tom Priestley. *players:* Linda Blair, Richard Burton, Max von Sydow, Louise Fletcher, Paul Henreid, Kitty Winn.

As feared, this turns out to be one more example of the foolishness of follow-ups, even making nonsense of what has gone before. Linda Blair is forced, poor girl, to blot the memories of her meritable performance in the original, and Richard Burton looks embarrassed. The ghastly examples of television

sequels "based on characters created by . . . " (in this case, of course, William P. Blatty) should have provided warning enough—but it seems that in the film business anything which can crush a few more box-office drops out of an already squeezed orange is justified.

1977 **HOLOCAUST 2000.** *Dir:* Alberto De Martino.

Odd mixture of nuclear power and the Anti-Christ—with characters named "Caine", "Sara" and "Angel", and a mixed cast of American/British (Kirk Douglas, Simon Ward) and Italian players—resulting in the usual dubbing horrors.

1977 **THE INCREDIBLE MELTING MAN.** *Dir:* William Sachs.

Moral—keep clear of Saturn if you wish to remain solid flesh.

1977 **DEMON SEED.** *Dir:* Donald Cammell.

1977 **ZOLTAN—HOUND OF DRACULA.** *Dir:* Albert Band.

The Count has now dwindled to Mr. Drake (Michael Pataki) in this sad travesty.

1977 **THE CAR.** *Prod:* Marvin Birdt, Elliot Silverstein. *dir:* Elliot Silverstein. *sc:* Dennis Shryack, Michael Butler, Lane Slate. *ph:* Gerald Hirschfeld. *des:* Lloyd S. Papez. *mus:* Leonard Rosenman. *ed:* Michael McCroskey. *players:* John Brolin, Kathleen Lloyd, John Marley, R. G. Armstrong, Doris Dowling.

In a dull year, this stands out as a technically brilliant, action-filled and genuinely shuddersome horror story, with a really original menace—a large black automobile, apparently driverless but far from motiveless in its attacks. Underlying the enjoyable fantasy are hints of a darker allegorical significance. The final moments of devastating fire and explosion are awesome, climaxing in a demonic figure which forms momentarily—baleful and sinister—in the chaotic sky.

1977 **THE OMEN II – DAMIEN.** *Dir:* Don Taylor. *Players:* William Holden, Lee Grant, Jonathan Scott-Taylor, Lucas Donat, Robert Foxworth, Nicholas Pryor.

1978 **THE FURY.** *Dir:* Brian De Palma. *players:* Kirk Douglas, John Cassavetes, Amy Irving, Carrie Snodgrass.

INDEX